MADE IN THE USA

Made in the USA

Global Greed, Tax Laws and the Exportation of America's Future

Why and How You Support America

Barr McClellan

HANNOVER HOUSE
2010

ISBN 978-0-9637846-8-1 / UPC 7-61450-95552-3

Published by Hannover House
1722 N. College Avenue, Fayetteville, AR 72703
www.HannoverHouse.com

Text Editor: Debbie Self
Text Designer: John Coghlan
Cover Art Design: Lindsay VanBeck

Printed in the United States of America

Library of Congress Cataloging-in-Publication Data

McClellan, Barr.
Made in the USA : global greed, tax laws and the exportation of America's future : why and how you support America / Barr McClellan.
p. cm.
Includes bibliographical references and index.
ISBN 978-0-9637846-8-1 (alk. paper)
1. Free trade—United States. 2. Globalization—Economic aspects—United States. 3. United States—Foreign economic relations. 4. United States—Economic policy. 5. United States—Economic conditions. I. Title.
HF1756.M325 2009
337.73—dc22

2009029636

For Cecile, always

CONTENTS

PREFACE

Middle America provided the inspirations for an in-depth look at globalization and what has happened to the United States during the past sixty years of ever-expanding free trade.[1] Many friends and associates provided the necessary insights.

This book resulted largely from a remarkable cooperation between publisher and writer. After presenting a bestseller in *Blood, Money & Power,* we realized there was a mutuality of understanding about what was needed in the world of words, or more accurately, the ongoing wars of words.[2]

This overview affirms the cooperation possible, indeed necessary. Friends, business associates, family and more in our networks reflected the ever-rising interest in globalization. We took a look at the issues and the many disconnects. The subject was among the most active on the book publishing list.[3] The Internet traffic was similarly overwhelming.[4]

Something needed to be said about the assault on America. My experience with power politics and with world affairs prepared me for the writing of this book.[5] I saw that politics' adverse impact on America, on the citizens here, was too often ignored. Verbal assaults were—and are—unwarranted. Many of the wars of words are simply a cover-up for personal allegiances of the writers, their biases. The short recommendation—disclose all personal connections.

Efforts to obtain comments for this book from prominent economists and political leaders were nonproductive. We turned to individual experiences and then to what the leaders were saying, to quote them in their words.

Authors on key subjects of world progress, free trade and competition were reluctant to discuss the topic of globalization. All have takes on globalization spelled out in their own books. "Read the book" is a statement both author and publisher understand.

Special thanks to the many individuals and friends, some of many years, some of only a few weeks, who contributed their stories and added their comments as the research and writing for this book was underway. Thanks also to all those who agreed to share their experiences. For now, they will remain anonymous.

The basic facts are clear. Sixty years of ever-expanding trade, of globalization, have had an enormous impact, good and not so good.

Changes are needed.

To summarize, fair trade trumps free trade.

Even more interesting, the policy issues—the politics—are also changing.

From beginning to end, this research centered on what free trade was doing to America. We saw the impact of greed, outsourcing, taxes and immigrants. We also saw the need to do something.

What does Middle America want? Peace on our globe, good will among all peoples. During the many realignments in global politics and the global economy, we have been and are and will remain good neighbors.[6]

But we should no longer bear this burden alone.

Barr McClellan
New York City
January 2010

INTRODUCTION

Globalization.

Everywhere.

Unhappy with high prices at the pump?[1] Consider the explosive demand for gasoline around the world. More and more people have cars. There are only so many refineries. Only so much oil is being produced and refined. Demand is growing with no foreseeable leveling. Prices go up. Supply, demand and price work together. We have a supply shortfall.

Toys for children are made in China and imported to the United States, followed by reports of lead content and then recalls. What else is dangerous? How about prescription drugs? What other regulations in America are not required for products made abroad and imported here?

The manufacturing plant provided employment with a retirement plan after forty years. The company suddenly closed without notice. The former corporate administrators are reportedly building and staffing a similar plant in Pakistan. There were no benefits for the workers at the defunct plant. The promised training was only for computer webmasters. Senior employees were left with nothing.

An overloaded 18-wheeler speeds down the Mass Pike with only one front light, no tail lights. The driver has been behind the wheel from Laredo, Texas, almost nonstop. Quickly unloaded and reloaded in Worcester, Massachusetts, the truck is heading west when pulled over by state police. The driver does not speak

English and when arrested has no employer to report. The investigation into the delivery point and the truck ownership begins but is soon lost in paperwork and delays. After a weekend in jail, the driver is released and never seen again.

Annoyed by helpdesks for that expensive computer because the expert is unintelligible? This is a product of outsourcing, of sending computer support plans abroad to inexpensive call centers that serve no good purpose. Corporate planners, however, find the lowest wages possible, no matter what. When a call arrives for support, the customer and the employee will waste still more time looking for an understandable answer. An intelligible answer takes two minutes in America and is less expensive than an outsourced call taking twenty minutes. We also have a global wage problem. The Filipinos and all the others in India, Pakistan and elsewhere work at 10 percent of American wages.

Try getting a construction team together. The unemployed Americans hired yesterday do not show or are late and too hungover to work. Hire the available immigrant group waiting at curbside downtown. See the dangers on the job as no one understands the power tools. We have a workforce problem in America. We have a communications problem with this in-sourcing.[2]

Time and again, crimes are committed by illegal immigrants. While on probation pending release approval, an immigrant, now desperate and faced with few options, robs a convenience store and murders the clerk. Arrested and tried, deportation will follow a twenty-year term, typically reduced to five years.

There are many more examples. Every Middle American has their particular bad experiences.

Globalization is the basic problem. The adverse impact is felt in these examples and in many more cases. The total impact is much deeper. We face long-term problems for our USA that are totally unacceptable, costing us multi-billions of dollars. For a typical family of four, the cost is in the tens of thousands.

This adverse impact on Americans and America should not be happening.

The United States has carried the losses since 1980.[3] We should no longer bear the cost alone.

No More War

"Globalization" has been underway from the beginnings of human wanderings but it has had serious consequences since 1945. At the same time that the "greatest generation"[4] was winning the war, careful planning was underway to develop the best means to avoid future wars. We did not want any more "we regret to inform" letters to be sent to mothers. We had won the war. We set out to win the peace. No more war was what many considered a basic policy.

We knew "isolation" was not possible. By 1945, we had learned and were convinced that the world was linked together. We acknowledged the global connections. We also knew our economy had worked, that we had produced what was necessary to win the war. We knew nuclear warfare was simply unthinkable.

We resolved to rebuild from the devastation, to build as lasting a peace as possible. We developed a new dedication, in today's terms a vision and a mission.

The vision the greatest generation had was world peace with a renewed value on human life that required full protection and promotion. To prevent wars, we needed systems that would improve people's lives. To protect the peace, we needed military power.

The mission was world peace through political and economic systems. The hope for peace rested on substantial changes in the pre-1939 world order. We committed to a renewal of the American values we had learned and proven through experience.

In a very deep sense, the greatest generation understood that, on the global scene, new political and economic systems needed to be in place. Based on our experiences and way of life, we planned, again, for that eternal dream and hope for world peace with progress, for that shining city on the hill.[5]

A Political Plan

First and foremost, we planned new political organizations to preserve world peace. There was broad thinking outside the box. Unlike the failed League of Nations, we had to have something that worked. The immediate political plan was for the United Nations to bring the world together and keep it together. Starting in 1943, planning began and decisions were made.[6] With the new world organization, the United Nations, procedures were in place to bring nations together to discuss and resolve disputes, and to better promote world peace. We even provided for a joint military command with the Soviets.[7]

A deeper motivation was that, like the United States in our beginnings as the Thirteen Colonies, individual nations could join into a United States as still another state, a stronger state, a nation. We had united independent nations into a United States.

In 1945 perhaps other nation-states could unite. There would be no question about following the "American Way." We were basically an economic and political union. Democracy was the best choice for organizing the United Nations. Nations would join together in an agreed charter. Procedures would be in place to enforce world peace through democracy.

Our ideas carried the day.

In 1945 in San Francisco, based on the war-time planning for peace, for a new world order, the Allied nations joined together as the United Nations with a dedication to political systems designed to preserve the peace.

Unfortunately, the United Nations and its related international organizations did not work.

The first big realization that global peace was a long way off was when the Iron Curtain descended.[8] When the Berlin Wall was built, the divided world became all too real. Brick and iron blocked any hopes for democracy.

The Korean War started with a military invasion by North Korea. The Soviet Union did not attend meetings for peace and a United Nations command was put together. Aggression was contained but any progress to world peace was halted.

Human rights violations by too many nations were placed in the hands of those same nations and their dictators. The notion that Cuba's Castro could be responsible for American human rights was blatantly repugnant. Recent amendments only continued a ridiculous program.[9]

When the United Nations voted with near unanimity, with only two dissenting votes, that Israel should be condemned for defending itself, the injustices were all too clear. The world organization was predominantly anti-Semitic.

Efforts at world peace by serving as the policing authority crumbled when the United Nation's police, the so-called "blue helmets," were prohibited from fighting back except in situations of immediate and personal self-defense. These police totally lacked any authority to enforce the peace. There was no law and order.

Without an effective international army, units from national armies were enlisted to maintain peace. Not fearing the use of force and intimidation these military units too often engaged in deprivations of the local populations under United Nations sanction. The United Nations was ultimately responsible for countless innocent victims of localized wars.

When stability for world commerce was reestablished after the Gulf War, Iraq was offered food and other necessities for its citizens in return for payment with oil. Under UN overview, vast sums were illegally granted to private individuals and organizations. Instead of brokering food for Iraqis, many UN agents and representatives were unjustly enriched. This corruption was never corrected. Investigations were blocked by a code of secrecy no one could open.

With these examples and so many more from 1945 through 2000, the UN was clearly a failure. The high hopes and the careful planning for a world organization dedicated to peace were not fulfilled and did not work.

A greater sense of injustice was that the end of the cold war in 1989–1991 meant nothing to the United Nations. Too many international organizations—and the United Nations in particular—were shown to be corrupt to the core. This massive "corruption" was unequivocally stated by a key employee of the secretariat.[10] He also emphasized that most employees had secret, offshore bank accounts for the ongoing corruption. Human beings remained greedy and self-serving. This fact of the real world was reaffirmed again and again. The high calling of employment by the UN was not enough to guarantee public service. There was no pride in service for peace.

The careful plan by our "greatest generation" for a lasting political solution was ruined. Instead, there was greed that yields to nothing, not to pride in doing a good job or in service to a better world. Money and personal gain became the sole objective. There was no justice. There were no apologies.

Not everyone at the United Nations was corrupt. For those who retained a sense of pride and of public service for peace, a culpability remains. Self-righteous support for statism,[11] meritocracy and the cult of personality prevented your halting the corruption.

If you do nothing, you become no better than your corrupt colleagues.

Overview of Conspiracies

If you wish conspiracy thinking, consider the real conspiracies. There are two kinds: criminal for personal gain and political, to impose a new governance, in secret.

First, understand that a conspiracy is an agreement between two or more people to commit crimes for personal gain.

There is no known great subterranean planning group that has been around from the beginning of time to control and rule the world. The Illuminati are not to be found. The Masons are not actively governing through puppets. The Rothschild banking system does not control all financing, not even through the gnomes of Zürich. There are no grand conspiracies.[12]

There are plans that are public; however, the significance of those plans is well concealed and the appearance of a conspiracy remains.

There are small conspiracies among people in power, usually with their attorneys participating, to improve their bank account and to reassure their reelection. Consider the example of our Congress. Legislation called "earmarks" is passed to keep key supporters in line, in return to receive their campaign contributions, and to be reelected. Failing that, we see our elected officials leaving office with a big investment account. Small conspiracies are widespread.

The political conspiracies are more widespread. Consider the "vast right-wing conspiracy." That is political organization. The secret plans will emerge with "governance" at the United Nations. That is a conspiracy.

A Business Plan

Fortunately, the greatest generation and its successors, its children, did not stop with political organization. Along with planning for the United Nations, a more practical solution to promote world peace and to prevent "we regret to inform" letters was underway. By 1947, economic systems formally commenced to bring progress, to improve peoples' lives, to take care of family, to curtail the ravages of poverty and helplessness that were major causes of war.

While global political organizations were failing between 1945 and 2000, national and international economies were making significant gains.

In 1947 when the Iron Curtain was in place, we faced a cold war with the Soviets and their communist allies. We did not stop efforts at world peace. We continued to rebuild the war-torn world, starting with the conquered—Germany and Japan.

Incredible economic victories from 1945 through 2000 included a dedication to free trade and democratic business principles based on law and order. The world political order set up in 1945 was gradually ignored. We accomplished our secondary plans for world peace through international trade with new agreements and organizations. Under our leadership, those regional groups produced and are producing what was promised—progress for every nation willing to participate. Our example of the original thirteen colonies uniting into a single economic unit worked for us. Similar regional organizations should work for many other nations.

They did.

They still are as the downturn corrects.

With the exception of a few nations still mired in the cold war we have produced the greatest progress for business, for nations, their individual citizens and their families ever achieved.[13]

The rebuilding of Europe centered on the Marshall Plan. All of Europe was invited to participate but the Soviet Union rejected that proposal, setting up its own plan for its puppet governments in East Europe, behind the Iron Curtain.

Today we have a European Empire[14] taking more and more nations into its boundaries while declaring ever-more assertive global leadership. Built with help from American leadership, we welcome the new, still-evolving European Union.

With Japan, we started economic reconstruction along with a new political structure. For a nation without democratic traditions and with an economy almost totally destroyed, we were able to help reorganize and rebuild a powerful nation and economy. Several generations of young men were lost in Japan's wars of aggression.[15] The extent to which the success of democracy rested with the scarcity of alpha-males is a question still needing research. The overall result is clear. The Japanese system is a striking example of what we could do, and it was done in full cooperation with Japan.

There are many more regional organizations moving forward successfully under the American Doctrine for Globalization.

The Greatest Generation Continues

Consider again the powerful legacy of the greatest generation, 1929 to 1945. What happened to the greatest generation in the years following the world war?

Many children of the greatest generation were in total awe of what America had accomplished in those critical years from 1929 through 1945. But the greatest generation made mistakes. They had passed restrictive legislation to keep foreign goods out and that worsened the Depression. They also avoided the European and Asian wars until Pearl Harbor "awoke a sleeping giant [the United States]."[16] We would go from isolation in the 1930s to world leader in four short years.

The "greatest generation" did not stop in 1945. The same men and women continued the war to win the peace. Their children joined in the basic vision and mission, in the doctrine of globalization, in promoting peace while containing a belligerent force promoting statism, communism, socialism—and terror.[17] Our policy was containment enforced by the most powerful military ever developed to prevent global war. That defense force did the job.

The children of the greatest generation, destined to assume

leadership in the decades following 1945, gradually continued the globalization. During our high school years we were the "silent generation,"[18] so-called because of this admiration for what our parents and grandparents had accomplished. Many of us had this deep sense of responsibility to our parents and to our nation, to the legacy of the greatest generation.

Anyone active in politics and committed to the success of our democracy was all the more impressed with the American system of government and law as we entered the 1960s. We knew that, where change had to be made, we would get the job done. We confronted and resolved many glaring violations of human rights and civil rights.[19] Dissent over Vietnam resulted in unacceptable violence, but the war still ended with a peace treaty and abolition of the draft.

In an era of nuclear warfare, the hope was more powerful than ever for peace and the plans were as specific and practical as possible, to deter war and build business. No one needs to imagine what world war three would have meant. Simply stated, nukes could not be used. There would be only one nuclear war.

For those of us entering adulthood in the 1960s, the concern for peace was all the greater as our children became a vital part of our lives.

During the 1970s and 1980s, the cold war stumbled ahead with recurring threats of a nuclear holocaust. The recognition of China and the establishment of commercial relations represented a major step for peace. On the home front we witnessed outstanding progress in science, health, technology and communications. The use of the Internet for defense and academic purposes led to global information and contact, to pure globalization.[20]

Success and the Critics

Still in the hands of the greatest generation, the cold war came to an end with the dramatic and highly emotional pictures of the

Berlin Wall being torn down by private citizens. Shortly after, the Soviet Union collapsed. The decision had been made by millions of people that the communist example of statism did not work, that the American system of government and business had worked. Containment worked. No nukes were launched. There was no global war.[21] Our lives changed from cold war preparedness with red alerts and bomb shelters to a world of peace and economic progress.

Hopes and dreams that were necessary in 1945 for political solutions, like the United Nations, proved totally useless. The secondary mission for globalization was based on specific and very practical plans for commercial progress, like the European Union. Eight more economic unions are underway. The backup plans for economic-commercial unions worked.

Despite the great victory over statism with the end of the cold war, the world's political organizations were worse than worthless. The statists were dangerous because they became enemies of America and all we stand for, all we did to prevail in 1945, all we did to maintain the peace against the Soviets, and then all we did again to bring economic progress to the globe.

Victory in the cold war, however, has not been enough. The statists and socialists refuse to accept a key fact—their systems for government control of the political and economic systems do not work. America won the cold war and excellent results were achieved, results that should be accepted and routinely applied.

The hard facts are ignored by many in the media who look mainly for lurid headlines and confrontations.[22] Success by capitalism is too often ignored. Too much is done in secret to advance statism, resulting in the 2008 downturn.

Similarly, the academic world attacks the results. Despite the continuing failure of the great universities to develop systems that work and to confront human suffering in the real world, the American system of democracy and business has worked. The critics only raise problems; real solutions are beyond their limited interests. The protestors are active and partisan. Even today, they glorify domestic violence and terrorism; they propose destruction of the democratic system that decisively beat their statist system.[23]

The current batch of welfare and socialist states oppose us. Many societies prefer secrecy and oppose our liberties. From time to time a few militant groups jump up. Reduced to a handful, some return; they have no future.

America's Dedication to Peace

American values directly contradict violence and killings.

We do our level-headed best to promote peace and law and order. Thanks to our military, we are relatively successful under very difficult circumstances.

In an imperfect world the USA stands for values of peace on our globe, of good will among all peoples, and of support for each other, the good neighbor.

There are problems. We have solutions that must be constantly renewed. We have done so consistent with our most fundamental values.

Huge sacrifices were made to overcome the Depression and then to the win the war against fascist dictators in Germany and Japan for freedom.

Those sacrifices left a legacy.

The greatest generation upheld that legacy and won the cold war, developed incredible technological progress and brought economic improvement to billions. We also defeated the statist dictators on the left, again for freedom and democracy.

From 1945 through 2000 a new legacy developed, one of political and economic victories.

We should never turn our attention from those legacies. In a rapidly globalizing world, the successes we have achieved with our system of values should continue. Those values are fundamentals common to all peoples, to all families and businesses. American values are universal values.

Letters to Leaders

The results of globalization since 1945 prompted this book, to be a review of what our current leaders believe. We requested words of wisdom from several key participants in the global war for power, prestige and money.

Letters were also sent to leading economists and policymakers, requesting comments on where globalization is taking us.[22]

The usual answer, however, was delay and then more delay. At the same time more and more cautions were appearing—jobs declined, poor products appeared and were rejected, extensive in-sourcing and outsourcing continued, and other imbalances hurt our international standing. The results were not favorable to America and its citizens.

Government has proved unable to take action. The national political agreement is for free trade. We continue what we started. However, adverse results continue, and we need time for a pause and review. A broader and deeper inquiry into globalization is all the more necessary.

Even without direct responses from leaders, the answers we requested are still available. We have spoken and written records. We abandoned the request for interviews and comments. We needed only to uncover what these leaders are saying and doing, to disclose what is happening.

In addition, discussion with friends and associates revealed a deep interest in speaking up. Plans expanded. We would feature not just the words and actions of leaders. We would include the experiences of Americans in their daily life within the global community. We would look at the success of those generations following the greatest generation.

What Is Happening

The chapters that follow review our findings and conclusions.

What we first affirmed was that those who followed American leadership after 1945 remained part of the greatest generations.

In the second chapter, we address what key participants are saying about the great success of globalization. These leaders proved to have one element in common. They are very wealthy. Results count for everything in business. What the leaders do is as relevant as what they say.

The business results and political policies demanded an analysis of the broader and deeper economic trends. Economists are the so-called experts in the huge economic progress of the years since 1945. In the third chapter several issues are examined to show there is no real agreement among the experts—except to globalize.

In the fourth chapter the statistics of globalization show several key results. The real world of cold, hard numbers shows that globalization and American losses are underway at an accelerating rate. Our position in the world is becoming ever worse while other nations show great progress.

The results include

- corporate greed (whether business, government or other);
- taxes (including all forms of government charges);
- outsourcing (job migration out of the United States); and
- in-sourcing (economic inroads from outside).

Once the problems are considered, solutions are needed. The simple rule in business is

"problem, solution."

A look at alternatives show that the key for solutions is based on parity, on a level playing field and fair competition.

In a democracy, how leaders are selected is vital. The sixth chapter reviews our election process and highlights policies such as globalization that need change. Candidates may or may not adopt the new policies. Compromise should happen in the fascinating American process of democracy. Because globalization is so very successful and because of powerful interests supporting free trade, changing course is not likely. Selection of leaders who are aware of America's decline relative to other nations is required.

Finally, we turn to our values and their renewal. The powerful legacy of the great generations, those tried-and-true values the greatest generations continued to follow in 1929 through 1945, those renewed in 1990 and renewed again in 2000, are restated with suggestions for achieving a fair balance in the new global world.

The new balance will be political as well as economic.

That balancing is underway but is threatened by determined enemies.

Fundamental Changes Underway

In a political and media frenzy driven by extreme and too-often vicious rhetoric, underlying problems are easily overlooked. The deeper problems and the deeper perspectives are necessary to develop the vision we need. They have been overlooked. The major changing point in the global economy and politics has not been considered.

There are many valid reasons for extreme caution as the world becomes ever closer. We have to direct all concern to our children, in my case six, and for our grandchildren, ten and still expanding. The family must remain the foundation for our policies.

We need to assure law based on democracy, on the American system.

The warnings say we have to change the severe impact on Americans. Again, fair trade trumps free trade.

One major change is apparent: The world's leading nation is no longer America.

There are ten major economic groups—the United States, the European Union, China, Latin America, India, Russia, Japan, Southeast Asia, the Muslim nations and the emerging African Union.

This progress is based on our economic policies. The result is at a heavy cost to us. We have ample comfort in the developed world and yet we still bear the burden. The nine new regional groups need to pitch in and help.

The global peace continues at an unfair cost to us.

Greed has resulted from this imbalance. The world's economies need a new relative balance, a new "parity."

We have created a model for the world economies. Apologies and compromise are not needed; withdrawal and still more cash giveaways are not needed; ethical and professional standards *are* needed. Once again, we have to commit the world to the new system for peace and progress, one with law and order.

A new paradigm is necessary.

The new paradigm is necessary because contrary changes are underway in new proposals for "governance," for a new world order based on the United Nations, a corrupt institution with new world control proposed by corrupt nations.

If public disclosure were in effect, there would not be a problem for those dedicated to government control. Too much is hidden. We need government to disclose all, to live in the feared "goldfish bowl."

Assault on America

Even though we are in fact on top of the world, the assault on America and Americans is never-ending. We remain the target of any and all critics or commentators even though we are the refuge and the dream for the vast majority of world citizens.

Consider this: were our barriers to immigration removed, much of the world would soon be here.

Success makes us what we are and we are successful because of a capitalist business and commercial economy and because of a democracy based on law.

The two ideals of democracy and commerce, not necessarily compatible at all times, make a powerful combination. We are envied and from that envy springs an unfathomable fury, mostly from alphas and type As, typically men.

We also have too many in media who delight in comforting the afflicted and afflicting the comfortable. And we have a batch of factually challenged professors who promote statism without meaningful peer review.

These many doomsayers forecast woe but provide few new solutions. Their plans, if any, always include more statism, more government and more taxes.

What Is "Made in the USA"?

A fair resolution to all this rhetoric remains in our hands. "Made in the USA" covers all those things we have done in America since our beginnings. We have our values and we have our goods and services. We then need a renewal, to sell America, to promote our ideas and ideals. We need to recognize universal values. Most important, we need to resume leadership of this critical competition of market economies, this war of ideas and words now occurring on an unprecedented, apparently disorganized scale.

The economy must be included in planning for our future. What happens to Americans is based on the economy. One seemingly trite remark is, "It's the economy, stupid."[24]

No matter how trite, the statement is accurate. All polls show a continuing and overwhelming interest in the economy. That means business.[25]

There are some agreed-upon desires. The vast majority of people the world over want peace, a living income and a safe home for family. These basic desires are too often distorted and corrupted by greed, typically by personalities intent on statist controls, not democratic freedoms.

The problems we face and the vicious attacks we have sustained, while comforting the socialists, only compel us to do better. We do. With a level playing field we will continue as the pacesetter as well as the peacemaker. Our values have prevailed for a reason. They work. We are ready for fair competition.

With a careful identification of the values that have produced the greatest economic advances ever, renewal of those values will result in change for the better.

The overall objective then becomes not a hope, not just a vision, but a firm plan, a vital mission to make the system work far better while easing the undue and unfair burden placed on our businesses and our families.

What change is needed? A renewal of values based on what has been proven to work: democracy and business.

The big picture is what has changed. New ways to look at the world are necessary. Any system for solid planning must be based on the new paradigm.

The economic values making this possible include several obvious rules. Our founders adopted the values that have defined American business success.[26] Hold a sound dollar, avoid deficit spending, keep inflation in check and maintain sound monetary policy. We need law and order, not corruption. We need open governments, not conspiracies acting in secret. Simply stated, we have to follow the rules that make commerce and government work.

What Is Globalization?

The meaning of globalization is still wide open. Many limit

the process to international trade. Free trade is their word of choice. Others see a broader impact, with the free movement of people. They call for open borders. Still others include all communications crossing national borders, acknowledging what the Internet has done and seeing a need to monitor the freedom the World Wide Web provides. Some recognize the penetration of borders by a *de facto* system of openness and seek balance to free trade, in favor of fair trade. Some consider the total impact of international activity on the nations and the peoples of the world. This broadest interpretation is the most effective way to understand the most fundamental of changes, of the progress of the nation-state to regional organizations, just as we did in that critical period from 1776 to 1800.

An interesting definition is provided from Stanford University:

> globalization refers to fundamental changes in the spatial and temporal contours of social existence, according to which the significance of space or territory undergoes shifts in the face of a no less dramatic acceleration in the temporal structure of crucial forms of human activity.[27]

Huh?

What does this mean? As usual, academia must mystify what they say. Gives them wiggle room when a question is raised. What they need to understand is that old business value called KISS:

> "Keep it simple, stupid."[28]

As should be expected, the Stanford definition has an ulterior purpose. The definition says that in an Internet world, new developments are widely and rapidly known worldwide, globally. Change happens much more quickly. The definition also implies local values may be lost.

The concern is losing local values. The benefit is bringing the world closer together. If local values are challenged, the freedom must still be there to make that choice. The choice must be by individuals, by voters. Be for democracy.

We have to understand the choices. Then we have to make a choice. If a majority decide to make a change, they should have the freedom to do so. We call it democracy.

Globalization is everywhere. The issues now underway need to be decided with an understanding of globalization and where we are going. Profound changes are already underway. The statist plans those changes with as much secrecy and as little disclosure as possible. Democracy is denied.

What has happened?

Where do we go from here?

The answers rest with the success of America and Americans. For the international, globalized world the universal values we first proclaimed in 1776 need to be renewed. The values made the greatest Americans what they were and what they still are. The values that won the cold war and brought the globe to the greatest progress ever recorded must be maintained and renewed.

We have things of value, great value.

The promotion, protection and support of those values remain a noble calling for the American people.

We did the job.

Now we have to keep doing it.

Fortunately, we have the freedom to make that decision. That decision is very personal and individual, the way democracy and voting work. We do not need a government making the decision for us.

We do not need Big Brother. The world George Orwell forecast in *Nineteen Eighty-Four* (*1984* hereinafter)[29] is not happening. That book remains a work of fiction.

We only need the details.[30]

The details, the hard facts, include

- a look at the greatest generations since 1945
- our national leaders and their vast wealth
- the globalized economic results
- how greed has corrupted globalization
- a solution in fair trade and fair competition
- selecting leaders to change policy to favor America
- renewing our universal values.

At a personal level, we need to promote and sell America and our values because they work and we need to buy America, we need to buy what is *Made in the USA*, our own goods and services, until fair trade is in effect.

ONE

PAX AMERICANA

World peace is a fundamental ambition.[1] After the wars to end all wars, after the development and use of nuclear weapons, and during an ever-rising value to human life, global war is not an option.[2]

The initial words that promoted peace among nations came through the revolutionary ideas of the Christian faith.[3] For the first time there was a way of life that rested on peace, on being a good neighbor, on respecting life itself, or, in today's terms, on having a life. Peace on Earth, good will among all people became the new standard. The contemporary era began with that philosophy, that religion of peace.

At the time there was a Roman peace, the *Pax Romana*. That great era collapsed, mostly from weakness and destruction within the Empire. For some three hundred years there had been a secure political system to do business and take care of family. Then there was none.

Rome's peace was not worldwide. On the opposite side of the globe, the Chinese Empire was prospering. That empire of relative peace would endure some three hundred years.

The next major era for world peace was *Pax Britannica* when the British Empire ruled the waves and protected commerce globally. The sun never set on the British Empire during the golden years that centered on Queen Victoria's reign. This era lasted some 120 years.

The combination of commerce, military might and a commitment to peace was successful until terminated in the massive destructions of the first and second world wars.

In 1945 we took that mantle of peace and worked ever so closely with the British to maintain the current peace, the *Pax Americana.* Our peace has been around for less than twenty years, since the Berlin Wall was torn down and the Soviet Union collapsed. There have been local wars but world progress has moved forward during this current era, bringing vast improvements in living conditions to the majority of people.

There is still a long way to go but we are making progress.

At this time we are turning our peace into a worldwide system where we are one among many. We are globalizing and it is working; however, after two thousand years we are still "fighting" for world peace and progress founded on the family.

The current era of world peace is the result of the greatest generation continuing a unique dedication to peace as a calling, to unparalleled technological innovations and to free markets.[4] In the United States we survived the Cuban Missile Crisis with all its preemption. We also settled through our democratic procedures the great national debates on preventive war and civil rights. We maintained the overall peace with no nukes fired, placed men on the moon with all the accompanying technological advances and witnessed a world economy grow to unprecedented benefits for so many.[5]

Recognition has been given the generations of the Depression and the Second World War. Those generations were remarkable in their achievements and in the changes they undertook.

The Greatest Continue

The generations that were tempered in that period from 1929 through 1945 did not stop their efforts to find world peace. After defeating the dictators on the right, they proceeded to confront dictators on the left, the communists of Russia and China, and they prevailed. They tackled unprecedented opportunities in technology, bringing wondrous progress to the world. They dedicated themselves to helping as many nations as best they could.

There were serious problems but the majority confronted those problems and resolved them through democratic processes consistent with the traditions of America.

From 1945 through 2000, the United States won the cold war, protected and promoted world commerce, assisted much of the world in recovering from wars and in advancing progress everywhere, and promoted commerce in the democratic tradition that extended a better life to more and more people.

At the same time we confronted a fundamental review of our policies for containment of the communist world and made peace abroad and at home through the same democratic processes. We also advanced the proven system of political and economic organization called business with free trade agreements and regional economic groups.

During this time there was a community spirit that we were all in the good fight together and that we had to do something to protect and promote the American Way and to block communist takeovers. We proceeded with preparedness and deterrence based on what the greatest generations learned about appeasement and failure of will. These experiences and values were passed to the next. Perhaps one feature of the American Dream, the world dream, is that when we have a problem, we must solve it.

We did.

The same personal qualities that prevailed during the "greatest generation" continued. Naiveté would assume the greatness ended in 1945 or that all good things happened then and were resolved then. The greatest generation had many injustices that carried forward into the eras of civil rights and war protests. Those same generations still guided the succeeding generations to bring down the Berlin Wall, to end the Soviet Empire and bring democracy to Russia, and to lower the wall imposed by China, bringing commercialism to a communist political system, truly opening a closed society.

We see success in those efforts by our former opponents.

With our American system as a guiding example, worldwide progress and world peace that should last many more years is right here, still in our hands.

What has happened to these generations since 1945 is best understood in very personal terms. Interviews with fourteen Americans shows a dedication to our national values—personal, business, economic, political and civic. The very practical result has been and remains the driving force guiding the world or perhaps more appropriately, the globe.

Remarkable stories are told by our sampling of middle America for those greatest generations from 1945 through 2000. One became a millionaire by playing by the rules and even bringing jobs back home. Another more directly assisted in containing communism at every turn, by being alert and fully protective of America. Another showed entrepreneurs in other nations how business and the economy work best. An exemplary family stood up for our basic values in an often antagonistic world. Another contributed in her unique way to that entertainment so vital to any political system.

The lives of these fourteen Americans are examples of over three hundred million of us who developed and still maintain the world of peace and progress we now have.

The names that follow are fictitious. Their names are changed to protect against an expected backlash. Some disclose national secrets. Others present important confidences. None is perfect. These men and women are a cross-section of our greatest generations.

CLAY MCNAIR

To start with five of those from the "greatest generation" who survived the Depression and the Second World War, one standout is Barclay McNair. His "fancy" name was chosen by an impoverished mother having high hopes for her child. Once in school, Clay would become his preferred name.

One disappointment after another drove the woman to despair and the edge of sanity. She did the best she could under the awful depression.

Clay's youth is stark witness to poverty in the 1930s. He was born in an impoverished community near Harvard University. He survived grueling circumstances when the nearby prestigious academics had no solutions that were convincing to our democracy. Arriving when the stock market boomed and then collapsed, he would take his personal world of less than nothing to follow the American Dream and become a multi-millionaire. He worked hard, competed in the American system of business, followed the work ethic and "made it."

The onset of Clay's experiences were in the winters of the Depression. The bitter cold of poverty in Boston, and specifically in the Somerville section near Harvard, could not have been worse. With an ill mother and an absent father he was the man in the house. When only nine years old he went out in the bitter cold to scavenge food wherever he could find it. After all, his mother and baby sister had to eat. Taking a few bites from the garbage he searched, he took what he could back home.

The next few growing-up years were hardly better, but the situation did improve until that day his mother announced they would take a trip to New York City, to the World's Fair. The train ride was thrilling, the view of the skyline fascinating, and the trip to the Fair . . .

"Well," Clay later said, "it did not happen."

Once at Grand Central Station, his mother took Clay and his

sister off the train and, seeing all she knew about the city, perhaps believing Grand Central was the Fair, she said, "Here it is." In a few moments, they were back on the train, returning to their tiny apartment. For far too many women in those awful years, an unsettled and often desperate outlook was a part of life.

When Clay turned sixteen, the opportunity offered by the Army was irresistible. A regular job with pay and extras like food and a bed was easy to accept. He was underage, had barely enough education to pass the exam, and was not in the best of health; however, as the nation prepared for the final battles in the Pacific, any volunteers were welcome. The available manpower pool had been severely depleted by 1944. Few questions were asked. Into uniform he went and, for four years, he served with the quartermasters, taking care of supplies and moving wherever needed. His most difficult assignment was returning coffins to families. "I guess I saw the worst of war," he said, shaking his head. Like most Americans, war was never welcome and was to be avoided except as the last alternative.

During that time while the nation cleaned up after the shooting ended, Clay had time to learn. His demand for knowledge was powerful. He took the many empty hours to read, starting with the encyclopedia.

Clay also made lasting friendships. Today networking is the way to do business. For Clay, meeting people was the way to find work and make money.

After the military stint a friend convinced Clay to join him in home-building. The results were the sprawling neighborhoods known as Levittowns.[6] The team started with a few homes and quickly learned to meet the huge demand for homes.[7] Subdivisions went up across the Northeast. Clay and associates made money, lots of it. Nothing special about their training or salesmanship. Construction and homebuilding were something men did anyway. The sell was easy. The demand was met. As Clay would remark, "Easy as wading in a cranberry pond looking for cranberries."

A new demand arose. Buildings in New York City needed roofs, new roofs, repaired roofs, removed and replaced roofs. In 1962 Clay joined in the effort, this time as his own boss, and with his own money he made still more money, this time all for him.

By 1980, with careful attention to business, Clay had mastered that dedication to business and to capitalism that was so essential. He had the ability to meet the payroll, a hard fact of business too many political leaders still do not understand. Practicing inexpensive living for himself, he saved his money and was soon a millionaire. Now having money, he could reinvest.

He stayed in the roofing business until New York City became so corrupt and lawless that the need to change was obvious.

After the breakup of AT&T, telecommunications was an emerging opportunity. Like so many stories about success in the American economy, the phone business was recommended by Clay's friends and contacts. Networking, having friends and staying in touch, was the way to know what was happening, where the opportunities were.

A major two-way radio company was having difficulty. The business and its building in New Jersey were for sale. Clay moved quickly. In business, when opportunity knocks, at least answer. Follow the old rule that "if you don't ask for it, you don't get it"; he made an offer. The closing came within a few days.

That business was giving way, at the time, to paging and mobile phones. Clay, after cleaning up operations and turning the two-way company into a moneymaker, stayed in touch with friends, got a name in business as a major investor, and was contacted about "cell" phones.[8] Learning that a car phone could go from one cell served by a transmitter to another without interruption, he could see a nation talking all the time.

Clay purchased a small retailer in the Boston area, a few more around the nation, and soon had the offices for a major national company. His "new company" was set up with friends and neighbors. New investors brought in technocrat managers with squads of pencil pushers (also called analysts or accountants), and they spent the net income on new offices, travel, expense accounts, higher pay and other schemes. When Clay protested, they wanted him to leave. He did.

Within two years, the company was ready to close the doors. The new managers were desperate and took the easy way out; they disappeared. The few remaining investors called for help. After reassurances from key investors of total control, Clay took over what was left.

The first step, again, was to cut costs. He fired the remaining pencil pushers, brought in new management, and again turned the company around.

By May 2003, Clay looked over a vital national cell phone operation with over seventy offices in forty states. He even faced the reality that outsourced helpdesks abroad and the operators overseas did not help. Just the time wasted in talking and trying to understand was not good practice. The time studies were not needed to convince him the loss of goodwill was not good business. He brought the call centers back home.

Clay knows his accomplishment was possible because of the American economy and its rules of business. In short, Clay was a certified member of the greatest generation that reversed the Depression and won World War II. He had taken the hard lessons of those years to grow by the same rules of business and capitalism to become a millionaire many times over.

ZEKE DUPREE

Another in the greatest generations grew up in the South, in a region then recovering from the Civil War and still shackled to a tradition of slavery and racism that in turn shackled economic progress.[9]

Zacharias Dupree grew up in Alabama, in a red-dirt area that was, to state it bluntly, no way to make a living, let alone make a profit. Plowing the infertile and dry fields with oxen offered no prospect for a better life.

After the Civil War, many in Alabama faced the same desperate life without a future. Impoverished, not able to see progress until the early twentieth century, still deeply divided, dedicated to farming, without plans for a future, Zeke had no hope.

In those days children, and especially boys, were seen as workers for free. Semi-slavery was their lot. Many a son would leave home to seek a better life. There were no goodbyes.

Zeke was denied even a basic education because his father refused to pay the book fees. After all, the son was to work the fields. What education was needed to plow a field? While others learned, he was set by the wood stove, required to keep the firewood in good supply, stacked and ready to burn. Most days he plowed the fields with Dick and Red, oxen yoked and driven over a hard, nonproductive land. He would spend any spare time with Sweepea, a black his age and for many years his only friend.

The one thing Zeke had was laughter. He knew one moneymaker he set up for city slickers, and he had a good laugh telling friends. When autos finally came to central Alabama, he would sit by the creek, waiting for drivers trying to make the grade. First, he would wet down the grade down to the creek. It was always too slippery to escape. For a few coins, he would help. As the thankful driver would move on, Zeke could only smile and tell his friends. When he reached sixteen, the ability to tell a humorous story or two endeared him to others. They had the autos but needed him to keep the conversation going with the girls. He kept the passengers laughing.

Zeke had many setbacks growing up but one was particularly

painful. Seems he had "a terrible hurt" in his stomach, so bad he would have Sweepea stand on it to ease the sharp attacks.

When the Depression started, Zeke never noticed. His personal economy was always depressed. In early 1934, he heard of jobs available and food being provided nearby. Some new fangled "gummint" project called the CCC, the Civilian Conservation Corps, had moved into the county with all kinds of promises.[10] He walked to the location and there, under huge tents with long tables piled high with food, he knew he was in heaven. Loading up a plate and eating, he was amazed to find the pain in his stomach was gone. For Zeke, a whole new life began.

Marrying and moving away from Old Salem and his father, he set up house in nearby Petula and was hired at Brookley, the military base in Mobile. There he finally found opportunity. Hired as a common laborer, he found he loved machines and could work them. With his humor he was able to win friends and "politik" his supervisors just enough to learn more and more about the equipment and machines. His lack of education kept him a laborer, the lowest on the pay scale. But he moved up.

Pay was regular, children were born, and Zeke was able to build a small, two-room home not even fourteen by fourteen. As the country neighborhood grew, he helped set up a Methodist Church and even bought a car. Life was proving to be good, or at least far better than anything back home. There was only one problem. Beer was plentiful and too many weekends after payday were spent recovering from hangovers.

Pearl Harbor hit America and Zeke was drafted. He could not pass the physical because of stomach problems. He stayed at Brookley, now an army air base, and even as a common laborer, the demand for workers moved him up. He would become the senior crane operator.

During the 1950s, Zeke was able to enjoy life as never before. One day at the county fair, he entered the hog-calling contest and, on that hot afternoon waiting for the "calling," he listened to a new singer in town, a young fellow named Elvis Presley. Elvis was playing away when the fair director interrupted for the hog-calling contest. Elvis walked off as Zeke and the other contestants took center stage and went to work. Zeke won, took his ribbon, and let Elvis return. Soon after, Elvis was a national sensation and never returned to that county. Zeke would be the last man to stop an Elvis performance.

Zeke stayed at Brookley until Johnson was elected president. Because Lady Bird had been heckled by crowds during a train tour in the 1960 election, the base was closed to teach the locals a lesson.[11] Zeke worked the crane that closed the gates for the last time.

When offered employment at an air base in San Antonio, he refused to move. In those days most Americans never left their home county and Zeke had already moved two counties too far. He stayed, working odd jobs and finally landing a job as a tractor driver at the county dump.

Zeke would be saved by the values he accepted and had passed to his family. His daughter would not let him stay at that "awful smelling, viciously hot dump." She arranged a job for him and his wife managing a Western Union office in Pascagoula, Mississippi. There he learned to take and deliver telegrams and pay out cash sent over the wire. He even learned to use the typewriter.

One day an armed man entered the office and demanded money. Zeke had been in the back and the man did not see him. The crook pointed the rifle straight at his wife and yelled for money. Zeke struck quickly. Embracing the man from behind, the two fell to the floor as Inetta ran for help. The chamber of commerce honored Zeke for heroism.

Still later, his daughter gave him a fourteen-room house on four acres. When Zeke saw the new home, he and Inetta were like two children at Christmas, unable to believe their good fortune.

Zeke even met Donald Trump. Seems casinos were coming to nearby Biloxi and one day while Zeke was fishing on the pier, a man stepped out of the limo and looked around, then walked into the casino.[12] Zeke followed and still with his sense of humor and always ready to talk, walked over and shook the man's hand. When he learned the man was Donald Trump, he wore a plastic bag over his hand for a week. Convinced the local government was moving far too slowly, Trump never came back.

Zeke lived out his years on his "estate," enjoying the back porch and pool, taking care of the grounds, returning to religion by joining the Methodist church across the street, and making plans for his gravesite.

On a slope looking east where he would be able to rise to glory with the coming return, he was buried. His wife joined him soon after and there they rest, to rise some morning as the sun bathes their graves.

Throughout his life, Zeke had been firm to those fundamental ideals that made America what it would become during the greatest generations. And he witnessed it all. Firmly a Democrat from those days when he was for the first time fed enough, he was helped with government jobs for many years. Entering private life with Western Union, he literally grew up and prospered with America, coming from extreme poverty to a life of comfort.

THAD WASHINGTON

For blacks in the South the economic outlook was far worse than anything Zeke faced. There was always hunger, even starvation.

There was fear. Do not "git uppity." News of lynchings[13] spread quickly to the Green shacks, named for the old slave owner. Thad's mother knew one thing; she did not want her son in trouble, not in any way. And Thad knew it, too.

The little community lived in the old slave shacks only two miles east of the capitol building in Austin. The life the community eked out was what was grown nearby and what friends thirty miles west could grow on small tracts by the Guadulupe River and bring to town on a mule-drawn cart. The blacks also had "the holidays" when women in the white churches would give leftovers. Life was hard, even vicious, but they survived.

There were no jobs except what the slaves had done before 1865. Servant jobs, dirty work cleaning up, hard work in the fields with pay at a dollar a day on a good day. The money went back to the black community, centered on the church building. Thad could not run away to a better life. He was not like the "blue-eyed devils," the white boys.

Thad Washington grew up in that state of poverty, one step above starvation that was helped only by all blacks contributing to the group.

Obedient to whites, Thad worked at home or in the Green community. Those were his limits, strictly enforced by his mother. She worked for the "white folks" doing laundry or chicken "plucking" or whatever else she could find. He was kept busy learning to write with a pencil on scraps of paper. He could practice by tracing letters on old ads. His "learning" was at the school in the one-roomed church, barely more than benches on a bare floor.

When Thad turned twenty, the Green shacks were purchased by an oilman lawyer who bought the land there at Sixth and Dancy in East Austin. A new "big house" was built on the edge of the "green" where Thad's mother was "hired on" to do housekeeping. He would help there at the "mansion."

The kindly wife of the old man had a ready affection for the black woman and her son, in part because she had grown up on a farm in deep west Texas where women were but one step above slaves. Sons were born to work the fields; daughters had to take care of the housework.

Having made the way to the University of Texas where Dania had completed two years, she met the old man and they married to keep her child honest. Eddie was a beautiful child but was felled by "the fever" when he was only five, leaving him crippled, hardly able to control his bodily functions and given to outbursts of anger, especially toward little girls.

One hot, dry afternoon when the whites at the big house were resting, Eddie came out and assaulted the daughter of Dania's brother. Thad had been working nearby and he stepped right in, gently restraining Eddie while convincing him to let the little girl down. From then on, Eddie and Thad were the best of friends.

Dania saw that her son finally had a friend and she hired Thad to be the caretaker. The job was not hard. Eddie was confined and slept most of the time. As he grew older, his condition worsened and Thad did the dirty work, talking to him, entertaining him, watching as Dania worked with him and, during the rest of the day and night, maintaining the big house and grounds.

The old man died when "the fever" hit again and Dania took over a sizable fortune. To isolate Eddie from the town and the fact her son was crippled and his only friend was a black, she bought a sixty-acre tract in the far south of Austin and built a community to care for the handicapped. Thad became the caretaker where he lived in a three-room house next to the home Dania built for Eddie. There Thad started his family and kept them safe.

Dania kept the fighting roosters her husband had purchased, and Thad became the keeper of the "red terrors." The cock fights in the seven-county "war zone" meant Thad could travel by pickup outside the county. He was getting to know the world.

Eddie died an early death, and Thad stayed on, now the sole confidant for Dania. When she died, the sixty acres became Thad's property. Dania favored him over her brothers and sisters. She knew how much Thad had done for the only child she ever had, and how much he had done for her.

Thad lived into the 1970s and when he passed on, his son Edward was given the property. After all, Thad had made certain his first-born had an education. Edward set to work developing the property as a subdivision.

Thad was part of that greatest generation that did the job that had to be done and that took care of business as well as possible. He found a true friend in Dania and could give his family a good home. He left his son a fortune. Severely limited by prejudice and poverty, Thad survived and prospered in his own way.

Thad rests in the still-hidden cemetery in the Green community. Near a creek on a gentle slope facing the rising sun, Thad waits for the "jubilee day," just like Zeke waits.

MILLIE DIETRICH

Women fared no better during those awful years following the stock market crash. Mildred Dietrich, known as Millie, had married a JC Penney manager and enjoyed the good years of the 1920s. For many, those years meant a comfortable living.[14] The retail company, an example for the later Wal-Mart, paid well. Millie's husband opened new stores in small towns across America, and her family was dedicated to American business—family, education, Christian values and more.

Marrying in Indiana and moving across many states as her husband set up stores, she reared a family from Tucson to Atlanta. There she met Margaret Mitchell while *Gone with the Wind* was still in the typewriter. The name Millie gave her first child made its way into the manuscript and then the book and movie.

The market crash wiped out the family income and the impact on her husband left Millie no alternative. She divorced and left.

Moving to Los Angeles, she was hired by a private school as a math teacher. With the help of her sister Ledora, she was able to survive that shock for any divorced woman on her own in a strange city.

Mildred proved to be an excellent teacher and a very good storyteller. After all, her family had a long history in newspapers. Her sister had married the director for the port of Los Angeles and the city was booming. During the war years, the sisters prospered. After the war, they thoroughly enjoyed the fascinating life in Los Angeles.

Millie was finally able to afford her own car, affectionately named Grundoon for the character in Pogo, her favorite comic and editorial strip. In the 1950s in southern California, even women loved their cars.

Wit and wisdom combined in Millie's always optimistic outlook on life, and there were times when the breakfast crowd at her home were laughing so hard they could not stop. In those days she was a Johnny Carson to start the day.

Millie's youngest child, a son who graduated from the very prestigious Cal Tech, was employed at the famous "Skonk Works" designing advanced facilities for aerospace.[15] Rennie made the first moon-base plans.[16]

Survival had seemed impossible when she divorced. By hard work and a prospering economy, she made it and did well, always with a smile and with those warm eyes that always seemed to have a tear, always enchanting to everyone.

Millie never remarried and lived out her life in Bellflower. In her final years she moved to a retirement home in Santa Barbara where she stayed with her beloved sister. There she died and was cremated, with her ashes distributed over the Pacific. She too had come home in her own way and on her own terms.

Millie grew up with tragedy, rededicated her life to family, and was able to see the results, of a son reaching into outer space, to go where no man had gone before.

BELLE UNDERWOOD

Belle Underwood also exercised her rights when there were supposedly no rights for women. She would take a different path from Millie, going where some believed no woman could go. Belle went into business. She was a stunning success.

Belle was born in Minnesota into a family that would be relatively successful. Her later success was all the more remarkable because she started life with polio. The cure for polio had not yet been discovered by the great medical institutions of America, and Belle was struck down. Only four years old when she contracted the disease, her legs were permanently disabled. The personal tragedy only added to her determination. She rejected the verdict that she would never walk again. With braces required for the rest of her life, she came back stronger than ever.

During the Depression, Belle's family moved to Westchester County just north of New York City. By that time, because her father had good income from Ford as a vice president, she did not encounter the severe economic problems faced by Clay and Zeke or by Thad and Millie.

As a teenager in the later years of the Depression, the family business took her to Virginia where she became, literally, the belle of the ball, pursued by men in training to serve their country, and by many other men as well. She describes the time as "those fast days," saying that, in today's terms, she would have been "grounded."

When war was declared, she did not hesitate. She saw the need to help her country and went to work in the war industries. As we turned the tide in Europe and the Pacific, life improved for her and, when the war ended, she met and married a British royal, one of those among the "be-knighted." Actually, her husband was even more; he was the "peerage." His family had an estate very near Westminster Castle, a location that had resulted in its utter destruction during the blitz.

Following the marriage, Belle started an idyllic life in the Virgin Islands. When the marriage failed after a few years, she worked at a nightclub on St. Thomas, enjoying the casino life with a girl friend. She also learned the ins and outs of business. The two women met the piano players there and struck up lasting friendships. What we now call "networking" was standard procedure in those days.

As Belle describes her situation, she and her friends were finally "bored" with life on the islands. They returned to New York where the unsinkable woman married her piano player and took a job. She also landed modeling jobs back when beauty was everything. Belle was a remarkable woman; even with braces she made the grade in the cut-throat world of New York City fashion.

Belle had learned business and was determined to start her own company, to pursue the apex of the American dream—be your own boss. Do all those steps business required—get some money, set up an office, get customers, provide excellent service, meet the payroll and all the rest. Starting a business is seldom a dream, too often a nightmare.

Opening in 1955, she soon had an answering service that was strictly limited to celebrities, to those people in the limelight who demanded utmost privacy. She found her niche. She provided the necessary assurances of absolute confidentiality, and, by meeting people and seeking their business—"sell, sell, sell" in today's terms—she prospered.

Shortly after hanging out her shingle and opening the doors, the Broadway play "The Bells Are Ringing" went into development.[17] Judy Holliday learned how to work at the answering service under Belle's skillful eye. "Very good operator," Belle would later say. "Could have given her a regular job."

The press picked up the story. Soon the word was out all "about the town" that "Belle knows." Belle smiles, adding, "A bit of luck helps every opportunity, especially with Judy Holliday."

Going into business in Manhattan is not just opening the doors and providing excellent service. You have to deal with suppliers and other vendors in a city as corrupt as Clay had discovered. Existing suppliers already have many clients and pay little attention to newcomers, especially at the "suggestion" of their paying clientele. The phone company was notorious for being hard-headed. If you had a rush job, the phone representatives would delay even more. Belle had to be tough, and she was. She got her vendors in line and kept them there.

Belles Celebrity Service was not for just anyone. She had her clients and knew who she wanted to serve. Sticking with her niche, she prospered. Because she provided excellent service and kept the faith—the secrets—she would grow with that very best of advertising, word of mouth. She was also tough enough to tell her clients how to behave. She did not tolerate fools.

In a city that Clay had the good sense to leave, Belle was tough enough to stay and prosper.

The business was always demanding. Ten "telephone boards" with calls in-coming at any and all hours, with messages to be taken on paper pads and placed in the pigeon-holed cabinets above the boards. Connections could be made with other phone lines at other boards in front of the bank of operators. The work was often fast and furious. Twenty-four hours a day, seven days a week—today's "24/7"—the calls were answered and relayed.

The demands of celebrities are well-known and Belle knew and served them all. Early morning calls were required. Do not miss a wakeup call. Help at a very personal level was needed at all hours and particularly on weekends or at times too late for the employees. One famous playwright even called for a "wee loan." He was just arrived from London and at the airport in those pre-ATM days, he was without cash. A cab and some weekend money were just absolutely essential. Belle sent Rob, her piano player husband, to pick up Noel Coward and advance the needed funds.

Belle knew, as so many forget, that celebrities may have unusual lives but they still have the everyday problems of the rest of us. Warren Beatty needs a call back from sister Shirley MacLaine, Ali McGraw is looking for Candy Bergen (she leaves the party invitation with Belle), and Paul Newman has a new project for Robert Redford. All hot information that the press would love, and what today's ever-present paparazzi would buy.

Problems included fights between couples, often ending in divorce. Great care and caution were required. Belle smiles as she remembers some of those splits because both would remain with her, giving her two new clients for one. Problems extended to children who, Belle says, should have been grounded. All news the media would love but never heard.

To assure privacy, Belle did not advertise. In business advertising is essential. Without it, most fail. Except for word of mouth and personal contact (sell, sell, sell), Belle maintained the confidentiality her clients had to have. The main number for Belles Celebrity Service was for many years unlisted. Prospective clients were not welcome without a recommendation. Some just did not make it to the telephone boards.

Belle was tough and smart with her suppliers and employees as well as her clients. Even clients were kicked off her service.

Problems for celebrities never ended. Extra keys were kept at the office for absent-minded clients. Her central location was a place for deliveries to be made should the client be away from home. She took care of Imogene Coca's dog when the walkers were not available or did not show. She gave Al Pacino "evacuation" plans. Seems he had been pursued home by three female admirers who insisted on "hanging out" around his apartment. What was the best escape route?

The secrecy was challenged by Burt Reynolds, who accused Belle of giving out his phone number. When the media broke the story, he at first denied ever using the service. A ledger record of his payments for the phone ended that false accusation.

A radio show host lost his job and left town, owing Belle money. When he returned with a new call-in show, one call from Belle demanding—on the air—that he pay up resulted in her being cut off. He was one of the few men to hang up on her. The check arrived the next day.

A true measure of Belle's character was her very high-profile client, Swifty Lazar, the man in New York City who could do anything, like get a play produced.[18] Swifty opened offices in Los Angeles where he became the one man who could approve a movie or cast a star or get a beginner a role. He called Belle, saying he had to have some inside information on another client. Belle refused the $20,000. Swifty persisted until she told "motor-mouth" as he was known, "Do you want me to tell what I know about you?" He promptly hung up on her, either mad because she would not do his bidding or humbled because he knew she was right. He stayed with her.

Today, Belle loves to tell how she woke Robert Redford every morning, whispering in his ear, "Time to get up, darling." The same wakeups would be placed to Al Pacino, Liza Minelli, and Candice Bergen just to name a few.

Even now, Belle is always energized, "feisty" as Rob describes her. She established and led a business that played a central role in the entertainment world of New York City, the nation and the globe. Celebrities were her calling and she did the job the American way—with excellent service. The work was always demanding, she says with a tinge of regret, because she too often had to ignore her twin boys to maintain the service required. Still and all, there was devoted attention for her family, with the extra benefits of a suburban home in upstate New York, annual ocean cruises, many other trips abroad and the income needed to enjoy the good life.

Retired after more than fifty years in the middle of music, drama and comedy, she is being courted for documentaries and books on her life and the lives of her clients. They still want the story Swifty Lazar wanted, and the many more stories she knows and does not tell.

Surrounded by the client records and the hundreds of photos of her celebrities, all endearingly signed, she struggles to recover from post-polio syndrome, a weakness that results in great pain.

Despite the problems, Belle is having more fun than ever. Her book is in the works, *Belle Knows and Belle Tells* with, of course, the permission of her ever-loving clients.[19]

Contrary to many assumptions, this woman and many more women were deeply involved in the greatest generations. Women have always played their vital roles in America, motherhood and homemaker included, and that role has been constantly and relentlessly expanding.

It is unjust to belittle those many roles our parents had as part of the greatest generation, of the wisdom of our fathers and mothers.

A Second Look Back

These members of the greatest generations of 1929 through 1945 did not give up and change their ways after 1945. They did not all of a sudden become less than "great." The end of the war was not the end of their roles in America. They continued on, keeping their values and making America the world leader of today.

A couple of footnotes.

The "greatest generation" was not limited to the years 1929

through 1945. Strictly speaking, that period of seventeen years would be only one generation. The reality is that the greatest generation included their parents and then they, as parents, continued their ideals and values and passed that culture to their children.[20]

The greatest generation included all Americans in several generations from 1929 through 1945, when greatness was required. That greatness continued after 1945. A "generation" is but a "stick" or "cohort" or "data set" in statistics. Any survey must extend through at least a lifetime of seventy-five years, necessarily including several generations.

The "greatest generations" included many stories, those of Clay and Belle, of Millie and Thad, and of Zeke. They were adults during the Depression and the war years. They kept their values in those highly visible, terribly trying years and then participated in far more significant success stories in the decades that followed. The successes from 1945 through 2000 would be far less visible but far more dangerous and profound.

Any limitation on what they and their generational partners did is not only short-sighted; it is an insult to the preceding generations of Americans and to those who followed.

Before taking a look at the younger generations, the children after 1945, take a critical look at what remained undone. Economic access to the American business machine was limited. Civil rights were too often viciously denied even during a time when they were being peacefully championed. Generally accepted standards for wages, food, medicine and more were only beginning to include effective legal protections. Compared to what we knew in 1945, incredible advances in technology were still awaiting fulfillment. Compared to what we would learn in the post-1945 era, medicine was still in the dark ages. The great academic and teaching institutions of America would begin keeping up with America and taking the lead.

Most important, peace was not won in 1945. The war that

ended in 1918 did not end all wars. Similarly, the war ending in 1945 was not the end of war. Much was still to be done to prevent Armageddon.

The greatest generation, from 1929 to 1945, was not perfect.

The task for the remarkable progress from 1945 through 2000 remained with that generation and with their succeeding generations.

The Greatest Generations

What the extended greatest generations would accomplish was completed without the huge publicity given the Depression, of its soup lines and suicides. Similarly, the press covered the world war with huge headlines. Those events met the criteria for comforting the afflicted. They missed the virtually miraculous success of the extended generations.

The far more significant events of the following five decades were virtually unnoticed.[21] Only problems were covered. The motto for the media became, "If it bleeds, it leads." These limitations to understanding were a major failure of our cold war victories and the peace and progress of *Pax Americana*.

CURT SANDERSON

Curtis Sanderson grew up in the great Northwest, born in Washington State on the eastern side. Curt had a brother, a non-identical twin who would become a rock band player in high school and beyond. Curt proved to be the more serious of the two.

He attended Sacagawea High School and graduated, well aware of the historic attention Native Americans and women deserved. From there service in the Army took him to Vietnam where he was responsible for something he did not publicize in his later years, serving as a flamethrower for a short time, responsible for killing the enemy in a gruesome way. "Better than dead buddies," he would grimly observe.

Curt also went to a small island in the middle of the Pacific where he inventoried our defensive supplies of chemical weapons and began the process of eliminating them.[22] Long rows of bunkers housed the American arsenal there. As the weapons aged and the cold war cooled down, the time arrived for their destruction. Never a safe job, Curt took care of gradually depleting the nation's ability to counter in kind, biological or chemical.

Following his military service, he completed a degree in civil engineering and went to work building America's infrastructure. An interesting event intervened. After college, while awaiting an engineering job, he managed apartments in Seattle. One location included Bill Gates and Paul Allen as tenants. Curt remembers the two computer globalizers hurrying out early every morning with the skeleton computers in hand, to load them in the car trunk and take off for another install. They were determined in what they were doing, their products worked wonders and within a few months, they moved.

Soon after, Curt also moved, working with engineering and construction companies across America. In Arizona, he met and married Marge and the two traveled to Dallas and to Orange County on assignments, mainly building highways and bridges. Curt expanded into light rail, the sensible way to move large numbers of people from destination to destination in metropolitan areas.

Success in Los Angeles led Curt up the supervisory ladder until he was chief for the light rail system in Houston. A political hot potato, the project needed "kid glove" treatment. Curt completed the first phase between downtown and the medical center with migrant help for his workers. Legal or not, they did the groundwork under his supervisors' watchful eyes, and his success was measured by the results—the project came in ahead of schedule and under budget.

The trains were a sight to behold in a crowded downtown

that did not expect trains on rails to be in operation. Accidents happened as the car-riding public went their merry way, racing trains or not even looking for them, and causing wrecks. One fatal collision occurred in the late evening, early morning hours as the saloon crowd made their way home. One happy driver tried to outrace the engine. That did not happen.

The equipment was purchased overseas from Germany. The engines met every test, including the wrenching stop while going full power. Whistles. Brakes. Smoke. And a full stop. There was damage to two units, requiring extensive repairs.

But they stopped.

Curt's duties included the design and construction of several major buildings, that of the "roundhouses," repair shops, passenger platforms and more.

Rails were laid in a continuous ribbon and well grounded to expand and contract without popping loose. Swiss watch accuracy was essential. Careful planning for the pair of parallel rails installed flush with the pavement was successful, passing the acid test, the very hot afternoons.

Now a well-recognized project manager and planner, Curt remains in Houston with support services for his train while the city debates adding more light rail. Approved and then not authorized, local "politicos" were in control of the rail project and mayors were elected or thrown out of office as the ten-year project moved forward and then stopped with the same wrenching results the trains underwent when they were stop-tested.

A city dedicated to cars and petroleum continues to struggle with a roughneck's history and the opposite demands for lowered gasoline consumption and fewer cars. One key answer is light rail. The politicians cannot accept that fact. The Houston system remains a one-route rail.[23] Congestion and pollution get all the worse.

Curt is prepared to continue his plans to make Houston an ever-more modern city, ready for the twenty-first century. Yet the city stays behind in a twentieth century that is gone forever.

A measure, again, of Americans, their resilience and their willingness to put themselves on the line, Curt served his country, grew up in an open society and contributed in important ways to making *Pax Americana*. He was not involved in the decisions to contain the Soviet Union and to enforce that policy in Turkey, Cuba, Korea, Greece and Vietnam and other faraway places. He did not make sure nukes were not fired. Curt understood and supported the American democracy far better than our detractors understand. Debate the issues and decide, for or against light rail or any other issue. He supported the decisions made and remains still another American making and keeping this nation the greatest and most powerful ever.

Always early to bed and early to rise, Curt enjoys beer and playing pool, is an excellent cook, and is a lover of history and motorcycles.

As a working member of the American democratic system, he understands and accepts the necessity to draw those lines in the sand or mountains or jungles. He does his job supporting what is decided to be done.

The decisions made in a democracy demand no more and no less. If the losing side fails to make the case, then accept the result and go forward.

For our greatest generations, Americans did not expect recognition. They completed their job according to our finest traditions, made sure the results matched the plans and called "next" for what was still to be done. In a democracy such as ours, the acceptance of the decisions by the majority through our lawful processes works.

We proved the process time and again during those years following 1945.

Some protest and that, too, is not just accepted and duly considered; dissent is encouraged.

There is one exception. Violence is outside our accepted traditions and results in rejection rather than agreement.

Some Americans fail to understand that democracy and the ballot, whether in the precinct or in Congress, replace violence. If you lose, look at the failure of your advocacy and do a better job the next time you try to lead.

The simple test is whether advocates are able to convince a majority. Barring that, accept the final decisions and abide the law. Live in peace and proceed to "next" on the agenda.

Most Americans bring this dedication to do what they decide. Only a few resort to violence, to terror.[24]

Those who do not maintain the peace have to pay the price. Civil disobedience and violence have their penalties.

TOM ANDREWS

Thomas Andrews was southern-born, to a pecan farmer. The usual tensions existed between father and son. In Tom's case, the big issue was the one that decreed children were to work the farms.

Tom's father was T. J. Andrews and he went by the moniker Jeff.[25] Southern-born, he was the founder of very large, very productive pecan orchards. Successful in his calling, he made "a young fortune" every year the crop was good. Of course, when the pecans were in short supply, usually two out of every three years, the cost of living continued. During the "tight years," Jeff covered family expenses by contract work, construction and similar odd jobs, any odd jobs.

He worked every day of the year but Sunday, the one day committed to his faith.

He was not only close to the land. He was dedicated to family and community, those key American and universal values.

Jeff was also a businessman. Learning the hard way, by some very rough early years, he knew what was needed to make a living. Get up early, meet with your friends and neighbors at the nearby coffeeshop, compare notes on jobs and whatever else was going on, check out the day's prices on the products of the land and get to work. Land the job and get the work done and pick up the pay. Take care of family.

Tom's father brought this same determination to his wife, caring for her into old age. Jeff also knew to teach their children, by example and by talking to them, telling them when necessary. After all, he would shrug and remark, "They gotta learn and who else to teach 'em." He did not rely solely on the county schools. He continued the teaching at home.

Abide the law. Serve your country when needed and support your country against all enemies. Show the flag.

Simple guidelines for a hard life as a farmer and a contractor.

Many a story is told of the easy life on the farm. The old country fence-sitter could always take money from a city slicker. Zeke showed how it was done, just fool 'em. That part was easy. You had to be a smart trader. The old "country lawyer" was the perfect example. He never lost a case.

The apparent "simple life" was far more complex. Rearing his children was the hardest part. "You raise chickens, you rear children," he would say with a whack of his hand and a smile. He would add, "Give 'em their roots and give 'em their wings."

Jeff should know. After finishing high school in Arkansas, he embarked on a new career, away from home. During the Depression, he ran off late one afternoon, headed for the state line to start a new life. He never looked back.

Jeff's son had the same restless feet and that streak of independence. The American tradition remained strong.

Tom left home for college and did well enough to attend medical school and became a doctor of medicine. From there, he served in the Navy and rose to serve as chief medical advisor to the commander of the Pacific Fleet.

The Navy's basic mission was to keep the sea lanes open and safe. An immediate problem was piracy in the Indonesia and Malaysia areas. Navy ships kept the murdering raiders in check.[26]

The military presence also maintained the peace between China and Taiwan. Some suggested the fleet be withdrawn. National policy kept this particular threat of war from happening. The bloodbath did not happen.

Another major strategic interest is to keep the peace in the South China Sea. Several island groups and archipelagos, known collectively as the Nanhai Islands, are there—the Spratlys, Paracels, and Pratas plus the Macclesfield Bank, the Scarborough Shoal and the Reed Tablemount. Huge oil reservoirs are underwater. China disputes ownership of the islands with Vietnam, Taiwan, Malayasia and the Philippines. Indonesia and Brunei also have claims but only to sea areas, not any islands.[27]

The disputes extend back in time many centuries and remain active today.

The Fleet maintains the peace over the vital territory of oil reservoirs and the always important sea lanes. The task is for peace, keeping the competing nations buffered from one another.

With the huge investment America has in its Navy, the peace is kept, not only for Southeast Asia but worldwide. There have been limited wars in Southeast Asia. For many years, no major confrontations have been necessary because of the American presence and show of force.

Tom was with the Navy for the Persian Gulf War. His task—get the hospital ships ready to evacuate and treat injured soldiers. "You know when the war begins," he said before the shooting started. "We attack when I have the advance hospitals ready." Our forces have a long-time military tradition of being as well-supplied, supported and served as possible.

Tom did what he had to do. He would know exactly when the first bombs could fall. When his medical support was ready, he would be the one to say, "Go anytime." He literally called the shots.

Perhaps some in the media knew about this vital preparatory step. Sometimes the reports of when the attack would begin were disclosed by the press.[28] These reporters would be first to deprive our forces of the fundamental combat advantage of surprise. The press seemingly cared little about the harm done to our troops. Get the news first. Do not be scooped by someone else, not even by our own military.

The years in the Navy as director for medical services gave Tom excellent organizational skills. In medical services, the facilities back home had to be ready and Tom improved several veteran hospitals in the United States.

He left the Navy before Iraqi Freedom and settled into a medical career as an advisor, still able to organize, administer and command.

Tom or his father were not "great" in the sense of making history. They did not fight in any great wars and they did not survive any depressions. Instead they did their jobs to prevent wars and to avoid depressions. They just did their jobs, out of sight from the front pages and the history books.

Their successes were far less costly than the expensive Depression and war of 1929 to 1945. The results were of far greater consequence. Their efforts are part of that overall effort that resulted in *Pax Americana.* The United States became the greatest military and economic power in history and presided over the greatest period of commercial progress ever. The peace was hard-fought with emphasis on diplomacy and, only when necessary, limited wars to contain our enemies.

When there are no great headlines, analysts have problems seeing what really happens. They miss the individual level, the micro-level. They also miss relating the local level to the big picture, to the macro-level.

Tom is part of what these "greatest" Americans did. They were active at the individual level. They made us what we are. They got results.

Jeff and Tom. Like father, like son. Both independent. Both "good men" and both good Americans.

SANTO DE GUERRA

Life began for Miguel Jesus in Mexico, in a small fishing community on the Gulf of California. An "indio," he was in that caste system in Mexico where the Spaniards, the heirs of the conquistadores, ran the state for the wealthy, the landed gentry, the "caballeros."

When Jesus turned fourteen, he learned what the system meant. Yelled at by a store owner, he ran. The federales[29] were soon looking for him and he headed east, into the rocky plains that led to the mountains, the rugged uncharted peaks on the horizon, far to the east.

Pistols were fired as he ran, barefooted but knowing how to avoid the rocks. The federales soon gave up. Jesus did not. He kept running, until the darkness was complete and he could reach up, so it seemed, and touch the mountain peaks.

There he rested and then kept moving east, ever higher into the ridges and valleys, knowing what to eat and where to find water, going ever farther from home. He knew not where he was going, but he trusted his instincts, that he would find someone.

He did.

A rugged indio called for him. He told the rescuer he was on the run, a fugitive. Welcomed to the campfire, he was taken into the small group of banditos.

With them, Jesus learned of the quest for the "taza de oro," the cup of gold. The mountains had hidden this treasure trove.

Rainwater streaming down the steep slopes fed into a valley with a cupped formation. The water washed down the gold and the cup trapped it, just like gold miners worked the streams with pans.[30]

When resting from raids on wealthy Mexicans, the banditos would scale the mountains looking for the elusive taza. There Jesus (pronounced Hay-sus) spent his learning years, climbing and crawling the rugged slopes and cliffs, seeking the gold.

When he finally realized the banditos were on a fool's mission, he wanted to leave but was told he could not.

Confinement was not for Jesus. Like so many, he had an independent streak.

One dark night he took off, heading north for the only remaining sanctuary available, the United States. He knew the mountains and valleys and he escaped, heading into the desert, resting by day and walking by night. He knew the ways of the wilderness and soon was deep into the dunes, always heading north, subconsciously looking for still another pot of gold, the one he knew, also subconsciously, los Estados Unidos had for him.

After an unknown time in the desert, he despaired. The sources for water had disappeared; the cacti were too barren in the section of the desert and his sombrero was a wreck, no longer protecting him from the blinding, blistering sun.

Still moving mostly at night, he saw a light in the distance and there he headed, arriving near the shack as dawn was breaking, exhausted, spent, nearer death than life, stumbling, then crawling.

The light went out and the door opened. A gringo stepped forward and, looking around, saw the small body near the fence. He walked over, lifted Jesus to his feet and then half-carried him to the shack.

Saved, Jesus had no idea what was ahead. He spoke only Spanish. His savior could speak the language and tell him he was near Douglas, New Mexico. He was in los Estados Unidas, the United States.

The two men talked for hours that morning, learning about each other and where they were. The cowboy was riding fence for the ranch and lent a hand in the form of good advice, sending Jesus to El Paso to work out a future.

There Jesus, determined never to return to Mexico, worked odd jobs, dirty jobs, for several years, learning English and learning about food service. He had fallen into the career that would later serve him well.

El Paso was no point of prosperity. The work was hard, the town was dry and the weather was either too hot or too cold. Jesus knew he had to move on, and the word among his new network of friends was to head for California, to the land of gold.

Laughing at the description, knowing there were no tazas de oro anywhere, he hitched a ride on a big rig and, in January 1967, he entered California's Imperial Valley. Work was easy, papers were not required, and he made some extra money.

Then he moved on, to San Diego where the climate was always right and the Navy brought prosperity to the citizens. Again he found work in food service, learned to drive a pickup, and was soon driving to Los Angeles to pick up supplies, those special tomatoes his chef wanted.

The lack of papers caught up with him. Again, he escaped, this time into the suburbs across from turnip fields. He moved furtively down the residential streets until a resident gringo stopped him, asking him what he was doing. The fuss started and soon turned loud. "Why are you here?" "Do you have a job?" "Are you running away?" "Where are your papers?"

Jesus had no answers. Fortunately, Millie lived in that small community and she came out to see what was happening. He asked for help. She took him in, promising her neighbors that she knew him and that her sister would help the man.

Two days later, Jesus was working in the Port of Long Beach, in the company mess, making more money than he ever imagined. Equally important, he was able to get papers. Temporary admission was okayed while he completed citizenship classes.

He changed his name, becoming Santo, explaining to friends that he could never live up to his given name, not in America or anywhere else. He added that he could never be even a priest but that, with luck, he might be a saint someday.

Within a year he was a citizen, had married a Latino and had started a family. He spent weekends making his special tomato salsa and selling it. All he needed to do was the one thing he learned from the gringos, open your own business.

A roadside taco shack was the first office and kitchen. He even had a picnic bench outside. The salsa was popular and a gringo offered to set him up with his own restaurant. Santo accepted the deal. Following the rules of business, he worked hard, provided excellent service, saved money and in a year owned his own store.

Business stayed good, the salsa was ever welcome, and Santo "had it made." His family grew to seven sons and two daughters. All helped at the restaurant for a time, and then they helped open other stores, a solid family business that kept everyone comfortable.

Santo had what it took and did what it takes. He was a success. The American system of business works.

Drawn into the migration debates, he shrugs, then gets angry and yells, "What do you do? Take over California and bring it to Mexico? What happens then? When the federales come after you? You flee to Canada?"

His advice to the fugitives: "Bienvenido; ahora trabaje!" Welcome and get to work! Santo provides the jobs, tells his new employees to learn the language, get on the citizenship track and make America your new home.

Santo did not, could not, forget the home he left behind. Four years ago, even though assured he could return, he declined. Instead, to return home he brought his ailing mother to Orange County and, with his two brothers and four sisters joining her, he settled them into a new home.

And he expanded his business even more.

Santo laughs, recalling his dedication to America and, at the same time, decorating his restaurants with Pancho Villa memorabilia. "You gringos," he says. "Love the revolutionaries." Shrugging his shoulders with a knowing smile, he adds, "Son locos." You are crazy.

One other secret. He named his restaurant La Taza. Until now he had not told anyone what it meant to him.

These lives our fellow Americans led are only examples. While much of Santo's story is unique, everyone in that time period after 1945 could tell similar stories, of hearing about Pearl Harbor and Kennedy's assassination, of watching the first steps on the moon, of witnessing the collapse of the Berlin Wall. There were many more vivid events from the greatest generations to now. Their stories are yet to be told.

SETH DONOVAN

Another person recounted his adventures for us but, like so many veterans, he at first did not want to share his stories. The reservations occurred again and again. So many soldiers did not want to or could not tell what happened to them in combat. Seth did not want to share what he knew except in the most confidential of ways.

Straight out of eastern Pennsylvania, from the Dutch (really Deutsch for German) Country of the Lehigh Valley, Seth traveled the world.

First there was his military time in Korea. In 1952 he enlisted with the CIA as a skilled small-arms sharpshooter. He retired in

1968 on pension for meritorious services rendered. During his seventeen years, he had many an adventure and was later in contact with the CIA with an on-again, off-again status as he traveled the world.

"The CIA," he says with a smile. "Those days were, well, interesting." Still carrying secrets not to be disclosed, he is able to detail what is public, but not generally known, about several key men with "the Company."[31]

Colonel Al Heine, now deceased, was in charge of the "PB" for the Panama Paramilitary Battalion, keeping an eye on that strategic nation and our Panama Canal.

Another was William "Rip" Robertson, "among the best," says Seth. Part Cherokee, Rip played football for a small college before signing up with the Marines for the duration of the Second War. He then went into Japan and later Korea where he headed another paramilitary battalion. After that stint he was with Heine's "PB" in Panama.

Rip's tours of duty included Nicaragua where he had good relations with Samoza and obtained gold concessions in the "bluefields" area. After a brief time in Nam, he was back in time for the Bay of Pigs invasion, and he would be the only CIA advisor to go ashore. After that failed adventure Rip returned to the Far East and then back to Nam for his last tour. He died at the Houston airport of a heart attack, ending what Seth described as one of the most diversified and interesting careers in service to America.

Seth worked closely with and particularly admired Tony Procearia, now deceased. Tony joined the Marines at an early age and was active in the Second War and then Korea. He craved action and went to Nam and then to Laos where he met and married. After working with the CIA, Tony retired to California with his family.

Studs Sterbel was another dedicated American who served as

a sharpshooter with the Marines. He was later an advisor for Colt, the weapons manufacturer. He was completely and unequivocally dedicated to America but out of that dedication to our ideals, he became very disillusioned. After leaving the agency, he produced *Renaissance Man* as his commentary on the failures of our surveillance activities abroad. He was particularly critical of our activities in Cuba and Guatemala. Leaving the agency, Studs went to Mexico where he had a small business and then went to Chile to open an artists' colony while Allende was in power.

"One smart man," Seth says of Sterbel, "and a true American."

During his sixteen-year stint, Seth served as a deputy under John Sherwood, a middle level officer in Berlin. John would later write *Legacy of Ashes,* a very critical appraisal of the CIA. In 2005, John committed suicide at his retirement home in South America.

Seth's career, much yet to be disclosed, covered some of the most critical assignments for the CIA. The many areas he visited provided the foundations for his later globalization work.

One day, soon after leaving the agency Seth was in Argentina for only a short visit when he was called by a friend. "Get to DC," he was told. There Seth was introduced to the CEO for a textile company in Pennsylvania with an unusual complaint. "Our people living near the plant are too hide-bound to work abroad." Determined to outsource, the CEO named Seth vice president for international operations. The two traveled to South Africa as well as much of Latin America—Argentina, Colombia, Ecuador and Mexico—where they outsourced America, taking textiles and the company equipment all over the world.

This outsourcing lasted six years before the company was bought out. The new owners closed their last American textile plant.

Seth had one more stint abroad, this time to Saudi Arabia to assist in contract negotiations with an overseas staffing company.

With that adventure, Seth's travels ended. Retiring from international jobs, he became a banker back home, thoroughly knowledgeable about business and how to outsource. He also had a special appreciation for the still untold and unknown dangers in world commerce.

In short, Seth's foundations in the CIA took him around the world, guaranteed him those contacts needed to land good jobs, and introduced him to the dark side of the globalization underway in the sixties and seventies, that same globalization occurring now with far greater frequency.

FRED-RICK WORTH

Frederick Douglas grew up in southern California and moved with his parents to Baltimore to inherit a business there.[32] A funeral home was one of the few ownerships available to blacks in the 1950s. "After all," his father remarked, "who else gonna plant us?"

There Fred changed his name to Rick in the turbulent racial equations of the era. As Rick, he was vaguely aware of the Supreme Court requiring an end to segregated schools, not from the opinion but from the scenes of little black children escorted by soldiers in battle fatigues through crowds of screaming whites to the public schools.

In the spirit of cooperation and persuasion promoted by the NAACP, he decided he wanted to be in law enforcement, to be on the side of the whites enforcing rights for black children. As he advanced in school, his priorities changed. The victories for blacks in the South were coming from the courts and he understood what the judges were saying. He wanted to be a lawyer.

He refrained from travel to the South, "probably," he says on looking back, "because I was afraid." Instead, he worked in his neighborhood and church to assist freedom riders and to get candidates to run and voters to register. He wanted elections to win power for blacks, the peaceful way in a democracy.

He proved both committed and vocal about the tasks and was selected to run for city delegate in a nearby suburb. Maryland was still a southern state that had not seceded. In the 1960s, there was still a racist clique and it was very vocal and very strong. Rick had been warned; the election was vicious. When Rick was elected, the courts intervened, denying him his position for the two-year term. By the time final approval came around, Rick was out of office. He was still paid for the term in office, for the service he did not serve.

In the meantime, his ambitions had advanced.

The church and political leaders had taken notice of his even-handedness, and they made him a prime candidate for the training and attention needed for him to advance their very peaceful cause, that of getting blacks elected. Just as some young blacks trained hard to be football and basketball players, others were encouraged to advance, to get professional degrees. Supported from early on, Rick went to Law School where he completed the degree and obtained his license.

Now a certified attorney, he was selected for the district attorney's office. There he followed the usual career of handling drug cases, advancing fraud investigations and then getting a murder case. The defendant was black but Rick pulled no punches. He won a jury verdict of guilty. And he continued to win the trust of the white community.

After three years Rick left the district attorney's office to enter private practice in a white law firm. He was the only black and was never comfortable. The partners never could take him into their deepest confidences. Rick was ready to move on when one partner asked if he was interested in a civil justice assignment. He was. A few months later, he was selected to a district judgeship, to run unopposed and to become the first black district judge in the county.

As "your honor," he practices the same even-handed justice

for everyone. As he says, "I treat everyone equally bad." Of the blacks who have successfully navigated the racist traps in America, the honorable Judge Worth took a path to success that more and more navigate. In doing so, he is a vital part of our legal traditions.

With his family of four, he still lives in the Baltimore suburb where he started. He knows racism and candidly admits part of his feelings are internal to him. He understands his legacy only too well and for it he participated in the million-man march. But he pushes on and is eyed for every higher positions in the judiciary.

Now in line for a federal judgeship, his long-term goal remains the Supreme Court.

JON RODGERS

Jonathan Rodgers was born into a farming family in Colorado with parents who were not only farmers but teachers dedicated to education. If ever a man stood for the faith of his parents in America Bubba as he was called in childhood was that person.

Among the stories from members of the greatest generations, Jon's is particularly compelling for the compassion he brought to the values Americans cherish. Jon has the faith of his father and his mother. Most of us have that same faith, often with unmentioned but special thanks to our mothers.

Born in a small town near cotton fields that grew no taller than shrubs, Bubba lived in the hard scrabble life of the flat, dry plains of eastern Colorado. "You could drive forever and never see a soul," Jon would say. "That old ribbon of asphalt stretched to the horizon, straight as an arrow and," he added, "no speed limit."

The first born of Wayne and Marcia, Bubba had the bedrock values of Americans taught him by parental example and at church. His father was a solid representative of the men in those days, hard-pressed to make the money they knew their family needed but unable to find good-paying work when school was out. The college degree was just not enough. The cotton crop for the year had to be good, or else.

Wayne was hard working, with big, leathered hands and a permanent tan. He also had excellent common sense, able to distinguish good from bad. He was determined to do his best. At times, the task appeared too difficult to undertake or to complete. Binge drinking would be a weekend escape.

His wife was from a Kansas family with the qualities we expect today from "Dorothy-land." The one quality she had above all others, Bubba fondly and emphatically remembers, was understanding and forgiveness.[33] Never one to say a bad word about anyone, she not only forgave her husband but also, Bubba was proud to say, "Just about everybody else." She literally radiated this spirit of love.

Jon's parents were excellent students, both decided on teaching as a career and both later taught in the public schools. For Wayne the teaching had to be part-time, as a substitute. He could teach after working the fields, handling construction jobs and finding odd jobs wherever possible. Both mother and father had hard-working careers to care for their family and see them through college. They knew what Jeff knew. "Give them their roots and give them their wings."

In high school, the prevailing attitudes for Jon were "old fashioned." Whenever divorce hit a family, the children were often belittled. In those pre-pill days, abortion was unheard of, something that happened in those strange places in America like Hollywood and New York City. Any pregnant classmate had to leave town for one of several "homes for girls" to have a baby and leave it for adoption. These new "political" issues and many more were so foreign to his way of life that they were meaningless and irrelevant; they were just ignored.

When Bubba went away to the University of Colorado, his professors tried to teach him about the political ineptitude of the greatest generation. Back home between semesters, he told his father what he had been taught.

Wayne quickly spoke up. "Is that what they're teaching over there?" Bubba nodded a yes. The father's advice was simple, "Quit! Just leave." Bubba persisted and earned a degree while encountering the new issues, the new problems and the new criticisms of America after 1945, attacks that worsened as each of his college years closed.

Bubba also learned a few "new things" on his own. While on a beach trip in 1957, he and his friends found what appeared to be marijuana in a bottle. They turned it over to the police but heard nothing further. They never knew for certain what they had found.

When Vietnam turned hot and the draft beckoned, the former Bubba—now Jon—enlisted and was soon on Navy ships carrying supplies from the United States to the battlefronts.

Jon saw no need to question the fundamental lessons from his father and mother. Their examples were guidelines for the life he led. Unlike too many children, he had solid values for life. He married his childhood sweetheart, and the new family followed those values his parents taught him. He says, "We are doing just fine, thank you."

For Jon, charity is an important value. He travels to Costa Rica regularly to support his church's mission there, to lend support to building hospitals, installing and maintaining radio and telephone systems and providing support for the impoverished citizens. A faith-based life is the "foundation for a very rewarding life," he says, "for yourself and for all those others in need."

One other observation. Wayne and many did not take the SATs. There was no such thing when they left for college. The current "meritocracy" of too many colleges is not for Wayne or

Jon. The kids scoring high on the SATs and believing they should run the country without debate, disallowing dissent and avoiding fair and balanced discussion, were dismissed with a shrug. In his view those living in their "ivory towers" are the naïve ones.

Jon remains faithful to America, accepting the democracy provided even though many policy decisions are not to his liking. There is no violence associated with his objections. In so doing, he presents a model of the highest values of our greatest generations.

His family and their lives are the heart in our heartland.

BILL AND MARIA YBARRA

America's southern borders have always been ambiguous, full of holes, much more a sieve than a wall. After all, we have been and are at peace. Our major neighbor, Mexico, was as warily friendly to us as we were to them. Friends respecting each other's boundaries, avoiding forts or war.

Immigrants who today are "illegals" were openly encouraged in the 1940s and 1950s and even before, to come on in, to work the fields, dig the mines and take care of households. The local citizens were delighted to have the visitors. "Legal" was not an issue. Just ask Santo.

The borders let far more pass through than were restrained. Cross-boundary travel was easy, particularly away from the more populated areas. In the deserts that long, invisible border was not seen as Santo showed. Peaceful transit back and forth was unquestioned. The locals on each side of the imaginary line or river paid their taxes to their governments but traded freely, as needed.

A similar tranquility, a shrug of the shoulders, reached across the seas separating us from Cuba, Haiti, and the other island areas. We were at peace. Coast guards, local police and even military bases were nearby, ready as needed for duty, usually for disaster and relief work. Little attention was given to a defense from our southern neighbors or to enforcement of any restrictions.

One person who often crossed the borders was from Cottonwood, Arizona, a hamlet next to Smelter City and about two hours south of the Grand Canyon. Guillermo, known as Bill, was born into a rugged area that was slow to produce a decent living. There were no competing lifestyles. He grew up learning what his family and neighbors could show him. Life was hard.

Bill wanted to move up and he did, graduating from Arizona State with a degree in business followed by his MBA. He decided to take care of his military obligations. Water was never present in abundance in or near his hometown or state so he enlisted in the Navy, "to feel some moisture," he said. After basic training, he was assigned to the aircraft carrier USS *Princeton* as a communications/cryptography officer. He was later assigned to Guantanamo as an instructor with the Fleet Training Group. He left the military in December 1960, heading for New York City and then private business.

Little did he know that his bride to be was leaving Havana that same month.

Bill's career would take him into the Central American countries and he would later travel the world, an interest reflecting his broad experiences and his global outlook on life. The early travels started with Costa Rica, Guatemala, and Honduras, and included time in San Francisco and New Orleans, all with United Fruit.

In 1970 in New Orleans Bill met Maria. She had fled Havana as Castro was entering the city, about the time Bill was leaving Gitmo. She left with few belongings, knowing the dictator would soon be replaced, her family properties would be returned, and she could safely resume her life. Her mother and father carried her to New York City but she would stay only a few months. Moving to New Orleans, she became a secretary and later met and married Bill.

The couple traveled wherever United Fruit took them. Their longest stay was in Honduras for a thirteen-year assignment.

During those travels two children were born. The son would become a doctor and marry a nurse, continuing a family tradition reaching back many years. A daughter was born who grew up to become a nurse, marrying a doctor. The two children are still in New Orleans with their families.

The medical tradition is from Maria's family. Her great-grandfather was from Scotland and was a member of the British contingent fighting alongside Simon Bolivár for the liberation of Venezuela. After the successful liberations and the end of the fighting, Edward passed his medical boards in Trinidad. Also educated in Germany and France, he was fluent in the languages of the four areas where he had learned and practiced medicine.[34]

Edward's son was born in Cuba and educated in Scotland, France and Philadelphia where he earned his medical degree. Despite many offers, he returned to Cuba, to practice in Matanzas and then Havana.

The good doctor would twice make recommendations regarding epidemics. When Havana was hit by cholera, he warned about the drinking water. Tragically, he was ignored. Soon after, he studied yellow fever and its incidences. He concluded mosquitoes spread the disease. This time, his efforts led to a successful sanitation program in Havana. Walter Reed proved the theory was correct.[35]

Cuba would later name a park for the doctor, across from his home in Havana. His statue still stands in the park but his home across the street was confiscated by Castro. With renewal of diplomatic relations, Maria may yet recover her ancestral home.[36]

During the Castro years Bill and Maria traveled throughout Central America. Bill served in key financial and purchasing posts with United Fruit and also made important bridges between the local communities and the United States. Business relations were excellent and Bill can say that there was no corruption in the work he supervised. He adds, however, that corruption was a constant problem in Latin America and that it is a serious burden on business with no easy way to publicize or disclose the conspiracies.

Bill adds that in Nicaragua the United States both supported Samoza and helped Ortega overthrow the dictator. A colleague was implicated in the arms trade with the Contras in Nicaragua, all part of the successful effort by the United States to contain communism. Bill's friend paid a steep price for his small part in national policy.

For Bill, a highly successful career led to continuing advancements and a final assignment to set up the purchasing office in Gulfport, Mississippi. The port is the major point of entry into the United States for most bananas sold here.

Now retired, Bill and Maria continue a gracious life of helping others and visiting the world. He is typically the life of the party and stays up-to-date and very committed, not only with "current affairs" but with everything. He even provides a web service for friends while trading stocks and bonds for family.

Bill is globalized.

Several years ago he went by sailboat to Havana, to relive memories and to try to answer his curiosities. The entry was a bureaucratic nightmare. Almost twenty agencies had to be visited for approval. Each required a payment, in cash, dollars required. The land and people were dismal but pleasant. He felt he had traveled back in time, to the same country he left in 1960.

The most dramatic and emotionally draining part of the trip was on the way home. They encountered a flooded escape boat, little more than inner tubes tied together, with five Cubans desperately clinging to the collapsing "boat." Looking for freedom and a better life, the refugees were in terrible shape, nearer death than life. Rescued, the worst part was yet to come. Bill and his companions had to contact the Coast Guard and send the four men and a woman back to the prison that is Cuba.

The Ybarras are committed to family, to friends and to their community in the finest traditions of the greatest generations. As a family between Cuba and America, they are truly world citizens; at the same time they are globalizing citizens.

SETTIMIO SAM VALORI

When Abraham Lincoln was getting started in business, he took off with some friends down the Mississippi to see the heart of the United States and to make some money. The trip was a success. He returned with a better understanding of America and especially the one and only New Orleans. He also made a good profit.[37]

Almost one hundred years later Sam Valori made the same trip, canoeing with two friends down the Ohio and Mississippi Rivers to New Orleans.

Among great Americans and globalization, Sam stands out for his classic heritage into America and for his unique service as a point man in those critical years of cold war, technological innovation and unprecedented economic progress. During his career in those turbulent years of progress, Sam remained a dedicated citizen, promoting American values when they were assaulted to the core and then seeing those values prevail.

His family is part of that wonderful, very emotional tradition of Ellis Island, of welcoming migrants yearning to be free. In 1920 Sam's mother and grandmother arrived at Ellis from Genoa after a month-long boat trip. They quickly found menial jobs in New York City but wasted no time moving inland where opportunity presented itself.

Sam's maternal grandfather worked in the coal mines near Pittsburgh with many other Italian immigrants. To get by, he also dug graves at the local cemetery. His wife took in boarders in their small home for needed income. Her most important daily chore was to carry buckets of water from the outdoor well to the home. There was no running water.

Sam's father was born on a farm in central Italy. The seventh of twelve children, he left in 1920 for a better life. With a sense of adventure and fifteen dollars in his pocket he came to the United States, landing in Philadelphia. After working in the Navy shipyards, he moved to Kennett Square, Pennsylvania, the mushroom capital of America. There he met Sam's mother in the Italian community where he lived. They married a year later.

While growing mushrooms, the couple had friends with a tavern in Wilmington, Delaware, and when the opportunity to purchase came up, they acted. During the course of a day's trip over and back, they owned their own business.

Working sixteen-hour days, with Sam's father running the tavern and his mother waiting tables and taking care of the paperwork for the business, the couple made good money. His grandmother moved in and cooked for the family in the back of the tavern. Attracted by the aromas, the "bouquets," customers asked for a taste and soon she was serving her pasta to more and more visitors. The little tavern became a restaurant serving her dinner menu.

The family's true entrepreneur spirit and hard work paid off with their very successful neighborhood restaurant. During this time they also learned English and became American citizens.

Sam was born two years before Pearl Harbor and his earliest memories were connected to World War II. The rationing of gasoline, tires, butter and sugar was a problem for their business. He also recalls the blackouts. And he was there the day the authorities removed their short-wave radio; after all, Italy was allied with Germany.

Vivid memories of George Martin's barbershop include listening to the GIs who were lucky enough to return, recounting their experiences. In particular, Sam fondly recalls Joe Schofield who lost an arm in the war but who was always neatly dressed, the coat sleeve for his missing arm tucked into his coat pocket.

Sam began helping in the family business at a young age, running errands and doing odd jobs. When he turned thirteen he found work at the nearby country club as a caddy. Pay was an unheard of five dollars for a round of golf. His next job was at a local supermarket, earning seventy-five cents an hour stocking shelves and working as a checker. Later, he delivered groceries in the store's panel truck.

First he had to learn to drive and this lifetime passion started with his bicycle. Riding and racing soon became a favorite pastime and progressed naturally to his purchasing his first car. For two hundred dollars, he owned his very own 1937 Ford convertible. The next year he purchased his first Triumph motorcycle. Racing became a very serious passion.

He attended one of the finest boys' schools in Wilmington where discipline, loyalty and human values were instilled along with high-level academics.

Then, a few days after graduation in 1957 he did what Lincoln did. With two classmates, Sam put a nineteen-foot fishing dory in the Ohio River at Pittsburgh, Pennsylvania. With only "a Texaco road map, a guitar and lots of canned tuna and Spam," the trio rowed and drifted two thousand miles down the Ohio and Mississippi Rivers for a forty-seven-day "trip of a lifetime."

The three young men followed a strict schedule, with at least one on watch during every twenty-four-hour cycle. Sam knew enough about maritime customs to set up this rotating system of four-hour shifts with one a captain, the second a rower and the third asleep. The team successfully lived off the land and the rivers. They rowed all the time as they went through twenty locks on the calm Ohio River. Once they reached the Mississippi, the rowing "was smoother and easier," but they weathered one hurricane and twenty storms.

There was a difference from Honest Abe's travels. Along the way the press picked up the story. The team received extensive newspaper coverage as well as radio and television appearances.

They did not make a profit but the trip was a success, an adventure for a lifetime, one few ever experience.

After high school, Sam began drag racing at local strips in Pennsylvania and New Jersey and then graduated to national events in Texas and California. His love for racing progressed to Corvettes. He purchased his first in 1971 and has since owned six more.

After graduating from college in Wilmington, he landed a job with the best wages in town, at the Chrysler assembly plant in nearby Newark. He earned $3.13 an hour on the assembly line and was soon promoted. As a transportation administrator, he had a salary that included overtime. He worked twelve-hour days, seven days a week.

The job continued for a year, until he received a letter from "Uncle Sam." Discussing the situation with a friend, they quickly chose to enlist.

Sam was accepted for Army Intelligence. After basic training and covert intelligence collection training Sam was assigned to Fort Bragg, North Carolina, with the Eighteenth Airborne. His first armed conflict was during the Cuban crisis. We were ready to strike preemptively to block plans to install nuclear missiles there.

The following year Sam served briefly in Korea and then went to Fort Benning, Georgia, and Officer's Candidate School. He graduated as a second lieutenant. He continued his education, receiving a bachelor of science degree from Hampton University in Hampton, Virginia.

Subsequent overseas assignments placed him in command of highly sensitive units in Europe, Korea and Vietnam. He also served on special assignment to the CIA and provided support to joint FBI, Department of State and Secret Service operations. During this time a special mission was to interrogate Cubans turned loose by Castro during the "Mariel escape."[38] One key question was carefully reviewed at the highest levels.

"Did Cuba still have A-bombs?"

The questioning was not conclusive. There is no way to know what is really in enemy territory "until the boots are on the ground." The consensus was that Cuba still had nuclear weapons, violating the subtle agreements from the Cuban missile crisis. Castro was not to be trusted. Diplomatic relations and open trade were not possible.[39]

Close surveillance continued. Dictators are never predictable. Because of that fact, they are always dangerous. After all, they answer to no one.

The United States still respected the unstated agreement not to invade, to leave the "ultimate leader" alone in his misery, able to continue trying to stir up the Americas but unable to see any results, except the misery of his nation.

After twenty years, Sam retired as a major. He had received numerous medals, including the Legion of Merit, a Bronze Star, four Army Commendation Medals and a Joint Service Commendation Medal.

His background in intelligence and surveillance landed consulting work as a private investigator. He handled strike security, insurance fraud, undercover operations, executive protection, fraudulent real estate transactions and asset searches.

Sam's worldwide travels led to an ongoing, insatiable curiosity about other countries, their cultures, foods and customs. "The food was always exotic," he says, "and the customs always unique." Other travels included the outback in Australia, campfires in the "bush" in Zimbabwe, the diverse culture of Pakistan and gauchos in Argentina. More recently, he spent six months in Alaska working and exploring.

Most important, his particular love for Italy means annual visits to family and friends "back home."

Sam's love for racing has never waned since his "foot first found the gas pedal." He has raced Corvettes all over the country, most recently at the Texas Motor Speedway in Fort Worth, only a few miles from home. He has several national awards for autocrossing, drag racing and economy runs over his thirty years attachment to "his" Corvettes.

Sam led a fascinating life on the front lines of our national defenses, had adventures around the world, and embraced a commitment to travel and friendships. As a good American, he is a key example of the globalization that is happening under our leadership for peace, that peace he helped maintain.

Like many Americans, Sam is truly globalized. He knows that when our many friends overseas benefit, we do too.

Our National Commitment

What else?

We won the cold war, saw statism in the form of Soviet socialism fail and collapse, developed technologies that took us to the moon and gave us a whole lot more, produced an economy with huge benefits for more and more people, and maintained world peace and global commerce.

The era was and is truly *Pax Americana*.

The men and women portrayed here and millions more

- assisted the vanquished after the war
- soundly rejected "better Red than dead"
- tolerated the fear of nuclear attack
- adopted broad civil rights
- abolished the draft and maintained peace
- promoted international "giveaways"
- lifted millions out of poverty and
- won the cold war

During these sixty years and more there was this community spirit, this American commitment that we were all in it together and we had to do something together. Perhaps one feature of the

American Dream, the world dream, is that when we have a problem, we solve it.

Our Universal Values

Some rules emerge from this greatest generation and personal values define what these men and women did in their most intimate lives.

One value was that the whole was greater than the parts, that the individual was part of a greater good that was the guiding light for a generation. Some would easily recognize that value as patriotism. Others would agree and carry the value even further and deeper into the fabric of their daily lives, to a Supreme Being.

Respect for family is a basic value, the cornerstone of life in America. The values of a man and woman caring for their children during the growing-up years is a worldwide value, reaching back to community and state and nation and upward. Families have their problems and ignoring your best friend and your children is done only at your peril. Facing them and understanding them is far to be preferred. Families have to know how to get along with one another and most do. If help is needed in this day and age there are far too many "experts" to consult. They will provide that understanding and forgiveness Jon's mom practiced.

A respect for life is another value. We value life far more than most other nations. We do not easily choose to take life. This value extends across the board, to whatever life-threatening or life-ending activity we may face. We love life and place that love high on our values.

We honor and respect property. This key value is founded on the individual; what a person does with his or her own efforts is to be rewarded, protected and promoted.

Respect for family includes respect for women. This basic value is well recognized in the United States and is protected by law in many ways.

With this system of respect for family and community comes the value of being a good neighbor. We have endless examples of being a good neighbor to the family next door, to the people in another part of the city, to those in need in the state and nation, to being a good neighbor to the world.

Do not bear false witness. This is expected from presidents on down to spouses and children. Accurate facts have to be a foundation for our way of life. In most cases we say it the way it is.

We pass laws to reflect our basic values. And we abide the law, or learn not to break the law. Far better to follow the law than to break the law and be put in "the system."

We are not always successful but we keep trying.

Each of the fourteen Americans are witness to our values. The values practiced by these greatest generations were guidelines throughout very challenging times, for them and for America.

The sources for our common values are easy to locate if an open mind is willing to consider foundations of our civilization. Many will recognize biblical sources for what we have done.

More "Great" Stories

The greatest generations have continued these values and seen them sorely tested. At the same time they have struggled to enforce and enlarge them despite vicious attacks by enemies of America.

There are many enemies, external and internal.

What have Americans done to realize these high ambitions and powerful values? To achieve these greatest results?

A great deal.

We need those experiences.

The enormity of the progress in our post-1945 years needs still more attention, and not from just the successes. We invite anyone to submit their stories. Tell us what you did and what happened during these years leading to world peace.

Send the letter or manuscript to us. The addresses are in the Appendix.

Include in your communication any particular comments on the major events of that time from 1945 through 2007. Many memorable days went by.

Send in your stories for our sequel to the greatest generations—1945 through 2008. Key events in the sixty-year period are listed for comments. As an outline you might recall what you were doing during some of these major events:

- the attack on Pearl Harbor
- D-Day at Normandy
- news of the atomic bomb
- the Berlin blockade and the Berlin Wall
- integration in Little Rock schools
- *Sputnik* chirping from outer space
- the Cuban missile crisis
- the Kennedy assassination
- Martin Luther King's "I have a dream" speech
- landing on the moon
- the oil embargo
- Nixon's resignation
- the Iranian hostage crisis
- the fall of the Berlin Wall
- 9-11

This list is only suggestive and covers what the headlines proclaimed. Tell us what was important to you. There are many, many more big events, particularly in the entertainment world of Elvis, the Beatles, *I Love Lucy* and so many more.

These events represent the transformation of our thinking. These were "future shock."[40] With Pearl Harbor we knew we had to go to war after doing our best to stay home. With Kennedy's assassination we knew that our presidency and our nation were not protected. In 1969 we knew we could reach the moon. With the dramatic destruction of the Berlin Wall, we witnessed the collapse of an enemy dedicated to our destruction.

With your comments and suggestions, the sequel to *Made in the USA* will chronicle what happened to so many more of the greatest generations, from 1945 through 2008.[41]

Also, unless the disclosures in this chapter result in personal problems for the fourteen, we will tell all about the very real people behind the assumed names.

Stick with us.

The going just gets better.

There is one special dedication to the greatest generation, those who served and sacrificed for us 1945 through 2007:

Military deaths
99,585
Military injuries
433,306
Total serving
17,689,000

This personal commitment by our military and for America occurred in Korean, Vietnam, Panama, Haiti, Lebanon, Somalia, the two Gulf Wars—on all those fronts where America committed our military power.

Another powerful legacy by our greatest generations.

The result has been, is and will be *Pax Americana*.

TWO

TRILLIONAIRES

Globalization was a roaring success in the 1990s. Great wealth was generated. The Net was the name of the game, and by August 1999, the dot-coms were doing better than ever and the betting began. Bill Gates would soon be the world's first trillionaire.

The gamble did not pay off. The over-inflated, deliberately under-regulated dot-coms dramatically collapsed over a few days in March 2000.[1]

The trillionaire tag is not lost. The United States has a trillionaires club with 129 members.[2] This very informal club includes the top billionaires on the list until a total value for those billionaires reaches one trillion dollars. The final cut leaves Stephen Spielberg and Donald Trump tied with several others at their level in the club.

Bill remained on top of the lists until 2008.[3]

There is, of course, no formal club; however, the members share a very mutual interest, that of the incidences and privileges of wealth.[4]

More important, they represent what is possible in the American economy, in the American way of life.

Most important, these billionaires make globalization work.

The wealth developed by our business leaders also works in the international economy. In most cases, the economies of the free enterprise nations have improved. In the world economy, there is a trillionaires club. The international billionaires list includes seventy in the top one hundred who are not Americans.[5] Again, we have individuals who realized the opportunities provided by a free business system dedicated to rewarding personal achievement and worth. We do not hoard our wealth nor do we go to war over loss of this top status.

The number in the top group has increased dramatically in recent years.[6] In 2007 there were 1,125 billionaires from all nations, representing an increase of 3 percent over the prior year. The diversity is revealing. Europe has twenty-two top billionaires in the first one hundred. Russia has sixteen. All ten global regions have several members. For the first time Africa is included, with two in the top billionaires group.

The United States does not have a lock on admissions to the club. We expect and welcome new members. What is exceptional is that the world is moving up on a parity with us.

We welcome the additions to the trillionaires club.

Globalization works.

More Greatest

In *Pax Americana* we saw what happened to fourteen members of the greatest generations. Those men and women, and millions more similar to them, were and are the foundation for American success. The top producers, our trillionaires club, are remarkably similar to the fourteen. Their growing-up years included many of the same experiences—school leadership, Scouts, military service, college, marriage and children plus direct experience with business as an owner.

Personal values between the wealthiest and the rest of us are remarkably alike.

Based on and measured by the economy, the trillionaires club represents the leading members of the greatest generations.

BILL GATES

One person stands head and shoulders above the rest. The man most responsible for modern globalization is Bill Gates. He is the "great globalizer" and he did it the American Way with hard work, dedication to the job, innovative thinking, fast implementation, and solid business ethics.[7] Recall that Curt witnessed Bill's hard work in the beginning. Gates and his partner carried computer frames or skeletons from an apartment to the trunk of their car, building and selling computer programs and desktops to interested companies.

Admittedly, few will lament the massive loss of money that Bill Gates suffered when the dot-coms went bust. At the same time that loss only underscores what this man did for globalization.

For Bill everything started with tic-tac-toe.

By the 1970s, with the Net already started[8] and with huge computers doing the big jobs, mostly for government, the digital revolution began. Computers had to be down-sized, to fit on desktops, to be personal computers, ultimately to allow individuals to communicate directly with each other.

Many were already working in the field and simple games were on the market to teach young people what was underway. Gates became intrigued as a gamester and developed a program for tic-tac-toe. He saw the potential and began the global expansion that became Microsoft.

Talking with the high-tech companies, he began developing software. Unique programming resulted that would lead to the DOS system and then to Windows. Even IBM used his talents in those early years. Most of the groundwork for Microsoft was done in New Mexico, and the vital energy among the original team members must have been very exciting, even intoxicating.[9]

From Albuquerque, Gates returned to his hometown Seattle and became the biggest player on the global scene.

How does the great globalizer feel about globalization? As

might be expected, Bill endorses the progress machine. His recent recommendations to Congress emphasized another key element of successful business, competition. He started:

> Any discussion of competitiveness in the 21st century must begin by recognizing the central role that technology and innovation play in today's economy. The United States has a great deal to be proud of in this respect. Many of the most important advances in computing, healthcare, telecommunications, manufacturing, and many other fields have originated here in the United States.[10]

Then he cautioned that his feeling of pride is mixed with a "deep anxiety" because, he said, we are too often "content to live off the investments previous generations made" and that "we are failing to make the investments needed to be sure the U.S. remains competitive in the future."

Urging Congress to take "necessary action," he recommended three important steps:

> First, we must equip America's students and workers with the knowledge and skills they need to succeed in today's knowledge economy.
>
> Second, we need to reform our immigration policies for high-skilled workers so that we can be sure our workforce includes the world's most talented people.
>
> And third, we need to provide a foundation for future innovation by investing in new ideas and providing a framework for capturing their value.

Bill is all in favor of globalization. His suggestion to others is to educate yourself then outsource, with "in-sourcing" and innovation, basically for the rest of us to do what he did. In other words he had already done what he recommended to Congress. Those left behind have to get educated and catch up. Many have done just that. This is small comfort for many now unemployed by globalization.

Bill's views on competition on the global scene are particularly relevant.[11]

Recall his experiences in reaching his unique position. First, he educated himself to innovate a new game. He then took the lead, getting out in the business world and selling his DOS program, the digital operating system. He networked and made sales. He then developed Windows to improve and bring the desktop to the customers, to the globe.[12]

Interestingly, Bill did not complete college. He dropped Harvard to pursue what he believed would work. Universities were not needed.

Now, when he makes a great donation to charity, he deliberately stays away from government as the beneficiary or administrator.[13]

Most recently, his innovative suggestions include staying away from charities because "all they want is money." He recommended expanded charitable efforts by private business, the companies that know how money gets results.[14]

One seldom-stated rule of American business is that if you want to learn how to do something, listen to the leaders in business who have done the job. Some business leaders have regular programs on business success and many have written books on what to do.[15] Others give their time and effort to make solid recommendations based on their experiences.

Listen to Bill.

Listen to our business leaders.

WARREN BUFFETT

Bill Gates is not alone as a leader. He is one among many and, according to the latest projections, one friend, Warren Buffet, happened to overtake Bill and become the most wealthy in 2008. The race was on. The stock values of each were fluctuating. Whose stock holdings would be worth the most on the closing date?[16]

Warren Buffett is from the center of America, from the cornfields and cattle ranches of Nebraska, from middle America and our heartland. Home was Omaha where he learned with a father who was both a stockbroker and an elected representative. Money and politics are always an interesting and very educational combination, especially for globalization.

Warren's early foundation was math. He read math books, reflecting an interest that Millie taught her students and her son. Bill noted that far more of today's students should appreciate math and learn the subject. Math is fascinating and it is vital, for you MP3 lovers, to music.

Warren learned math, which gave him a vital foundation to understand the stock market like few in the investment business. In addition to being a math bookworm, Warren was a "doer," intent on going into business, getting the job done and making money. He understood and loved America's business system. What he did was fundamental; he got out in the neighborhood and worked. Starting at an early age with that great American tradition, a newspaper route, he soon opened a "string" of vending machines (all three of them) and then used the business income to buy some farmland and then lease the farm.[17] Use the profits to make more money. Do not waste the hard-earned money to celebrate or to enjoy the latest fads.

This teenager's history sounds too good to be true. Perhaps the spin on the facts has been adjusted to promote the billionaire's legend. For example, the "string" of vending machines was only three; however, the newspaper route, so typically American, is true. As some media types suggest, if the legend is too much for the facts, at least go with the spin.

Warren earned the money from the very start. Almost too typical, the point remains that there is money to be made, work is required and you have to talk to others and find the opportunities. You cannot do it alone or sitting in a bedroom being a gamester or being "better" and "above" friends who have to work. There is money to be made. The way to do it is to meet people, to network, to get into business.

Warren was reluctant to go to college. He would have to forego the income he knew could be earned in business; however, he listened to his father, attended the prestigious Wharton School of Economics, completed college at Nebraska, and then studied at Columbia to understand stock markets and how they worked (this is an understatement). He knew how business worked, and he invested in companies that were strategically placed with a "durable competitive advantage."[18]

After completing college and putting in an intern's stint in New York, Warren went into the stock market, working at his father's brokerage house, then investing with family and friends in a series of partnerships. The investment interest was directed toward undervalued, safe companies. The strategy was very successful.

In 1962, he purchased shares in Berkshire Hathaway, a Massachusetts textile company, even then as Seth noticed, a failing industry. With excess cash from the company, he invested in other businesses and converted the textile company to a holding company.

Centering on successful but undervalued companies, he built up a solid portfolio and watched the investments grow with the American economy. He stayed on top of business, finding companies needing his backing and turning the management loose to get the job done with one exception. He stayed on top of the top executive, a policy he follows routinely.[19] Clay also followed this very good policy.

By the turn of the century, Warren was one of the world's most wealthy. With that mutual attraction between likes, between members of the trillionaires club, he became friends with Bill Gates. Somehow, including or in spite of the fascinating competition of the bridge table, they remain friends, now undertaking a major charitable venture.

Warren Buffett is an advocate of globalization. At the same time he is very concerned about the trade deficit and the decreasing value of the dollar and its impact on American assets. He has important investments in companies with substantial revenue from outside the United States. In his view the cost of labor is the main problem for global trade, whether free or fair.[20]

Warren is another business leader wise enough to invest in companies that will make him money in the form of value. He knows business in America and most of his investments are still with American companies.

Like Bill Gates, Warren provides important leadership. He is a leader for America, another member of our greatest generations.

SAM WALTON

Sam Walton was another outstanding business leader. He knew retail and made the family fortune bringing American products to rural America.[21] From there, he moved into the suburbs and cities, and then overseas. He went global.

Sam was from middle America. He followed the American plan for growing up. He became an Eagle Scout, played football as starting quarterback, was a high school leader, and graduated as an honor student. By current standards, he might not have been "cool" back then. On the other hand, based on his success, by today's standards he would have been "very cool."

In college Sam continued as a leader. Following graduation, he went to work with a variety store chain. His career was interrupted for military service. When war came, he enlisted and served in security units. In 1945, following discharge from the military, he opened his own variety store. There he developed the strategies that were the foundations for his success.

Here's a side note. In the 1950s, the growing-up years for the so-called silent generation, road travel would include checking to see if a small town had a JC Penney, more affectionately a "JCPCoInc."[22] If there was a store, the town had arrived as a "town"; it was no longer a hamlet. Goods and services would be available. Sam Walton had worked with Penney's, very much like Millie's husband started in the 1920s.

Sam had excellent work habits and he had the good sense to know that many work hard but help is needed so work smart and hire people to help you. He was soon recognized as a hard worker and an innovator and as being very intelligent in the ways of business. The point should be clear: business has its values. Sam knew and practiced them.

As Sam moved up he went to other stores and chains with Penney's but he would leave that organization after a few years. His objective was to open his first Wal-Mart, a small store in Arkansas, another out-of-the way place, almost too small even for JC Penney's. Moving from New York to that small, out-of-way town, he had the foresight to know that rural areas needed goods and services, that the center of America was an excellent place to start a national general store, and that there was a niche, some of what is now "blue ocean"[23] missed by others. In short, he had confidence in America.

Word was out. Wal-Mart had excellent prices and products.

Within a few years of opening the first store, Sam was expanding. Stores opened one right after another, covering the rural areas with much-needed products. Sam provided jobs to people not accustomed to economic opportunity. He delivered regular hours, assured pay and good working conditions.

The basics remained the same as Wal-Mart added superstores

and Sam's and so much more, blanketing America. Sam promised low prices and he delivered. The economic choice, the competition for customers with available goods at lower prices, worked. A remarkable business developed and prospered.

The always low prices should include other always—always open, always hiring, products always available, paycheck always on time, service always provided—all the requirements for a successful business.

From rural areas without stores, without secure jobs, and without needed products Wal-Mart did the job.

Well established by the 1980s, Wal-Mart moved into larger communities and maintained the many commitments, the "always." The efficiency was remarkable. Arkansas was in the middle of the country. Inventory controls were set up, with 18-wheelers ready to deliver from the center of the United States to all points, as needed. The central location meant efficient delivery, lower prices and needed products on hand and ready for sale.

Wal-Mart became the largest retailer in the world.[24] For a company first opening in 1962 in Rogers, Arkansas, the progress was remarkable. A Sam's Club opened in 1983 in Midwest City, Oklahoma. The first Supercenter was in Washington, Missouri, opening in 1988. Mexico City was the site for the first international unit. Now more than one-half million are employed overseas. Each week, Wal-Mart serves more than 176 million customers around the globe. Total associates are almost two million. Total sales annually are $349 billion.

Wal-Mart is an American company that is globalized. At the same time over 1,360,000 Americans have jobs here. Wal-Mart is localized.

Sam Walton was willing to bring the very productive American economy to rural areas where national corporations were reluctant to go. Wal-Mart also brought jobs to the rural areas left untouched by competitors. And Sam commenced highly innovative sales and delivery programs to reduce costs and get the job done. The venture was risky in the beginning but low prices and competitive wages worked, as always. Wal-Mart made money the old-fashioned way: with the same competition and innovation Bill Gates still recommends and with the management skills Warren Buffett looks for in chief executives.

Wal-Mart is routinely bashed by critics. Often the opposition is simply competition played out in the political arena. While anything and everything may be fair in open competition, too often competitors resort to political and legal challenges, not market competition.[25]

Sam Walton passed in 1992. His family continues his policies and when the four heirs are combined, they are atop the trillionaires club.

Sam Walton left a remarkable legacy. He is another leading member of our greatest generations.

WILLIAM BOEING

One of the first to arrive on the globalization scene was Boeing, of Seattle. People still shake their heads and conclude there must be something in the water up in Washington State where Microsoft and Boeing were startups.

When the business idea for Boeing first began, Congress was considering abolishing the Patent Office. After all, by 1900 all inventions had been made. A wasteful bureaucracy should be closed.[26]

In 1910, *Scientific American* proclaimed:

> To affirm that the airplane is going to revolutionize the future is to be guilty of the wildest exaggeration.[27]

Boeing had different ideas. In the very early years of his company, he said:

> We are embarked as pioneers upon a new science and industry

> in which our problems are so new and unusual that it behooves no one to dismiss any novel idea with the statement, "It can't be done."[28]

Today, the airplane is the most international of organizations, moving people globally. This global role started in 1903 when the Wright brothers made their first flight at Kitty Hawk, North Carolina. Aviation entered the modern era in 1927 when Lindbergh made his nonstop flight from New York to Paris.

Between those key years, Boeing was founded and prospered. Five men from those early years would form the airplane giant of today. William E. Boeing of Detroit began building floatplanes near Seattle, Washington. Donald Douglas of New York began building bombers and passenger transports in Santa Monica, California. James S. McDonnell of Denver began building jet fighters in St. Louis. James "Dutch" Kindelberger of Wheeling, West Virginia, began building trainers in Los Angeles. Howard Hughes Jr. of Houston set up business in Los Angeles and became the largest employer in southern California during the Second World War.

By the dawning of the new millennium, these men and their companies had joined forces to share a legacy of discovery and victory, competition and cooperation, hard struggle and high adventure.

Again, the story of William Boeing is one of American leadership.

Boeing left Yale in 1903 and headed for the financially rewarding Northwest timber industry. In 1910, he was in Los Angeles for the first American air meet. He tried to get a ride in one of the airplanes, but not one of the dozen aviators would oblige. Returning to Seattle, Boeing's boathouse became the factory for construction of his twin-float seaplanes.

From these small beginnings, a tiny airplane manufacturing company grew into a huge corporation of related industries.

There were problems along the way. When post-Depression legislation mandated the dispersion of the corporation, Boeing sold his interests and moved away. Fortunately, he never lost his interest in aviation. During World War II he was a volunteer consultant to the company and lived to see the company enter the jet age.

Following the war a new science glimmered on the horizon. The U.S. aerospace industry would benefit from "Operation Paperclip." At the end of the Second World War, masses of scientific data, tons of unused missiles and several hundred scientists from Germany entered the United States.

Development of our missile programs started.

The Minuteman was one of Boeing's largest, longest and most complex military contract. By April 1967, one thousand Minuteman missiles were operational and installed in six sites across the country. Minuteman established the company as a manager of complex systems and provided Boeing with a wealth of experience in propulsion and guidance systems.

A vital part of "MAD"—the containment doctrine of "mutually assured destruction"—the American defense policy centered on the Minuteman.

The program worked.

We never fired a nuke.

We won the cold war.

Boeing began with the air age and under American leadership, expanded from local to national and then global flight, including circling the globe from outer space.

Consider the hard numbers for a globalized company. Boeing is the world's leading aerospace company, the largest manufacturer of commercial jetliners and military aircraft combined. A major service provider to NASA, Boeing operates the Space Shuttle and International Space Station. The company also provides numerous military and commercial airline support services. Boeing has customers in more than ninety countries around the world and is one of the largest U.S. exporters in terms of sales. Now headquartered in Chicago, Boeing employment reaches across America and around the globe.

And this is where Millie's youngest child, the son she raised as a single mother, started with the "skonk works" in Los Angeles. After graduating from CalTech with the highest of grades, he got the job and joined the design team.[29]

High-level globalization is an important part of the Boeing story. For over five decades, the company has had a long-standing, cooperative relationship with Japan.

In addition, Boeing and China have worked together successfully since 1972. Aviation is crucial to China's economic growth, and Boeing support has been essential for training, safety, quality management and technical support. Also, billions of supplies and services are purchased by Boeing from China. In return, China buys planes from Boeing. Recently, China surpassed Japan in purchases from Boeing.

The government role is significant in the airline industry. Boeing leadership includes obtaining congressional approval for free trade with China and government approval of Chinese membership in the World Trade Organization.

Boeing is another major globalizer. Airplanes are truly a global connector for people. Boeing has provided that connection.

While looking at global aviation, there has been another major step toward "one world" or by current terms, "one globe."[30] For communication purposes, one language will clearly help. Aviation recently required all pilots be able to speak English.[31] Most spoke English already, and for obvious reasons. Now English is required.

The overall impact of Boeing going global has had mixed results. When the second world war ended, employment fell and Seattle suffered. Again with cutbacks in 1970, a Seattle billboard requested, "Will the last person leaving Seattle turn out the lights."

There is a pressing need to ease local problems. Support for local communities must be a part of globalization.

Globalization and Change

These four examples of American leadership by starting companies and then globalizing the world are in due recognition of what our greatest generations have accomplished.

The huge advances in personal wealth also underscore the advances in corporate wealth. Many Americans became fantastically wealthy during the successes of the greatest generations.

There was full cooperation between the nation and the individuals in developing wealth. The two successes—for individuals and for nations—happened together.

Each of their experiences is in praise of their dedication to the American business model. There are universal values or policies in making business work. Many are so fundamental that they are too often overlooked. Our leaders followed those values.

An important part of our business values is that our wealth has not been hoarded. The sharing of progress is apparent in lists of the most wealthy people worldwide. The international trillionaires club tops out with twenty-five members. The United States is not the only member. We are not even half the total membership, likely indicating a measure of sharing the wealth produced in America and of our progress sharing wealth globally.

We remain the most wealthy but our relative position, our parity with the rest of the world, is changing, and changing yearly. That change is not in our favor.

The Billionaires Club

Still another club for the wealthy is Congress. At one time the United States Senate was the most exclusive men's club in the world. Only ninety-six senators, all male, were allowed floor privileges along with the many hidden privileges behind the Senate chambers.[32]

But, since 1922 the club is not solely men. What many of the members have in common is wealth. None qualifies for the trillionaires club; at least none has publicly admitted to that high level of wealth. There are no billionaires. With the Senate and the House of Representatives, we have a millionaires club. The combined wealth would qualify many members for a billionaires club.[33]

Of course, not all senators and members of Congress are wealthy. A few disclose near poverty.[34]

The problem is determining that wealth. Senators too often complain of life in a "goldfish bowl." Even with all the "freedom of information" laws and public disclosure, no one knows for certain how much our representatives are worth.

Members of the Senate and the House of Representatives do not report their exact wealth. Do not expect financial disclosure. A yearly balance sheet and income statement are, in the eyes of Congress, totally improper. Tax returns would be criminal to disclose.

So much for "full disclosure" and "life in a goldfish bowl."

Instead, we have disclosure of a range of their wealth and some insights into their favorite investments. We know little else.

Interview Requested

With our letter for comment from the wealthiest individuals, we also requested comments on globalization from several political leaders.

None responded.

Most politicians are "ambiguous" and express reservations about hot issues like globalization. Silence should have been expected. No matter. Their positions are on the public record, both by votes and by comments.

The focus in our democracy is on the economy. This guideline is the way of life for Congress and for voters. A close relation between people with money and people with power is to be expected. In the final analysis, the connection is a necessity. The sooner that fact is acknowledged, the better both the wealthy and the government will understand each other. If we get full disclosure, they will also be understood by voters.

What do members of the billionaires club have to say about members of the trillionaires club? Virtually the same question is, what do they say about globalization?

These questions were directed in particular to three members I knew personally. The three provided a representative group in leadership positions. What was their position on globalization?

I contacted each.

A warning. Trying to pin any politician to a specific position is difficult, and for a very understandable reason. Until the specific legislation is presented as an issue to be voted up or down, they have to reserve the right to agree or disagree. This form of extended debate and compromise is a necessary tradition in our political system.

I contacted the three with that traditional approach in politics—true in elected offices as well as business, corporations, volunteer groups, churches, and everywhere—see the people up close and personal. In today's terms, advanced networking up close and personal.

TRENT LOTT

Trent Lott, now a retired senator, is a leading example of friends in big business.[35] Committed to globalization, meaning to him free trade, Trent had little to lose with his Mississippi constituents. Manufacturing jobs were not going overseas. Mississippi is so low on the national economic scales that there was nothing to lose.

However, Trent had everything to gain by in-sourcing foreign companies and their manufacturing plants, bringing them into Mississippi.[36] Landowners would sell land, local governments would add taxes, communities would have more business, and there would be jobs, many jobs. Everyone wins.

He assisted the process and the state prospered.

I met the good senator at his home in Pascagoula, on the southern coast where the vast Ingalls shipyards and one Navy base were located.[37]

On a warm afternoon, I drove up with my partner to discuss business opportunities on the Mississippi Gulf Coast. Behind Trent's home on supports twenty feet off the ground, I heard someone working. I hollered and around the side came a man with bush shears, no shirt, to all appearances a gardener.

"We're looking for the senator." I knew who the gardener was but, as they say, address the obvious at the outset.

"I'm Trent Lott," he replied.

"Hello, Senator," I replied. "I did not expect the gardener."

He smiled and we moved into a forty-minute discussion on bringing new companies to an area needing business and jobs; casinos, privatization, infrastructure and ports. We briefed him and went our own way.

Trent served as an elected member of Congress for thirty-four years. During his service, he developed a leadership style to bring differing groups together. A practical leader, he worked to get things done.[38]

His basic views on globalization were also his basic views on national defense. For example, he played a key role in bringing Poland, Hungary and the Czech Republic into NATO and the European Union. Defense and free trade were promoted in this union of economic and regional politics.

A leader working to get the egos of the Senate to agree, there was no need, in Trent's approach, to worry with policy. From the results, the final and true measure of the political process, Trent was an aggressive backer of free trade. There was no room for worrying about the consequences of removing barriers. He promoted free trade for the very practical reason he brought foreign business to Mississippi. If that commitment promoted international trade, very good. And very political.

KAY BAILEY HUTCHINSON

A letter also went to Senator Kay Bailey Hutchinson. Kay and I had worked together while I was finishing Law School. I was hired as a legal assistant and she was secretary to the same two members of the Texas House of Representatives. There was little to be done in the first few weeks of the session as the "lege" organized itself. Then, our first employer was killed in a car accident. We lost still more time awaiting a replacement. For me, this meant not only a paying job but also more time for Law School.

Since that short time we had with the same employer, there had been no direct contact. But, old friendships sometimes have benefits, so the letter requesting comments and an interview was sent.

No reply.

Follow-up calls were not productive.

What is her public record on globalization?

Kay knows elections.[39] With a Texas background in politics, she has participated in and survived the "heat in the kitchen" and is now a senior leader in the Senate. There she provides policy leadership for conservatives with a woman's insights.

Kay supports globalization with protections but has not taken a major role on the subject. On immigration she has a moderate position. The test for immigration has become a test for open borders. Strictly speaking, free trade includes an absence of border controls and free passage into America. Kay supports free trade but opposes open borders. She supports immigration controls.

LLOYD DOGGETT

Again trying advanced networking, I wrote Lloyd Doggett, a member of Congress from Austin, Texas. We had practiced law from opposite sides of the docket and knew each other well. Lloyd had provided clerkships for two of my sons when he was in the Texas Senate.

The letter and the follow-up calls were not productive.

Lloyd has been a political leader in Texas, holding many elected positions. He is also a millionaire and is thus a member of the billionaires club for Congress.

Where does Lloyd stand on globalization? He has taken a mixed position on free trade.[40] Sometimes more "global" than others but always for local subsidies to protect local communities from losing jobs. He has served as chair of the international studies committee and he works with a special committee for globalization. To restate his position, if there is subsidization for a local community impacted by globalization, he is all for globalization.

The positions of these three—one a middle-of-the-road conservative, one a dedicated conservative and one a liberal—have one feature in common. All supported free trade and globalization. Until recently, words of warning and concern were never enough to influence their votes.

OTHERS REPRESENTATIVES

I contacted other members of Congress, Senate and House, about their views.[41] After the request for an interview was ignored, their public statements were consulted. What did they say about globalization?[42]

Charles Schumer, a New York senator, favors globalization and supports the process. While he opposed the Andean and the Central American trade agreements, his position in New York City requires support for globalization. His comments are directed to improving features of current American policy.[43]

John Conyers is one of the longest serving members of Congress, and he represents Detroit, one of the districts most impacted by globalization. His interests are making adjustments to trade policy to help Americans. Specifically, he supports expanded free trade with Haiti. His official record does not otherwise mention free or fair trade.[44] More recently, he has taken leadership to promote more "fairness" for free trade.

Like many members of the greatest generations, John was in the military and served in Korea. He earned several medals. As a black leader, he participated in civil rights drives and employed Rosa Parks. He has headed the judiciary committee or been the senior Democrat on the committee for many years.

Senator Patrick Leahy of Vermont favors globalization, voting the same line Schumer supports. His main comment has been to tax the wealthy more, in support of "a more generous government."[45]

Do they have any interest in correcting the problems for America—our trade deficits, the open borders, and local economies impacted by free trade?

Each has expressed "concerns" for the specific issues but none has addressed the long-term problems of the deficit, trade imbalance and devaluation in any comprehensive way.

None has spoken about the new economic regions or the pending statist proposals for a new world government.

Congress is firmly committed to free trade and globalization.

Leaders among the Greatest

We took a look at the positions of other leaders. Comments and an interview were requested but none was forthcoming. Again, the public comments and speeches provided a measure of key leaders in the states, the cities and the private sector.

COLIN POWELL

Colin Powell had an illustrious career in service to the United

States, mostly for military and defense. As secretary of state, he led American efforts for a unified response to terrorism and apparently had little time for free versus fair trade.

His basic position on globalization is solid wisdom from a man with extended experiences in combat. Colin endorses free trade, noting that democracy flourishes when trade is free. His more direct suggestion is that we keep trading with China because "a person is less likely to shoot at you if you are trading with him." His advice is to "keep trading and talking."

ARNOLD SCHWARZENEGGER

The obvious candidate on the West Coast is Arnold Schwarzenegger. As governor of California, he is front and center on globalization. Forty percent of imports into America enter through California.

Arnie has spoken on free trade but not fair trade. At a conference endorsing open competition, the important issues of a level playing field and legal protections were not emphasized. At the same time Arnie approved legislation for extensive infrastructure improvements to support globalization—major highways to move foreign goods. His public statements show concern for adverse impacts of free trade; however, the money he is spending is all for expansion of free trade.

Count him in favor of free trade.

MICHAEL BLOOMBERG

On the east coast Michael Bloomberg, mayor of New York City, is another key leader. Starting business here as a stockbroker, he developed a market reporting system that included software to provide current information and added a radio program to keep his audience updated. A multi-billionaire, he has devoted substantial efforts to leadership of the city. He commands the support of the business community and has shown remarkable progress in most areas needing improvement or innovation here.

Mike is firmly committed to free trade. He cautions that "protectionism" is not something we need, and he has expressed concern that other nations will catch up and overtake us if we add restrictions on free trade.

Interestingly, the city has a program favoring business with local companies. In public procurement, city agencies are supposed to grant a 5 percent preference to city businesses and individuals. If two companies submit proposals, the city-based business gets a 5 percent adjustment downward to compare against the non-local company. This program started statewide at a time companies were leaving the state. Following 9-11, the favoritism saw renewed emphasis here.

Since the city's economy has improved, recent procurement results indicate the preference is not relevant.

Mike is a free trader. With a city as globalized as New York and with one of the most diverse populations on the globe, free trade is good business.

DONALD TRUMP

Another New York City leader deeply committed to the business of the city is Donald Trump. A native New Yorker, The Donald has developed major real estate interests here and in other locations. A natural born "celebrity," he makes a strong personal presentation and has the solid business sense to do things right. The Donald's "Apprentice" show presents excellent lessons in business, particularly that the bottom line has to be the objective. The best in business are those putting the most money in the bank, getting the results.

Fair trade is not an issue he has addressed often. Reportedly, he has contacts with the Reform Party, which supports limits on free trade, what could be called a policy for fair trade.[46]

The Donald has sounded warnings about China, stating it is "virtually impossible" to open a business there. However, China has "no problem" opening businesses here. He added: "Maybe you have to literally restrict trade because if it is not going to be fair, why should you allow it to happen?"

He is a powerful, very experienced competitor. When he says that China is "doing a number on [us]," we should listen.

The Donald supports fair trade, a sound approach when due consideration is given our growing trade deficit.

JESSE VENTURA

Jesse Ventura is an independent, an understatement if ever there was one.[47] As governor of Minnesota he generally supported globalization—a good thing for farmers and his state. After touring China he strongly endorsed free trade with that nation.

Although out of the political arena for several years, he has recently returned with suggestions that there are politics in his future. Still in prime time, his past association with Reform and Independent Parties gives him a base for campaigning. Many Reform Party policies oppose free trade. Jesse should clear up his basic positions.

Critics

The globalization juggernaut has not been without its critics. Not everyone in America fully supports free trade in all its forms. The basic consideration is the results. What is involved? Is the big picture more and more trade between nations with lower and lower tariffs and other barriers? Does free trade mean open borders? What are the details?

Free trade means lowering and eliminating trade barriers. Another part is making subsidies to American businesses and individuals. Still another is assistance we give to foreign countries. What is the total cost? What do we budget and pay?

There are some critics among those we requested for interviews. Of several expressing reservations, Donald Trump was both the most knowledgeable business leader and the most critical.

There are others.

JOHN BOLTON

John served as our ambassador to the United Nations.[48] He was critical of an organization insiders acknowledge is corrupt to the core. Still, he was attacked on a partisan basis for taking a hard-line against the acknowledged but ignored corruption in the United Nations, a corruption that includes the member states.[49]

Considering the hostile attitude by the United Nations to any public disclosures and considering its dedication to world-wide government control, substantial reform is needed. As a first step, we should abandon the discredited notion of sovereign immunity, that the king can do no wrong. We need full disclosure. We need substantial reform for free trade to work fairly.

Absent fundamental reform, the United Nations will remain a failed organization.

Congress has told the United Nations to reform or lose more support and money. The organization is blind to the idea.[50]

Under the circumstances the critics were flat unfair to John. He was trying to improve the organization; however, at the United Nations, dissent is not allowed. Some nations or at least their representatives might be "upset." The drive at the United Nations is always for a consensus, or unanimity, even though there is no unanimity.[51]

They resemble peer review at colleges. Disagreement is not encouraged in academia. They do not want to be "upset."

Some issues are not to be conceded; they have to be debated. The United Nations needs to encourage the free exchange of ideas, to be a true democracy. Unfortunately, in addition to corruption, the preference for state controls makes free speech impossible.

In the greater sense, with the current state of international corruption, there are many issues we cannot concede.

Although no longer at the United Nations, John actively promotes American interests. He has spoken on Iran, North Korea and the State Department. We need his continued contributions.[52]

Demonstrators

Some critics of globalization attack the entire process. Their demonstrations, too often violent, are not acceptable by American standards for peace and for meaningful debate.[53]

If you are for peace, your violence is self-contradictory and totally unacceptable.

A footnote on avoiding violence. Any person following the American Dream is entitled to law and order, to peace. The violence of the psychopaths, of the super-maxed alphas, has no place in a democracy. A democracy provides ways to make change. Make your case. If you do not make an effective case, who failed?

The demonstrators do not make an effective case. Until they make at least a good faith effort to debate the issues, they should be ignored.

Global Poverty

There are important issues about global poverty.[54] The problem is of major proportions. There are one billion people living below poverty levels as defined by the world court.[55]

One recent study asks whether globalization is good or bad. The report notes that hundreds of millions living in extreme poverty have been lifted out of poverty, adding that 25 percent of the wealthiest have also grown "proportionately richer."

The report concludes:

> The net is that on an absolute basis, globalization has had a truly

> phenomenal positive impact on reducing poverty (especially in the historical context).[56]

The report laments the wealthiest but acknowledges the "phenomenal positive effect on reducing poverty." As we have seen, the trillionaires club members run the engine providing the progress. Despite the violent protests and vicious critics, globalization is what works to reduce poverty.[57]

How effective are the statist worlds of the United Nations and the too many corrupt member nations? Look at the results. The United Nations and its allies have little effect on poverty.[58] Led by the United States, globalization does the job.

Give a person a fish and he eats for a day; teach a person to fish and provide him with food for a lifetime.

There is one additional critic, dangerous because of an impact on information but with an abject failure to deal with the facts rather than with political opinion and bias.[59]

The Media

Some journalists are obstructionists to globalization and democracy. They are the inbred meritocrats,[60] the experts who have never met a payroll, and the source of hostility for many years to democratic business and to free trade.[60]

Recall that the media always have to think sales in their very unusual way. To sell newspaper, the rule is

> Comfort the afflicted, and afflict the comfortable.[61]

This famous old maxim of the "yellow press" is still the rule, along with TV's favorite:

> If it bleeds
> It leads.[62]

For media reporters since the early 1960s, this has meant to attack America, to seldom say anything favorable about America, and to find the afflicted everywhere.[63]

They think like trial lawyers—find a deep pocket (the wealthy, the successful, the people and businesses with money, the people who disagree with government control) and attack. Do not worry about the facts. Say anything. Seek out the afflicted and spin the story.

For an America dedicated to helping others, this plea works wonders. We are the most charitable nation in the world and, as Jon noted, for the most part we do so through faith-based organizations.

Always quote the enemies of America and the enemies of business with whatever they have to say. Do not question them. Assume they are right. Make an effort, sometimes, to contact the target and get a quote but always question the response. Remember that whatever we say is "alleged." What our enemies say is never challenged.

Small wonder the media are among the lowest professions in the respect index, not trusted, not admired. Learn something. Present all the facts, be fair and balanced.

Business Values

The United States has come a long way since the 1929 market crash. The circumstances are unequivocal: we have taken leadership and we have been followed. Now we have a world economy—a globalized economy—where the nations and economic groups we have supported have caught up with us and are passing us.

Time for a slowdown and correction.

The time has come to level the playing field; however, to reach a fair result, the values of business have to be understood.

Consider what really works for business, for commerce and for the economy. We have seen what our business leaders say about where we are and where we need to go. What are the values for business that so clearly work?

The setting is the American Dream. That dream is not just "a car in every garage and a chicken in every pot." The dream is not just "forty acres and a mule," another failed political promise, or dream. The American Dream is not just a 401 account.

One real American dream, as Clay and Mary and so many more show, is owning your own business. To make a business work the owner of the startup must believe one fact: if you follow the rules, you will make a living. Ask Santo about this fact.

To follow the rules, excellent business ethics are required. You have to do what business requires.

Be prepared to appreciate the politics.

Consider the "big picture." As we have seen on the global level, America became world peace and *Pax Americana* with the collapse of the Soviet Union. The opening of Red China further underscores the success of our commercial model. These remarkable results were possible because of the greatest generations of that period from 1929 who overcame the impoverishment suffered by Clay and Zeke, went on in 1941 to defeat right-wing fascism, and then turned to their democratic traditions to prevail in the cold war and mark the end of socialism, of left-wing fascism, statism and government control. Our business democracy works.

In business, you have to vote in elections. You have to participate in the community. You have to "network."

How do we measure success? How do we truly say we are the greatest?

Donald Trump says the results are all that count. Getting there requires work, oftentimes 24/7.

Understand the values that make commerce work. There are some basics and the review of what these Americans did shows the business values required. Business has its demands. When those demands are met, prosperity will usually follow.

Listen to the leaders.

Some basic rules for starting a business:

- startup money is needed—have enough on hand to last at least three months without any income
- get some partners or backers—do some networking and find support with investors or at least lenders (security required)
- solid business plan—spend some time going over the cost of your business—get an accountant and put your plan in writing
- get a business organization—incorporation in some form or another is necessary—see a lawyer
- sales—advertise and get the word out that you are in business—join your chamber of commerce
- hiring and firing—help is required so understand the rules for employees
- meet the payroll—an absolute necessity: you do not get paid until your employees are paid

This fundamental model works. Just take care of the details. Follow business ethics. Listen to your accountant and learn about debits, credits and taxes. Listen to your attorney and learn about business law.

Always follow the rules. Be tough on this point. Do not compromise with customers, clients, suppliers, employees or anyone else. Do not let them compromise you.

A review of what our leaders did fits the basic model of the values for business. What Gates, Buffett, Walton and Boeing did is laid out. The rules are there.

Our greatest generations ended the cold war, sponsored economic progress for the globe, and advanced technology as never before, from men on the moon and on to the depths of space and to the depths of the atom and to the depths of our genes. Our greatest generations took us to places where no one had ever gone before.

We succeeded during important disputes to prevailing policy, all of which was resolved with peace toward the violent protesters.

Consider the wisdom of the greatest generation for 1929 through 1945: avoid wars, plan for peace, forgive enemies and work together. The accomplishments were quiet victories, largely unnoticed by the media, avoiding the sacrifices of Depression and global war.

The men and women making these silent accomplishments are truly the "greatest generations," also known by other names, including the cold war generation, the global generation, even the awkward and unworkable no-nukes generation.

How do we measure the success we have witnessed and are witnessing?

We need to take a look at the economics.

THREE

ECONOFACTS

Economic policy is guided by statistics. Numbers define the solutions. Buy or sell. Tax and spend. Cutback and grow. More sales or less. Hire or fire.

How much? When? Where? Who?

The answers are in the statistics.

Defining Statistics

The problem is summarized by a famous statement: "Lies, damned lies and statistics."[1]

The problems with statistics[2] are:

- the sources for the number are not always reliable or compatible;
- any comparisons depend on the same period of time, but some experts compare between a calendar year, a fiscal year and sometimes a guesstimated admixture;
- statistics compared over several years or decades or centuries are adjusted for current value but "corrections" over the years are also adjusted for six or more different variables;
- the "voodoo" expert is usually biased with the number "skewed" or "tweaked" to prove a point;
- polling statistics depend too much on judgment about the questions and the samples taken;

- to reach a desired political conclusion totals or percents or individual numbers are used; and
- these variables get bogged down in lengthy explanations that further complicate meaningful discussion.

The seven ambiguities compounded by six more adjustments are then subject to polling statistics. The margin of error, the sample taken, the questions asked, the sponsor's objectives, the use of push questions, and the variables used are still more problems.

For example, George Washington was paid $25,000 per year as president.[3] What would his salary be today? Experts will give you an answer varying from $550,000 to $23 million.

Or how much has the price of gasoline changed? In 1949, gas was 27¢ per gallon. Today, dependent on the indices used, we should be paying anywhere from 4¢ to $3.86 per gallon in "real" dollars, in what gasoline really costs us.

We have seven times six variables that make statistics worse even than the "running lie-dog."[4]

Call these numbers "econofacts" because they are special to economics. As "special" facts they have to be taken with a healthy skepticism.

Of course, statistics are useful and even necessary. For an "in-depth overview" of globalization, our statistics are taken from government reports that are relatively reliable. Dealing with bigger numbers will overcome at least some of the usual problems with statistics, of taking too small a sample.

The Economists

The front-line experts on econofacts are the economists. Note that seldom do economists agree on anything. There is an economic definition of a recession: "two or more successive quarters" (that's six months) of decline; however, half the economists will proclaim a recession with only a one-month downturn.

There are other definitions all saying standards are needed. Until then, there will be a variety of answers and we will know politics has intervened.[5]

Economists consider human behavior for their numbers and predictions and have profound differences. Psychologists also predict human behavior and have their differences. Unlike economists, the psychologists have developed reasonable definitions in the *Diagnostic and Statistical Manual* series, now on a fourth version.[6] For both professions, there are too often no easy answers; however, psychologists have at least some standards. Economists need better definitions and need to make their forecasts for economic behavior based on agreed-upon definitions. Economists must agree on fundamentals.

There is a caution: understanding economic theories is difficult. What economists propose for policy solutions is usually based on more government and higher taxes or less government and lower taxes. The difference sounds like the cold war: more government or more democratic freedom. This political division between economists influences their analyses and predictions.

Economists also tend to be divided into those who think, teach and write and those who are doers, taking responsibility for the economy and making decisions about how American commerce would work better.

There are several key economists, and their views on globalization are important. With due consideration for the basic philosophical difference, a brief review of economic thinking since 1945 may be helpful.

Economic Thinkers

In the realm of economics, Paul Samuelson stands out.[7] He produced the textbook for most economics classes; he analyzed economic behavior by consumers like you and me; and he attempted to bring the classic and statism principles together.

Using thermodynamics, he theorized that an economy behaves much like a boiling vat of different materials. Note that this sounds like the "aggregation" theory in politics, discussed in chapter 6, "Leaders." The parallel to the "skonk works" is unavoidable.

In full defense of Professor Samuelson, he was an extraordinary analyst and teacher. Nobel Prizes are not easily granted.

Regarding the definition problem he said:

> Economists have correctly predicted nine of the last five recessions.[8]

Samuelson favored globalization and could analyze the various impacts precisely. His belief in an "expert consumer" was often criticized. Consumers act for many reasons. Voters vote for many different reasons. Aggregation accounts for individual motivations that decide elections. Thermodynamics results from individual buying decisions influencing the economy.

There is no expert consumer. There is no expert voter. To predict human behavior based on one perfect, thoroughly educated person will not work. With government secrecy and the distortion of facts, there is no way to make that perfect decision either to select leaders or to make purchases.

On the one hand, classic economic thought is centered on microeconomics, on the well-informed consumer making decisions to purchase based on choice between goods. The anticipation is that competition provides a fair price and the expert buyer will buy at the lowest price. Sam Walton showed how this approach works.

On the other hand, big government thinking relies on macroeconomics, the big picture. John Maynard Keynes believes the big economy has to be regulated by government. Private enterprise had to work with government, and that means taxes and government control. The ideal is full employment and a stable economy, one without inflation. Only the government can do that job.[9]

John Kenneth Galbreath expanded on this alleged need for government guidance and control.[10] His idea was to tax for public-sector improvements such as highways and schools. During recessions big government would tax more to get the money to hire more people.

A favorite quote:

> It is a well known and very important fact that America's founding fathers did not like taxation without representation. It is a lesser known and equally important fact that they did not much like taxation with representation. [11]

This is one of my favorite quotes, not necessarily one of Galbreath's favorites. My interpretation is not that the founders were selfish and objected to paying for government. The founders knew governments were greedy so the less paid to them, the better.

Milton Friedman is another influential economist.[12] His approach was economic freedom. For social and political progress and a strong economy, he recommended reducing the role of government. His analyses of monetary policy, of how the supply of money would influence growth and inflation, are important contributions. Higher interest means less money and less economic growth. Lower interest means more money and more economic growth.

These competing writers on economics were also part of that greatest generation that survived the Depression. Galbreath and Friedman were in the middle of the recovery effort and their writings came out of their experiences. Does the economy need more government or less? Do we increase taxes or reduce taxes? Will raising or lowering interest rates by the Federal Reserve do the job?

Despite the hard evidence from the end of the cold war with

the collapse of statism, economists continued the debate of government control. Among the most significant was a belated recognition of Friedrich Hayek and his insights.[13] Opposing government control, he advocated more freedom. Well acquainted with socialism, Hayek knew that collectivism led to totalitarianism. He preferred the "self-organizing system of voluntary cooperation." In other words, reduce government control to maintaining the rule of law including police and national defense. Leave the economy to the people.

Another "new" entry in this world of economic academics, Arthur Laffer showed that a decrease in tax rates would stimulate the economy and increase government revenues.[14] Called "supply side" economics, the overall theory is to reduce taxes so people would have more to spend, to develop business, hire workers and stimulate the economy. His views are popular during conservative governments and generally rejected during liberal governments. Laffer's "supply side" was "trickle-down" by the liberals.

Again, the results show Laffer was correct. The economy responded.

The debate continues. These economist "thinkers" are cited by statists to tax and spend to provide more government jobs or by business to cut back and grow the economy by giving business the money to expand and hire more workers.

Someday economists may agree on the standards for their profession and reach agreement on the government role. My question: who runs the new government businesses, a bureaucrat or a business leader?

Many appreciate this simple quip by Ronald Reagan: "I am with the government and I am here to help you."[15]

Economists could also learn from accountants. Accountants keep track of the exact dollars and cents that a business makes and spends. They play a vital role in keeping businesses and the economy going. They do not produce "econofacts." They rely on hard numbers that tell what a business is doing.

At least accountants have prescribed standards for handling accounts. The GAAP (generally accepted accounting principles) states how accounts are compiled and reported by accountants.[16] Businesses will know how they are doing. In the aggregate the economy will be built on a solid foundation of real numbers.

There is room for opinion even among accountants. The United States Government has its accountants for policy purposes ("politics"). Unfortunately, budget manipulations adjust for fiscal years, budget shortfalls and more accounts, leaving the budget suspect at best. We would do ourselves a service by requiring that the budget be balanced. Funny thing happened on the way to the bank. We have the written requirement for a balanced budget but, Washington-style, we ignore the law.[17]

Pending that day of agreement, economists still have a key role in the economy by determining the interest rate.

Economic Doers

Some economists are "doers." The ones with government responsibilities, the ones whose decisions make a real difference, are those doers who serve as the chairs of the Federal Reserve. They determine the interest rate or more accurately the discount rate (also known as the cost of money).

Back in the 1980s Paul Volcker was the chair who commanded recovery from the stagflation years, when interest was too high for growth.[18] He limited the growth of the money supply, unemployment shot up, and the results included protesting farmers who drove their tractors to block government buildings in Washington, DC.

Still active in policy recommendations, Paul highlighted the current problems for the economy:

1. We do not save enough
—despite the advice of billionaires.
2. We are buying more than we produce
—trade deficits increase every year.
3. Healthcare is skyrocketing
—we should pay more even though many do not pay.[19]

From these problems he concludes "the world economy is lopsided." We are in trouble and globalization is at least part of the problem.

Paul was replaced by Alan Greenspan.[20] Alan would serve longer than any other chair and would help direct the economy through control of interest rates and obscure speeches that business experts would spend hours trying to understand.

Huh?

Alan was successful. His decisions were followed by two major recoveries and the economic progress of the 1990s.

During his term there were "bubbles" of economic growth in the dot-coms and in real estate where sub-prime mortgages flourished. Both "bubbles" fell apart. Greenspan's solutions were ever lower interest rates and continued progress, even after the dot-com bust and the mortgage crisis.

Globalization was recognized by Greenspan to increase economic activity while limiting inflation, and the growth in commerce meant outward capital flows for the United States. In other words, we were paying a high price for globalization.

On the one hand, Alan supported and encouraged the process. On the other hand, he also predicted serious problems. He predicted a slowdown, one that he stated was necessary. He said it would come when foreign nations decided to limit their risk with America.[21]

That slowdown has happened in an entirely different way.

The United States should have reduced the risk.

There is a new economist "doer" running the Fed. Ben Bernanke has his hands full, facing the current fall of globalization and somehow managing a "safe landing" with a healthy and growing economy.[22]

Globalization will not be halted by our leaders, whether elected or appointed. Some economists are looking at the overall problems of globalization and there may be a major change in thinking underway. Advocates of fair trade run into prompt objections. Free traders argue that problems with free trade do not support high tariffs. In a typical false statement, free traders accuse fair traders of being isolationists. The developing proposal is for fair trade, not free trade and not high tariffs and no trade.[23]

Since the Second World War economists have embraced globalization. All agreed that the stiff tariffs placed on imports by the greatest generation were not good policy. In a series of agreements, the United States reduced tariffs and globalization was on the way.

Progress has been virtually unlimited. No tariffs needed. Give us free trade, period.

To date, however, nothing has been done to improve the international balance for America. That balance worsens every year and is like a tax taking money out of the United States.

We need to correct the balance. Individuals acting as the expert consumer and the expert voter need to take action to improve the economy and make it work better for us.

In plain talk that's you and me.

Union Economists

One other economist must be heard. The unions in America have serious problems with globalization. The main attraction for outsourcing is the high cost of labor in America. High wages here are driving business abroad.

Unions have spoken against globalization but as a word of

caution, not outright opposition. Their leaders have not picketed the approvals of trade agreements.

Ron Blackwell is the leading economist for the AFL-CIO.[24] In recent testimony he urged full employment and protection of union rights. He did not attack globalization. He urged policies to protect "the living standards of America's working families." In earlier hearings on China and globalization, he did not oppose the process but urged regulations to restore "the health of the American economy."[25]

Perhaps the majority commitment to globalization is too powerful for unions to offer successful opposition. Lobbying might have effectively limited or even defeated trade agreements.

The results are otherwise. We are globalizing, period. The balance of trade is worsening against us. The results are what count. That count is running against us, in a very big way.

How bad are the economic results?

Expert Consumer

The real test of the economy is not the statistics or the experts. The real test is the evaluation by the aggregate of "expert consumers," the American buyer and seller. What do Americans think about the economy? What are consumers doing?

Poll after poll highlights our interest and our problems.[26] The questions are different but the result is the same. For us, apart from foreign affairs and national defense, only the economy matters.

Gallup routinely polls us and reports on many issues. One very specific issue or another is the most important. This may include war or global warming or any other subject. There are sixty specific subjects in the polls. No one issue could possibly command a majority.

However, when all the Gallup questions are reviewed, economic issues are the chief concern. Total the questions on the economy to get the picture. That total always has the same overall result—we are mainly interested in the economy.

We have families. We have to provide for ourselves and our loved ones. There is nothing more important than our personal economic situation.

To repeat, "It's the economy, stupid."

If the Gallup questions on the economy are analyzed further, economic issues relate to globalization. Our overall economy and all parts of it are dependent on world trade.

Globalization is everywhere.

For our livelihood, for taking care of family we have to have a good economy. A good economy depends on the success of globalization. Vice versa, globalization depends on a good economy.

Econofacts are used to analyze the balance, the economic balance and the trade balance.

There is a further consideration.

The business leaders run the economy. They know numbers that are better than statistics. They read balance sheets and monthly statements. They know how many employees are needed and have the duty to make sure there is income to pay them. Those in businesses know the cost of advertising and sales. They spend the money to hire, expand, advertise and take care of the business in every way. Better than anyone else, they know what their business needs.

Most business leaders support globalization.

The Globalization Process

What do statistics tell about globalization?

Two sets of statistics tell what happened to the world's economy during the last century.

The world's leading economies[27]:

In 1900

Austria-Hungary/**United States**/China/United Kingdom/Germany/India

In 1925

United States/United Kingdom/China/France/Germany/India

In 1950

United States/Soviet Union/United Kingdom/China/France

In 1975

United States/Soviet Union/Japan/Germany

In 2000

United States/Japan/Germany/China

The United States became the leading economy after the end of the First World War. Other nations came and went, in and out of the top list. Wars or political turmoil explain most of the changes.

War is not good for the economy.

Another comparison ranks by total product[28]:

1870: World—1.1 trillion dollars

Austria-Hungary/China/India/United Kingdom/**USA**/Russia

1913: World—2.7 trillion dollars

Austria-Hungary/**USA**/China/Germany/Russia

1950: World—5.3 trillion dollars

USA/USSR/Latin America/United Kingdom/Germany/China/India

1973: 16 trillion dollars

USA/Far East/Soviets/Japan/Latin America/Germany/China/France

1998: World—33.7 trillion dollars

USA/China/Japan/Latin America/India/Germany

Both reports show major changes resulting from wars. Note that the Austria-Hungary Empire disappears after the First World War. Because of its huge population, China is always a major participant. Latin America remains strong. Europe's individual nations move up and down. Russia has good times and bad.

A general comment on this long-term history: If political leaders would see the need to care for their economy and require business ethics rather than corruption, they would find plenty of work, national progress and no need for war.

The United States is the leader with a powerful economy. We have made great progress. By typical comparative statistics with the rest of the globe, we are the biggest, the best and the strongest.

A snapshot of some important statistics[29]:

USA population: 300 million

USA diversity:

White	66.9%
Hispanic	14.4%
Black	12.8%
Asian	4.3%
Native	1.2%
Multiracial	1.5%

Immigrant population—5,800,000
(over twice other nations)

Foreign-born—11.1%

Language other than English spoken at home—17.9%

Home ownership—66.2%

Total homes—124,521,886
(most of us have a home)

Equity ownership—50.3%

Total investors—91,100,000
(a majority have stock holdings)
Business establishments—22,974,655
(pursuing the dream, 24/7)
Education—
high school—80.4%
college—24.4%
(well-educated, with immigrants needing more)

Manufacturer sales	$3.9 trillion
Wholesale trade sales	$4.6 trillion
Retail sales	$3.1 trillion
Food and accommodations	$449 billion
Gross National Product	$12.4 trillion
Federal spending	$2.14 trillion
Total government spending	$2.7 trillion

These reports suggest some of the problems and the successes we have. One point about the numbers is that they show we work out solutions.

We are the major producer dedicated to meeting the needs of people, those of us, all of us, who are consumers and producers.

The top-ten nations based on gross domestic product:[30]

United States	$12.4 trillion
Japan	4.5T
Germany	2.8T
China	2.2T
United Kingdom	2.2T
France	2.1T
Italy	1.7T
Spain	1.1T

Canada	1.1T
India	0.7T

We are the world's leader. Our economy is strongest, still. Our military remains the sole power to promote and maintain the peace, the necessary global law and order. Based on our diversity, we are a preview of what is ahead for most nations. We remain the leader in so many other ways.

The rest of the world has also improved.

Because of the success of regional unions, we are losing the lead in many ways. The numbers show major changes are underway in comparisons with the evolving regional unions.

The Global Commitment

How well has America met its commitment to the world economy? The commitment was made in 1945 to prevent wars by building world peace.

Compared to all other nations, we have done an excellent job.

What have we done to maintain the peace and work to welcome the future in good order?[31]

Our USA has made the major contributions, both as the keeper of the peace and as the economic engine maintaining growth.

Looking at individual accounts, we are attacked as the world's worst threat because our defense economy is huge.

The top-ten nations by military spending:

United States	$277Billion
China	56B
France	47B
Japan	40B
Germany	39B
United Kingdom	32B

Italy	20B
India	16B
Saudi Arabia	13B
Brazil	13B

Military defense spending is necessary for maintaining world commerce. Tom Andrews made this fact clear based on his experience in service with the Pacific Fleet. We are the peacemakers and the peacekeepers.

What is interesting is totaling the military spending of each nation now a member of or in the process of joining the European Empire. Europe spends more, a total of $321 billion compared to the United States at $277 billion.[32]

Military spending for maintaining the peace and for many necessary humanitarian purposes is, as it must be, a national priority for law and order. Consider some of the services by the United States military—tsunami relief, food for Darfur, maintaining peace in the South China Sea, patrolling the Red Sea areas for pirates, assistance for ships in trouble, and much, much more.

If all financial efforts to maintain a world economy and to move globalization forward are considered, America is far ahead of other nations, as a percent, on a per person basis and as total investment and contribution.

The playing field is not level, and that lack of fairness shows up in many ways. The commitment to the world economy and to world peace is one comparative measure. Other nations need to pick up the tab in all sectors of the world economy.

Look at America's gain if we insisted on a level playing field. We would add $5,000 per person per year to our bank accounts.[33] These savings will be seen in chapter 4, "Greed."

Gallup polls show the greatest concerns for most Americans are the economy and globalism. Gallup conducts the poll for its weekly reports. Of sixty specific concerns, when the items related to the world's economy are grouped, global issues become the major concern for 45 percent of Americans.

We know there are problems with globalization.

The problem is that America is falling behind in the global competition. Our leaders continue to support trade policies unfair to America. The solution is we have to think America and we need to buy USA. We have to promote our values, not compromise them. Our leaders, too often enmeshed in "relativistic values," do not promote what has been "made in America." Some see a way to socialize America by agreeing to treaties and trade agreements that cost us our rights, our heritage, our economic future and our political future.[32]

LOU DOBBS

There are exceptions to the "accepted version" of free trade. A leading critic of unrestricted free trade is Lou Dobbs.[33] He is one commentator willing to take on the "prevailing wisdom" of our leaders and the media regarding free trade and open borders. The factually afflicted statist free traders have a worthy opponent.

First of all, Lou is an economist. He is also an author, a promoter of small-town America, a radio and TV host, and an advocate for fair trade.

Because of a back and forth career, Lou is unique in the history of cable television and specifically CNN. Born in Texas, he was educated in Idaho and was, like many of the greatest generation, a high school leader. Graduating from Harvard, he had jobs with an anti-poverty program and a cash management service, then went to radio as a police and fire reporter. From there he kept moving up, taking a position with CNN as chief economics correspondent. Clashing with management for its political bias, he left and then returned for news and financial reporting.

Lou opposes unrestricted globalization, outsourcing, illegal immigration, free trade and corporate influence. Critics attack him as an isolationist. This accusation against economists urging caution is misplaced.

Lou's views are outlined in several books. The latest is *War on the Middle Class*, a survey of the impact of globalization on individuals. He states:

> The cost of free trade is truly exorbitant. The United States is losing not only production, capital, and jobs, but our sovereignty, the ability to determine our destiny as a nation.[34]

Lou may disagree but his pro-American vision was developed by Goldwater, then Reagan, and now Bill O'Reilly and Sean Hannity, with solid support on Radio Free America from Rush Limbaugh and many more. The issue is not who your friends are and voting together. The overridding issues are the principles our leaders recognize and support.

The reporting of facts and the conclusions of these many individuals reflect the growing problems for unrestricted globalization. Lou's pro-American views are justified by remarkable changes in globalization. We have new economic arrangements emerging, new paradigms defining global economics and politics.

The Ten New Global Regions

The statistics show a huge American commitment to world peace in every respect, from keeping the peace to foreign aid and investment globally. Globalization began here and we remain the engine driving that progress.

We are not alone. The statistics show ten major economic groups worldwide. Several are drawing equal to and even ahead of the United States.

Consider the new global regions. One is the United States, the thirteen colonies who started as essentially independent nations and united to form our union.

The European Union is another, formed from the nations

most involved in World War Two with the exception of still another economic region, the Russian Federation.

Japan is one of the ten major powers.

China is a federation of sorts, the successor to the old Chinese Empire, with many diverse regions still held together by Beijing. That union in progress is a major new player on the globe.

Asia has several smaller nations, successfully uniting in the ASEAN group.

Latin America is another top producer now uniting into a trade region while developing political union.

Africa has a relatively new regional group. Progress is being made, particularly if the nations there will get together and take action over local wars, poverty and democracy.

The Muslim world is also well defined, centered on nations with Islam as the required religion. This organization is very loosely allied with major soul-searching underway to see how to pull together.

India has been a participant with the powerful economies of the world and is another of the top ten.

The new regional groups, the new emerging economic unions[35]:

Region	Population	Total Income
United States	300M	$13.5T
Europe Union	315M	10.8T
Japan	128M	4.9T
ASEAN	1.8B	3.5T
Latin America	0.5B	2.7T
China	1.3B	2.6T
India	1.1B	906B
Russia	942M	822B
Muslim	311.1M	71B
Africa	770M	49B

All nations within each region's general boundaries are included. Some small nations may never join the greater region but they are for all practical purposes members. A very practical suggestion: Join up. You are part of the globe. Get in. Cut the best deal and join.

In the past year changes have been made. Europe now has the world's largest gross national income. China has the world's largest carbon output. Others have moved forward with important economic progress. We are no longer the world leader in all categories.

Significantly, the United States has the worst balance of trade, dollar decline and national debt.[36]

These national realignments into ten world regions or supernations are flexible. Member nations join or participate based on their leaders' decisions.

Some critics recognize the emerging regions and predict a repeat of Orwell's forecast in his 1949 book about a fictional, futuristic 1984 with three major world regions constantly at war with one another and with the respective populations reduced to automatons.[37] The world of "big brother" ruled.

Orwell's work of fiction did not happen in 1984 and has not happened a quarter century after his fatal year. The new Orwellian analysis does not project a year. Out of fairness, give Orwell Junior until 2020.

Still will not happen. We will muddle through.

American Doctrine

America helped with two world wars and then practiced containment until the Soviet Union and its intercontinental nukes were taken out of service. We have not attempted to take over the world. Unlike the European Empire, we have not added territory to our national boundaries. We have no national goal or doctrine of taking over other nations.

We have taken the leadership in showing how business works

so that the economy makes progress. The nations have also learned to compete, another ideal we promoted. Look at our business leaders. The best example of getting out there and competing is Sam Walton. Many nations and more particularly their economic regions have made consistent progress.

Our national policies have been:

- promote globalization
- improve economies to improve individual lives
- stand for freedom of speech and press
- defend the world commerce system
- develop workable international organizations
- promote a healthy environment
- oppose waste and corruption

These policies developed with no preordained five- or ten-year plan. We have a vision for a better world through commerce and democracy and we have a mission of developing political and economic unions to achieve that goal. The plans are based on economic progress.

There is no fixed policy. We see immediate problems and we proceed to resolve them on individual and very specific terms, almost a day at a time. Our approach is very practical, based on actual results in the real world.

Underlying these policies are much more significant policies, results we hope to achieve in support of our overall goals. We never told the Soviet Union we would convert them to a Federation. We never broadcast to China that we would show them commerce works. We took over Japan and moved to set up a democratic business system with no blueprints about what would result. We made progress one step at a time, like you would teach a baby to walk or a child to ride a bike.

Europe was encouraged to rebuild with the Marshall Plan and then to unify into a common market. The resulting European

Union, now with greater income than we have, was never on the drawing board in 1947.

The results speak for themselves.

In business results are what count. Results may not be known until the end of the day, then the month, then the year. Many years may pass before results are significant.

Our very practical policies have worked. We showed they worked when we united our original thirteen colonies. We supported regional groups following the Second World War. We maintained world commerce and prevented world wars to provide ample time for the new economies to work.

Our policies worked.

At this time we have carried the burden too long and too far. Our main interest is to remain engaged globally. We have an unstated doctrine against isolation. Stated positively, our national doctrine is globalization.

From time to time we have adopted formal "doctrines" to define our international relations.[38] Avoid foreign entanglements, cautioned George Washington. Stay out of the Americas, James Monroe cautioned Europe. Establish organizations for world peace, suggested Woodrow Wilson. Contain Soviet aggression, urged Harry Truman.

These "doctrines" go on and on. We have our principles. Often they are never stated. Some are simply recognized for what they are. With the benefit of hindsight, the basic doctrines since 1945 have been containment and globalization. The end result was a stable world economy with progress to as many people as possible. We globalize based on our many values for individuals, for business, for the national economy, for competition, and for political freedoms. We seek no expansions of our nation. We welcome free trade.

The nature of politics, of power politics at the highest and deepest levels, is not to declare doctrines. Many develop in very practical terms, with one small success at a time. We have to wait to see the results.

In addition to supporting free trade, the doctrines have to be understood at deeper, very unstated levels.

We want world peace. We do not want to lose Americans to battles in distant lands. We promote the alternative, economic progress to prevent some of the causes of aggression.

A basic, perhaps subliminal understanding is that we trade on terms less than fair to us to help other national economies. At the same time we encourage economic and even political unions among the globe's nations for them to help themselves.

The results are clear. We have done just that.

Consider the trade imbalance, the deficit and the weak dollar. These three statistical results represent our contributions to the global economy. Any policy planner should understand that free trade would have benefits for us and for the other nations involved in trade. They have not considered what also happened, that we would go too far. We had the power and we assumed we could continue taking a loss position forever.

We cannot. We have a very large, very serious imbalance of trade compared to all other nations.

The same American leaders had to know that we would bear the burden and pay the price. Jobs would go overseas. Cheap goods would be imported. Recall when "Made in Japan" meant junk. The new meaning is "a better, less expensive automobile."[39]

With Japan and with Europe, we committed our economy to help, to bring them out of devastation. Our values have played a key role in that effort.

We continue to follow these policies.

We have to cut back.

The commitment is most striking in our trade with China. That trade is not fair and it is not balanced. We are supporting China to the maximum possible, firm in the belief that we will keep China at peace while we change the national policies there to support progress with business models.

We have gone too far.

Our trade balance with China is deficit after deficit, with the latest at 74 billion dollars.[41]

Consider the latest major trade agreement, NAFTA. The trade is not fair or balanced. Every year we have a deficit with Canada and with Mexico. Last year it was 127 billion dollars. That deficit is growing.[40]

Change is needed, to improve parity between the nations.

In all our globalized trade, we cannot keep making the big commitment. We have to level the playing field.

We are far beyond free trade now.

We have unbalanced trade.

We need fair trade.

Economic Values

We are what the greatest generations did to promote a better world order. The results are very good. Or a better way to express the results: our results with democracy and commerce are at least better than any alternative tried in the last century. Like democracy, our economic policies are not perfect but they are far better than any alternative.

Our economic system of commerce is part of what is meant by "made in the USA."

The primary test of politics and economies is the results. The beauty of our commerce and democracy is that what we have done is subject to criticism. Our standards for freedom of speech welcome criticism.

Honest criticism is needed. Too often that honesty does not happen.

Inaccurate criticism of our economic values is routine.

America works best because of well-established policies: a

sound dollar, avoiding deficit spending, keeping inflation in check and sound monetary policy. Those values are an "invisible hand."[41]

When we adopted our Constitution and became the United States with one regional economy, Alexander Hamilton knew what was necessary. As secretary of the treasury he was determined that we follow the rules of commerce.

Our Constitution requires Congress provide for our money and its value. Hamilton required we have a sound dollar. He wanted us to pay off the debt incurred by the colonies in gaining our independence. This was done. We avoided deficits in our commerce account with the globe.

Hamilton recommended a national bank. That idea was rejected for many years but evolved into the Federal Reserve system of today. We adopted his recommendations for tariffs on imports. The result was a huge expansion of the national treasury. We made money. The nation became very wealthy.

Hamilton's basic recommendations were adopted and we prospered. Our national economic union was a great success.

Over the decades we made changes. The fundamental change in 1945 was to adopt free trade. We abandoned protective tariffs and quotas. Instead we have the national doctrine of globalization.

There is one related issue, part of globalization. A feature of free trade is open borders. In the United States economic and political union, a citizen may travel anywhere, no passport or visa required, no questions asked.

What we have in America is not only outsourcing with free trade, sending jobs abroad. We also have in-sourcing, bringing jobs into America and still sending money abroad. Immigrants send their money home. We have the same result as outsourcing. The absence of effective controls means we are in fact following a policy of open borders. This unique practice, rejected by all other nations, cannot continue.

Because of globalization, there have been additional changes in our basic economic policies. We avoid tariffs and quotas to the maximum extent possible, opposing any fundamental change. We require full employment including government intervention. We fail to maintain a sound dollar. We accept deficits while trying to justify an ever greater debt. We have routinely welcomed immigrants and prospered; however, entry in compliance with our laws has not been required. We are not maintaining our international borders.

We are a long way from practicing these policies with one exception: that of eliminating tariffs. This free trade has to be adjusted. Until we get our other national economic policies back in line, we have to change from unprotected trade, from free trade, to a preference for America.

Until we get fair trade, we need a moratorium on new trade.

The lack of fairness is shown in the international greed that has resulted.

Our critics delight in the problems, find problems everywhere and have no solutions other than more statism. Some want a government job or even a government agency, preferably controlled by that same critic with a new, high-sounding position with excellent pay and such extras as an office and parking space, all with no fixed hours. For an example visit some of the top- and intermediate-level jobs in DC.[42]

Government jobs are different, not at all like any nine-to-five position or any 24/7 ownership position. Unlike any ownership position, no one in government worries about economic results. We developed powerful economic values, then compromised those values to our detriment.

Trade imbalances, budget deficits and a fallen dollar will not work.

We have to do better.

Consider the greed.

FOUR

GREED

Greed.

One of the deadly sins.

Inherent in human nature.

Unavoidable.

Unbeatable.

The founders thought so. The Federalist rings with their objections to government and power.[1] They knew from experience that power corrupts. Patrick Henry even left the constitutional convention because he was so opposed to governments.

Tom Paine, the revolutionary guiding some of the founders, said:

> Government, even in its best state, is but a necessary evil; in its worst state, an intolerable one.[1]

The old story of the emperor's new clothes speaks to the current state of corruption. Seems the emperor had purchased a new, very imperial garment. In fact, he had received nothing. Putting on his "new clothes" and going for a walk, he was pleased that his subjects spoke highly of his "new robes."Then a child hollered out, "The Emperor has no clothes."

The truth is so obvious that we ignore the role of power and greed. In England, the rule was that the king could do no wrong. The loyal subjects knew better but agreed their ruler did no wrong. Of course, they knew wrongs were done. They also knew the king was the law.

In the United States the rule was basically the same. You cannot sue the government because it has "sovereign immunity." If the government did wrong, there was nothing you could do about it. Same idea, the king (the government) can do no wrong. Do not even suggest otherwise.

The "fiction"[3]—as the law called the lie—persisted. There may have been a very practical reason. If the government could be charged with "wrong" in court, money might have to be paid. Keep the costs of governing low. Do not pay for mistakes. Say there were no mistakes; therefore, we are not paying.

In the minds of many in power, the rule is still there. Too many elected leaders agree with the rule and declare there was no crime so no payment should be made. They take us for fools because we cooperate. We shrug, say greed is part of human nature and overlook the obvious wrongs. The mistakes are forgotten.

Globalization shows the greed and how the greed is ignored.

The adverse impact cannot be okayed any longer.

Impact of Globalization

Our commitment to free trade has produced excellent results. Consider the wealth realized by the great globalizer, Bill Gates. He is the most wealthy—or close to it, depending on the stock market—because his global product works so well with the world wide web.

Great wealth has not been realized by everyone. In many communities, the loss of manufacturing plants and jobs has had very bad results for too many Americans.

Look at the impact[4]:

1. Since 1950, manufacturing jobs are down over 50% —as a share of total jobs:
   - manufacturing is down from 34% to 13%
   - service jobs are up from 59% to 82%

2. Job losses
   —textiles, from 924,000 down to 433,000
   —apparel, from 1,233,000 down to 522,000
   —metal, from 1,185,000 down to 593,000

As Seth Donovan showed, globalization has had an adverse impact on many people. Jobs are gone. They are lost throughout the economy.

The economy may be subject to the "invisible" hand of Adam Smith, the original economist.[5] Let the economy do whatever it does. Workers, however, are not invisible. Many new manufacturing plants have been built, with much more efficiency and with fewer jobs. Many Americans have new jobs and are doing well. Many are not doing well. Efforts have been made to ease the job losses. Some subsidies have been provided. They have not provided jobs.[6]

The total impact is difficult to measure but we see the overall result in the loss of trade. The period from 1980 shows an imbalance against America.[7]

The trade deficit since 1980:

- $6.193 trillion loss
- $80,000 per American family

The budget deficit is another measure of the impact on America. This impact hits the taxpayers, the American families covering the loss. Since 1980, we have been above the break-even point for only two years. The annual deficits have us down by $400 billion. An American family has lost another $520.

The declining value of the dollar is still another adverse impact. The founders insisted on a sound dollar. For most of our history, the dollar was the standard for commerce. Globalization has not cooperated. By 2008, the dollar had about one-half its value on international markets. Again, the value to the American family is a 50 percent substantial decrease in buying power abroad.[8]

We are paying a very high price under our doctrine of globalization.

How much have we lost?

Why have we lost so much?

Proof of Conspiracy

Because governments are so hidden and protected from disclosure, specific proof of wrongdoing is hard to find. Any plan to dig deeply into globalization will be blocked.[9]

The greed in the human heart and mind are hard at work in globalization. For greed to work, for government to take another person's property for personal gain, conspiracy is necessary.

Any conspiracy requires a secret agreement with at least one other person to take what belongs to others. Privacy is required. Working in secrecy with at least one co-conspirator, property belonging to others is taken.

The problem with corruption is proving what happened.

In the United States criminal greed and conspiracy are difficult to prove. Proof is far harder in nations without our systems for law and order. The emperor still has his new clothes. The king can still do no wrong. Today the dictator can do no wrong.

International organizations are even more immune. When nations join together for a new international organization, they add still another level of protection.

Going one step higher on the organization chart, to the super-organization at the United Nations, greed and conspiracy in support of greed is everywhere. In addition to the "human nature" we all know about, there is an interesting additional justification. United Nations representatives are on a mission of great importance. Personal enrichment should not even be suggested. The United Nations is so "vital" for the future of world peace that ongoing crimes should not even be suggested, let alone be revealed.[10]

Greed is there, still hard at work. The old rule remains in effect:

> Power corrupts and absolute power corrupts absolutely.[11]

The higher up we go on the new world order, the more absolute the power and the stronger the immunity.

How could corruption occur at the United Nations? How dare you suggest it?

Same as always. We know, then shrug and let it go.

There is one other consideration. To suggest conspiracy is an insult to the nation or organization. In the old ways of war before *Pax Americana*, the insult meant war. There are those who still hope political systems will work to prevent war. The organization cannot be tarnished. The emperor does no wrong. The tyrant is the law.

The newer organizations under consideration propose even more powerful and expensive government controls and are even more "perfect." According to the statists, we just need more government and no liability.

Perhaps explaining the dislike at the United Nations for free speech, the statists caution us to ask no questions. Trust them. Recall the old rule of equity:

> He who trusts most loses most.[12]

Trust us. Do not ask for records. Do not ask for any public disclosure. There is nothing to disclose.

For all these entrenched ideas, many from long ago, proof of greed and conspiracy is virtually impossible.

Proving Conspiracies

In the interest of fairness and justice, there are ways. Because more than one person has to be involved, for example just to sign the checks, one conspirator may break and confess. Insider disclosures are very helpful.

Even without "whistleblowers," an alert legal system has ways to follow up on suspicion and bring in the usual suspects. For example, the Internal Revenue Service used to go after taxpayers showing signs of increased wealth.[13]

We should keep an eye on the apparent worth of our leaders.

Law enforcement is doing better and better in tracking down deposits and uncovering questionable enrichment.[14] Offshore banks and the gnomes of Zürich have made "following the money" very difficult; however, new procedures in the war on terror are helping minimize this transfer of illegal funds. Technological innovations are also easing the burden on investigators.

The law used to make it easier to break a conspiracy. If one co-conspirator spilled the beans, the others were rounded up and compelled to prove there was no conspiracy.[15] This rule has faded. Now, if you want to prove a government conspiracy, you have to make your case from beginning to end.

Another new development has been the sheer size of the crimes and the related problems of proof. Internet scams are discovered; however, the crooks act quickly and the time required to locate the source, cross international borders for investigation and then gather facts and go forward block solid results. If one conspirator is caught and finally convicted, the rest go free. Just the time required for a trial to go from beginning to end prevents prosecution of the rest.[16]

The final protection for government is secrecy. You cannot see key documents. Freedom of information simply has not worked. This failure is not only at the super-organizations. It goes down the organizational chart to local agencies.

The many protections given government greed and the related conspiracies provide the protection the criminals need.

What do we do about it?

Results of Conspiracies

We cannot rely on conspiracies falling apart. Each member faces penalties, even that one necessary person willing to come forward and provide "State's evidence." Why suffer for ill-gotten gains? Why be a stool pigeon?

We are able to use our suspicions, not to convict for past wrongdoing but to prevent further taking of the public's money.

In business, there are ways to uncover greed. What is happening to the money? An alert accountant will ask questions, a good manager will see the losses and whistle-blower policies will encourage disclosures.

Conspiracies remain very difficult to prove.

We are left with the more general question, what are the results?

We have seen the adverse impact on America—imbalanced trade, budget deficits, a falling dollar.

The problems are our own doing. To state what happened in courtroom talk, we shot ourselves in the foot.

When political organization failed after 1945, we turned to economic rebuilding and that worked wonders. We promoted commercial union among similar economies wherever possible. We see the results with ten major global economic regions prospering from the business and economic values we developed.

The United States dedicated huge sums to the process. We have paid dearly. We are still paying dearly.[17]

Consider the balance of trade: since 1980, we are out of 14 trillion dollars. Each one of us is down $4,000.

Consider the national deficit: we are in debt to the tune of 3 trillion dollars. Each of us is in debt $1,000.

Consider the value of the dollar: because of an over-dedication to globalism, the dollar is almost halved. We are out a total of over $6,000.

That loss is per person.

Per family of four—$24,000 loss.

Some say there is no relation between international and national economies and individuals. Tell that to people without jobs.

In business, results are what count. We have paid heavily on the key measures of relative wealth. Huge sums have gone to other nations based on our dedication to keep the peace, for *Pax Americana.*

Our national doctrine for globalization has been a huge success based on the one overriding result: world peace; however, we cannot afford to keep bearing the cost of world peace and global integration. There have to be favorable results, not another thirty years of imbalances and deficits.

Huge profits are being made throughout the world by many citizens in other countries. Profits are coming to America but on balance we have passed any fairness. We are losing. We have paid the price in deficits, severe balance of trade losses and a devalued dollar. We cannot continue losing.

Since 1980, there has been a huge loss to America. That loss has enriched business, governments and international organizations. Some American companies have prospered; however, overseas companies have gained at our expense. Foreign governments have profited unjustly and we have allowed their ill-gotten gains. As a nation we have lost. Recall that one person's loss is another's gain.

Corporate Greed

First, leading members of the trillionaires club have taken good profits.

Bill Gates built a multi-billion-dollar fortune. He was and is at the top of globalization. The results are understandable. In business, profits must be available for owners, for growth and for research. Bill did just that and brought the globe much closer together.

In a tradition uniquely American, Bill decided to give back most of what he earned. He set up the Bill and Melinda Gates Foundation. Thirty billion dollars was his unprecedented and historic contribution to serve global interests.[18]

The Davos speech by Bill Gates is a remarkable affirmation of the American system of business at work. He highlights two key values: self-interest and caring for others. He notes "the genius of capitalism is its ability to make self-interest serve the greater interest."

After recounting numerous examples of corporate support for controlling and eliminating disease and showing how business principles work best to solve seemingly incurable poverty, Bill called for "creative capitalism" with a "twin mission: making profits and also improving lives of those who don't fully benefit from today's market forces."

These improvements combine the best of American commerce and American charity:

> For sustainability we need to use profit incentives wherever we can. At the same time, profits are not always possible when business tries to serve the very poor. In such cases there needs to be another incentive, and that incentive is recognition.[19]

What does this mean? That corporations should support needed programs for impoverished nations with appropriate publicity by advertising the good deeds. These are many of the examples of this creative process to reduce world poverty.

Speaking as "an impatient optimist" at the world economic forum about NGOs, Bill noted: "anything you offered had to be free so it was almost like a tar baby; as soon as you did it [contributed], then it was they'd want more than was reasonable."[19]

Greed is the problem. Creative capitalism is a sound approach to limiting its effects.

Warren Buffet also made a grand fortune. A concern for others undoubtedly motivated him to join with Bill and Melinda to provide funds to help others. He added 31 billion dollars to the foundation.[20]

The goals of the Foundation are exceptional and very revealing. Staying away from government control and avoiding cash donations to charities, the Gates-Buffett monies go directly into major international programs.[21]

Sam Walton made an unprecedented fortune. He also made a similar determination to help others in the usual course of business. Wal-Mart is the largest corporate cash contributor in the United States.[22] Charitable giving exceeded $300 million in 2007, more than $5.8 million per week. The global total exceeded $415 million. The contributions are local, where the associates and customers live. Another traditional American leader showing that same measure of charity Bill and Warren practice.

On the other hand the Boeing example is a measure of the problems with corruption and greed on the global scene. Doing business abroad as well as in the United States has resulted in illegal gifts. Boeing paid huge penalties for corruption. An interesting point—government has been the foundation of Boeing problems.[23]

At the same time and in the tradition of Bill, Warren and Sam, Boeing states:

> Global corporate citizenship refers to the work Boeing does in our diverse communities to improve our world. We know that what we do has a global impact and that our combined enterprise-wide efforts can yield sustainable improvement in the communities in which we live, work, and support. [24]

There is little to show that Boeing dedicates a meaningful net share of its global success to others.

The charitable work by Bill, Warren and Sam are a powerful legacy. They are also a wonderful comment on American values—get out in the world, work hard and smart, and enjoy life, that pursuit of happiness we cherish, then take time to look back and do what Americans have done throughout the last century and still do, share with others, be charitable. Again we see faith-based values in action.[25]

The profits made by the four companies are unbelievable. All are global. All represent outsourcing income. Profits were the game and now helping others is the ambition.

Corporate greed has limits. Bill Gates, Warren Buffet and Sam Walton reached those limits and returned huge profits back to the globe.

The world's billionaires have also made fortunes from globalization. Determining their contribution back is not readily available. The American tradition of giving back what you have been given is not a strong global value. For example, the largest charitable foundation in Europe is not included in some lists because of pending investigations into how much of its charity goes to others.[26]

We have a long way to go. Thanks for the leadership by Bill, Warren and Sam the guidelines are in place to promote world commerce and to return much to the global community.

With a special thank you to the leadership of our greatest generations, we have another powerful reason to listen to our business leaders.

America has followed these leadership examples. We have a long tradition of charitable giving and of setting up foundations to assist others. The United States has been a major contributor. For the most part, however, we have not learned what these business leaders have recommended, that government is waste and simply not up to the task of truly assisting others for the longer term.[27] Too much goes to corruption and the related conspiracies. Our national commitment to globalization and world peace needs major changes.

One major mistake is that we give to other governments.[28] Bill and Warren do not. We remain incapable of understanding that government cannot do the job. Socialism and statism do not work. We need to empower private individuals, not government bureaucracies. The mini-loan program by private individuals in several nations is a perfect example.[29] Help people by teaching them how to help themselves, to stand on their own efforts and not to be part of the "big brother" promised in Orwell's *1984*.

Keeping in mind the serious problems in proving conspiracies, how do we know about this global corruption? What can be done?

Government Corruption

The major reason for our failure to correct the corruption is that governments are not up to the task. Instead, the record for corruption shows too much has been taken. Greed has taken over too many nations.

Some analysts limit the cost of government to taxes paid. The cost of government is far more. Huge sums go into the national treasuries, never to be seen again, at least not by the donors. For our purposes "taxes" refer to all costs paid to governments to do business.

Two international organizations try to monitor corruption and integrity. The information helps companies find safer havens for business. Meaningful laws for commerce are a key part of global integrity. To avoid the bribes and related abuses avoid the more dangerous nations.

Transparency International has researched global corruption since 1995.[30] Reports are issued on in-depth studies, and annually a "corruption perceptions index" is compiled. The latest index covers 180 nations. The Appendix includes the latest summary.

The United States is in the top twenty deemed to be relatively free of corruption.[31] Other top-ranked nations include Singapore, Japan, Australia and the United Kingdom. Tied at number 72 at the very middle of the total are several of our key trading partners: Brazil, China, India and Mexico. Russia is near the bottom, at 143. Most nations remain corrupt.

Note that transparency has not been enacted into law. This is the fundamental test. Without open government we lose the integrity needed. Transparency International has a long way to go.

Corrupt leaders abound in some of our major trading partners. Why are we losing the balance of trade? Where is money appropriated for foreign aid being not just wasted, but stolen? Many of our major trading partners are corrupt, costing more for our government's assistance and more for American companies to do business. These "taxes" imposed on us by corrupt nations are taken from the taxes we pay to our government. There rests a good part of our deficit and imbalance. There is where change will have to be made. Individual citizens will have to do it.

The latest Global Corruption report covers judicial corruption, defined as "the abuse of entrusted power for private gain."[33] The report does not name names. Judicial integrity is a vital part of the law and order business must have.

The organization promotes "transparency" in the sense of full disclosure for judicial proceedings. The facts and the procedures for court decisions must be out in the open. Public forums, complete records of court trials, written opinions and more must be on the record. When we review a judicial decision, we want to know what happened. We have to understand the decision. Lawyers have to be able to advise clients how to do business in other nations. Based on court decisions, we predict the results and advise businesses what to expect.

These tests for integrity and for disclosure should be included in trade agreements with our partners.

Far too many agreements do not have this protection. After all, even our government does not believe in transparency. Ask any politician about living in a goldfish bowl. They complain about disclosure, insist they do not like it (implying they disclose) and they do not do disclose. Try finding out where "earmarks" originate and where they go.[34] Our money, our taxes are being wasted. No wonder the United States is not number one on integrity. The United States should do much better, to top the global integrity lists.

Another review of global corruption is conducted by Global Integrity, based in Washington, DC.[35] Their 2007 index covers only forty-eight nations. For the nations surveyed, measures of integrity are strong, moderate, weak and very weak. Only eighteen nations make the top level for integrity. The nations with good integrity include the United States, Japan, Colombia and France. The other thirty-one are less than honest; they are more corrupt. Some of the nations without "global integrity" include Russia, Mexico, China, and Nigeria.

Compare these separate reviews of global integrity. On the various reports, those nations in the bottom for disclosure and integrity are often the same. Leaders in these nations are benefiting from globalization as individuals. Our foreign aid, free trade and all other money transfers are still enriching the already wrongfully enriched.

Corruption is their game.

America pays the price.

We do nothing effective to prevent the abuse. We do not get the results needed. We do not insist on law and order overseas, we do not have transparency here or overseas and we continue to see our taxpayer money wasted and our global commerce out of balance.

The United States is top-rated; however, we know how much integrity our government leaders have. Small surprise that Congress and their "earmarks" keep our national deliberative body near the bottom of the job performance polls.[36] We have worked hard to set the example for the world and have succeeded in many ways. We still fail to do the obvious, to disclose what is going on in our government.

Where is the money going and who is getting rich at our expense? The question needs answers from the United States and from all nations.

The State Department in Washington warns of corruption abroad but names no names and provides no specifics.[37] The lists and index reports on transparency, global integrity and global corruption listed above are included with the State report.

The State Department has written objectives but few results. The State Department represents America overseas but takes no direct action regarding corruption. The compromises coming from State are not acceptable to our need for integrity, for balanced trade and for democracy and freedom.

With corruption so dominant on the world scene, proposals to globalize a new world government, a new United Nations, are not consistent with vital American values; however, those proposals are supported by our State Department. Not only in terms of greed and more greed but also in terms of vital American values, current proposals for a new world government are not acceptable. In addition, active support for regional governments is not on the agenda at State even though the economic unions are what work, not the political proposals for more international governance and control for more United Nations' power. It should come as no surprise that State is being investigated for alleged fraud and for blocking investigations.[38]

The corruption overseas extends into the daily workings at State Department offices abroad. Author David Casavis of New

York has investigated and, in his book *The Thomas Crowne Affair*, states the following about our career officers: "Their first loyalty is to their careers."

Surely some action is taken against the corruption at our overseas embassies. Not so. Casavis explains:

> Crime moves from Embassy to Embassy, continent to continent. When the perpertrators are caught at an American Embassy, it is easier to transfer them on to another Embassy than to prosecute. When they arrive thousands of miles away, they start up the same scam all over again in a new country.

Our local consulates are not immune from conspiracies. Again, drastic changes are needed at State.[39]

We do not have the needed transparency at State. Taking transparency as a vital measure of integrity, there is none at State or, unfortunately, through most of our government.

Quit complaining about being in a goldfish bowl. Just do your job. Our government leaders and all employees should be in a government goldfish bowl.

Our Agency for International Development has concluded that

> corruption and poor governance fuel state failure, deter foreign investment, and cripple economic growth and development.[40]

Forbes, once again, has a list, this one for corruption based on the one compiled by Transparency International.[41] Noting that corruption takes many different forms, *Forbes* is particularly critical of the vital integrity so necessary for law and order. The report summarizes:

1. The police and judges have "questionable enforcement" of commercial agreements.
2. Funds are diverted from critical projects into the pockets of government officials.

3. Corruption then filters into everyday life in the global community, too often in the worst ways.

These are our trading partners?

No wonder Donald Trump says we have been "had" by China. The results for integrity and transparency say we have been "had" by most of our trading partners.

These reports of government corruption are a measure of the "taxes" that seriously injure globalization and America. Our payments in the form of taxes or grants to governments only support the corruption.

We should not continue making corrupt government representatives wealthy with our taxes.

We know what happens to some of these leaders. They take the money and move to the United States. The irony is complete.

Consider the balance of trade with two of our most publicized trading arrangements. With China, we are way behind.[42] With NAFTA, the losses are also all one-way, against our national economy. The latest deficit to Mexico and to Canada was $127 billion.[43] This has been increasing every year.

The total trade balance with all nations shows the leader in the positive column is China with a surplus of $363 billion. The same list for 164 nations places the United States at the bottom, with a 2007 deficit of $747 billion. The numbers are for only one year.[44]

The chart in the Appendix shows the results.

International organizations from the United Nations on down the organization chart have highly questionable practices. The payments to those nations and organizations show a serious deficit of that most important quality of government, integrity. If the organizations had open records, that issue could be settled; however, transparency is simply not there. As a result there is arrogance.

The total lack of shame continues at the United Nations. Recently, after pleading poverty, they asked for more money. The world food program asked for more money even though they had more than one billion dollars on hand.[45] As Bill Gates said, these charities only want more money. Because they get away with greed, their claims never end.

Where is there any surprise in concluding the deficits and imbalances hurting Americans are being stolen by foreign leaders? Specific proof is lacking because corruption is so hard to prove. Nations are not transparent and law and order does not require integrity.

The results are overwhelming. Corruption governs half the global community, particularly at the top. Very few nations are even relatively corruption-free, high-integrity operations.

Charts in the Appendix provide necessary comparisons. We are the largest economy and have better measures of integrity. The rest are less and less honest as they move down the economic ladder.

The worst feature is not the taking of our money and it is not the arrogance. The worst feature is they take us for fools and we help them. The corrupt laugh at us.

There is more.

Exportation of America

The third major problem is outsourcing.

Again, no surprise. We are greedy.

America's jobs and manufacturing are going overseas. The impact has been summarized, that huge part of our trade imbalance, the one going down since 1980.

The most obvious is one every American has encountered. The overseas helpdesks are awful. The example at the beginning shows not just the total lack of understanding but also the waste. A typical call takes twenty times as long as one made by a U.S. operator. The flip side is some American companies are retrenching; thank you, Clay McNair. The overseas helpdesk is very attractive on paper. The time required to handle calls significantly lessens the apparent competitive advantage. The loss in goodwill is far worse.[46]

The flip side of outsourcing is in-sourcing. Friedman defines the term to mean American companies bringing foreign products here for the finishing work needed for a final product.

The definition is too narrow for revealing what is happening. In-sourcing is having American jobs and not taking them overseas but making them available to migrants.[47]

The issue is immigration. The exportation is the money going out of the United States.

Outsourcing has a major impact. The result has been billions of dollars gone. As part of our doctrine of globalization, we have supported and propped up foreign economies. The time has arrived for those economies to clean up their acts.

In-sourcing is possible because free trade includes open borders. In theory, if goods and services go freely across our national boundaries, then people should also move freely.

The fair trade versus free trade issue is revealed at a very basic level. First, no nation has open borders—except the United States. We have free trade and we have open borders. In a perfect and ideal world, the two should coexist. Our Constitution provides for that ideal within our borders. When we united the thirteen colonies, the new government meant for there to be free trade and free transit, period. The process works.

On the global scene, however, there is no perfection. The loss of jobs is both overseas and within our borders.

Forget the theory. The world is far from perfect and we are part of that world. Open borders and free trade do not work, not any longer.

With open borders, our migration exceeds all nations.[48] Our total is 38 million people. Russia is next with only 12 million.

The average migration population is less than one million. Our borders remain open to those "longing to be free." We remain too open. The need for balance is clear. A chart for comparisons is in the Appendix.

Congress tried to do something about open borders. Nothing was approved. We had no results. Whatever gets done on immigration, at least do something to control our borders.

To change free trade to fair trade, we need to do something. We do nothing.

America remains committed to the globalization doctrine. The cost becomes outrageous.

Look at the results. When a profit is made, you have a successful business. The opposite also applies; when the results run against you, something is wrong.

The balances—all of them—are against the United States.

Ethical Values

Business must be conducted with strict ethical standards. Business values require a company to have the highest standards for the key operations. High ethical standards also require a fair legal system with known rules for doing business.

In the United States we have those rules, basically stated in the Uniform Commercial Code. There are many other rules for business but our national commerce is governed by a solid code.

We also have a judicial system that meets most standards for fairness. These vital law and order values include

- courts with ethical standards that are enforced
- judges who disclose financial information and avoid conflicts of interest
- a judicial system that is well organized and that moves timely and expeditiously
- a review of decisions by an appellate system

There must also be an independent investigatory system with police and detectives available to protect business against corruption. The police must have access to the banking system to track corrupt payments.

Too many nations do not have these standards. We still do business with them. The expectation should be that we will pay extra for corruption. We do.

A New Government

With all the corruption and lack of trust, the most unacceptable feature of the current international system for government is not that the United Nations is a corrupt failure unable to correct known greed. The most unacceptable feature is not that so many nations do not provide legal systems to make commercial practices work fairly. The most unacceptable feature is not that global commerce is changing and still remaining the same.

The true shame is that the same proponents of an international political system believe a new, stronger world government is needed.

Progress is being made to correct corruption. The doctrine of globalization has resulted in a working economic system. We need to complete the unions of the ten regional trade systems that are emerging.

We are far from ready for a new organization with more corruption.

Ignoring the evolving regional unions, representatives from corrupt nations are hard at work, typically in private and with little, if any, disclosure. They are proposing a new United Nations, a new system for "a global neighborhood," what they call a new "global governance."[49]

What they propose is a new world order.

Representatives from several corrupt governments are recommending still more government. Of course, the obvious proposal should be that they clean up their own governments before going further. Instead, motivated by greed, they want more.

They are also intent on taking over the business systems that work within regional unions.

These corrupt governments plan to make the changes without democracy, without going to the nations and their citizens to obtain approval.

The still-developing attempt at a new world government is corrupt from the beginning and should be fully exposed in Congress and in the fifty states.

The same process is underway with NAFTA. Are you ready to buy with the "amero," a new currency similar to the euro?[50]

This planning is not publicized. Our representatives are taking no action to preserve American and universal values. Again, we have no transparency, no open records, no disclosure.

These leaders propose to take over our Constitution.

Many warn of this conspiracy. Unlike a band of thieves in a cave, the conspiracy is not hidden; however, there is no open disclosure, certainly not by our representatives. Directly contrary to democracy, the planners do not want to have a vote. The statists will impose government controls with no respect for democracy.

Again, the statists miss the point of democracy. One of democracy's most important values is open debate. The conspirators fear the public. If they had any understanding of what business knows and does, they would understand they have a sales problem. Talk about your new world order. Explain why we need change. Convince us with the facts.

They do not know how to promote an idea honestly and effectively.

Corruption and greed are everywhere in the global community.

When reform is needed, those same corrupt governments are

proposing even more controls, this time with taxation, standing armies and much more.

The wisdom of our founders must guide our policies:

> Federalists and anti-federalists both agreed that man in his deepest nature was selfish and corrupt; that blind ambition most often overcomes even the most clear-eyed rationality; and that the lust for power was so overwhelming that no one should ever be entrusted with unqualified authority.[51]

Even the master poet of civil disobedience stated the case against even more government:

> I heartily accept the motto—"That government is
> Best which governs least."[52]

We need to clean up the current corruption. Then we might have fair trade.

Until we have full disclosure and effective law and order, we do not need even more corrupt government.

What reform, if any, is underway?

FIVE

PARITY

Dogpatch was a backwoods community developed by cartoonist Al Capp, enlivened with unforgettable characters like Li'l Abner, Daisy Mae, Ma Yokum and many more. They were a cross-section of the United States with humorous, often-critical comments on the American Way. The Broadway play had an unforgettable line,

> . . . its parity no one understands.[1]

The next line said it all,

> The country's in the very best of hands.

During the Depression, "parity" referred to the government practice of paying or not paying farmers to grow or not grow certain crops in a prorate proportion to a test year so that prices would be stable or even higher.

Huh?

You see the problem Dogpatch had. So did the nation. Of course, parity was easy for the government. They just paid farmers or did not pay farmers for growing or not growing crops.

Same old circular, meaningless reasoning.

Strictly speaking, parity is a concept of "equality" or "functional equivalence." For economists in their world of "econofacts," parity refers to purchasing power made as an estimate of the exchange rate required to equalize the purchasing power of different currencies, given the prices of goods and services in the nations involved.[2]

Huh?

For globalization purposes, parity should be used to equalize trade balances in goods and services among all nations.

We need to measure the economies of the globe's nations and make each as equal as possible in their commercial relations with one another. The inequity comes from government. Government should remove the inequities.

This would not be government regulation. We are talking about government *de*regulation. Give American companies leeway in trading with other nations, especially those on corruption lists. If we cannot get parity, then a proposed 10 percent preference for America should apply. Leave it to the private sector. The government should clean up corruption abroad with specific lists of nations to target and with ample power plays to clean up those nations. We have to require law and order and full disclosure.

The balance of trade could become more equal or as near equal with "parity" for each nation and for all nations. There will be some differences. But not much. Not as that huge difference between China at the top and the United States at the bottom of the trade balance charts.

Level Playing Field

With parity, you move toward a level playing field, one with the same rules for the production and sale of goods and services here and there.[3] With equal conditions for doing business as the measure of equality, competition will be more fair.

With parity, global competition will be more equal.

Competition has to be fair and open. With parity, fair trade and open competition, America will have far greater success in international commerce. The balance of trade should improve. There will be less adverse results here.

With fair competition we cannot lose. We know how to sell and how to compete. We fully support the democratic business tradition.

What is needed is not free trade but fair trade, including fair competion.

What is needed for a level playing field?

Competition

Competitors, whether foreign or national, must have equal economic opportunity for business. Much like bidding for government contracts, companies inside and outside must be on an equal footing.

The competition should be for contracts

- available at the same time
- with qualified consultants and
- based on wage scales, employee benefits, and substantially similar local costs.[4]

The preferred way to reach a parity benchmark or guideline is with a level playing field. This means all trade agreements between these regions must be on the same basic costs of doing business.

Studies of the level playing field center on privatization. Should private enterprise provide a service now done by government because private is less expensive and more efficient?

The costs of doing business include[5]

- taxes
- wages, hours and conditions of employment
- job safety
- product safety requirements
- liability insurance
- air and water quality

- land use
- overhead

Omitted is a reasonable profit. The net income realized will depend on specific cases, on the success or failure of the business managers. There would be a profit.

This list is not to impose the costs of doing business on individual companies. The purpose is to total these costs among the ten regions and see what the regions need to do to produce a level playing field. Once determined and disclosed, each will be free to decide what to do to correct an inequitable playing field.

The anticipated solution is to reduce government intervention and government spending.

Open Government

The most important single need is full disclosure, for fair competition open to all companies and for unbiased judicial decisions.

Several organizations are working to assure fair competition. Wages and conditions of employment are core issues. The other costs are relatively minor or are already close to parity.

Until these issues are opened up in foreign nations, American companies cannot compete fairly and on a level playing field. Our ability to compete abroad is seriously hampered. Our balance of trade will remain unfavorable when we have to pay more than the local vendors.

American companies are traditionally in an exceptional position to compete. We know business and we know how to get business. Despite wage disparities, we compete. We only need to know.

For example, we continue to have the lead in computer technology, in innovation and in skilled technologies.[6] We have the keys for successful competition. Bill Gates emphasized these points in his congressional testimony.

Developing parity for business is one major step.

For governments and their budgets, parity also applies.

National Commitment

The United States has carried the laboring oar for globalization. We have done the job for over sixty years. All other nations need to help.

A brief recap. We believed the example of the American colonies would work. In 1789 the United States adopted the Constitution and became a common market. Our Constitution required that commerce between all states was equal. The experiment worked.

The value of a common market was also proven to work for Free Europe. The Common Market has advanced to a European Union with imperial expansion underway.

Similar projects were started to bring other nations together. Relying on what was in place and working, not on some vague theories of world government, we worked with the functioning commercial regions. The cold war slowed the process; however, when the Soviet Union was replaced by a Russian Federation, the cold war was over. Under *Pax Americana* additional common markets were possible. Those global nations already interconnected economically began to form trading regions.

The United States encouraged and supported these initiatives. During the *Pax Americana* that started in the late 1980s, economic ties between nations grew stronger and regional groups evolved. Those groups are now well defined. Further integration is ahead, both economically and politically, but the transformation is happening. A new global order is emerging, based on commerce.

This new paradigm is the outstanding example of what has evolved. The outlook is for a firm foundation for political union. Political union will not happen overnight. Europe has taken almost sixty years and is still incomplete.

The new regions will take time. One item on their agenda has to be supporting *Pax Americana*. If the costs of international peace are not mutually supported, we have to reduce our foreign commitments. We need parity in the cost of maintaining peace.

New Commercial Regions

When the globe's nations are considered individually, the United States remains the leader. When the economic regions are considered, the United States is no longer number one.[7]

By 2007 there were ten regional economies, ranked loosely by relative size of the economy:

- the United States
- the European Union (or Empire)
- Japan
- China
- Latin America
- India
- the Russian Federation
- the Southeast Asia association under ASEAN
- the Muslim nations (some requiring Islam)
- the African Union

These regions are outlined in the Appendix.

Some nations associated with each regional union may not be formal members. Typically small, like Switzerland, they are so closely tied to the region that they are included. They should join to share in the common costs. We need parity in the commitment to globalization.

In addition, the economic regions overlap. The United States is deeply involved with Canada and Mexico through NAFTA. The United Kingdom is joining the European Union but has close ties to the British Commonwealth and to the United States.

The United States also has close commercial connections with Australia and New Zealand.

- The United States must promote its values with stronger leadership and must reverse current economic losses.
- Japan's economy is closely linked with the United States. Japan and the rest of Asia could be closer except for lingering distrust for Japan's lost empire.
- Japan struggles to cooperate with its Asian neighbors and needs to continue efforts to rebuild relations.

China is one massive region still developing into a potentially huge super-economy. The economic region is well defined and is commercially progressive.

- China is actively emerging from undue controls toward democratic freedoms and needs to continue that progress.

Latin America is rapidly developing with increased trade and with renewed initiatives for combined national production. This region is fifth in size.

- Latin America has to loosen strict class structures and improve economic opportunity while maintaining confidence in business progress.
- Continue efforts toward economic and political union.

Like China, India has an expansive territory with many distinct regions and a large population. It is making good progress.

- India's stratified society should open up and economic parity should be improved in its society.

The Russian Federation continues to stumble with the

entrenched attitudes of government control but has such vast wealth that it should succeed.

- One necessary value needs serious attention and that is law and order for business to work better, much better. Follow that simple rule: solid business ethics.

The ASEAN group of Southeast Asia includes major economic engines like Singapore, Malaysia and Indonesia. Hong Kong remains an interested link with China.

- Long-term distrust must give way to disclosure with improved relations to resolve regional disputes.

The huge oil resources of the Muslim world should result in far greater economic progress. Serious inhibitions on freedom of commerce and innovation continue to limit progress. Reforms needed for commercial progress and political union are problematic.

- Muslims should encourage far better cooperation among the various nations with improved local economies based on freedom of commerce.
- Get the region better organized and united.

The African Union is developing and showing signs of progress. With many nations needing support, the area will command considerable attention from its more developed members and the other nine regions.

- Local traditions are giving way to major progress needing continued dedication to free commerce.
- Continue to unify the economies.

The business connections do not begin or end with these emerging regions. Substantial commerce already exists between these ten areas. They have evolved without government planning and controls.

Some critics of these extraordinary regional steps and economic projects see doom and gloom. One vision is straight from Orwell's *1984*. Orwell Junior projects world conflict and dictators. He believes the United States is unhappy because it is no longer number one. Militarily, we will be number one; however, we are not "empire-minded." We support the economic success of the regions we have assisted.[8]

This *1984* Redux will not happen. Economic integration is too far advanced. Globalization has brought freedom to the globe. Progress for citizens will continue. War at any level would threaten this progress. Nations dependent on each other will not allow *1984* to happen. Even a minor touch of Bill Gates's "impatient optimism" will keep things moving.

There is a new attitude toward war that lends little support to alpha-types intent on personal aggrandizement. If the military defense system maintained by the United States is needed, those warmongers will be restrained.

The Orwellian projections fail because the "three" regions overlap in all areas of commerce. Besides, just count them. There are ten regions in one global economy.

The evidence is everywhere. Democracy and commerce work well together. Statism is a proven failure. Continued attempts to rely on central control should be dead on arrival. Large-scale war is not an option.

The commercial progress now underway will define a far better political solution than the United Nations and its misplaced and unproven ideas for a new "global village," a new world government. Regional progress now underway necessarily precedes and overrides any precipitous enhancement of the United Nations and its corrupt systems.

The United States union was tested severely on several occasions after 1776. By 1920, we emerged as the world leader.

The process also took a long time for Europe. For long-term stability, ample time will be needed for the other eight regions.

There is no rush.

Patience is required.

New Political Organizations

The past twenty years in the relative peace after the end of the cold war offer important, realistic projections.

For now, these regions are still growing and solving birth pains. They are not equal but are becoming more and more equal. The outstanding example is the European Empire, the new big guy on the block. The United States has become number two in the overall rankings. We have done so without war. We have encouraged the Europeans to learn to live together. We welcome their success.

We remain the most powerful military force and serve as the international peacekeeper for the world. Peace is our profession. This became international policy during the first Gulf War. Conflict between nations is no longer accepted. The world will not tolerate the invasion of one nation by another. International borders are not to be changed by war.

The Iraq war will be seen as a reaction needed to assure limits on terrorism. The initial course taken against four nations has produced good results with three: Iraq wants to be and is becoming a democracy; Libya has made peace; and North Korea is making progress toward peace. Iran remains as a significant problem.

Internal or civil wars are left to work out their issues. Global intervention should occur primarily through sanctions. There will not be a military intervention. Regions may act to preserve their political progress toward union. Internal disputes will be challenged on a case-by-case basis. The United Nations with a failed history for its armies will be relegated to the background, to the sounding board or debating society it should remain.

Independent nations, uniting into economic regions, should have the final word in their regions.

For the United States, the time has come for the leadership and the national economic cost to be equalized. Parity is one step in that direction. The new organization of ten emerging political regions needs parity. The very expensive *Pax Americana* must be supported not just by the United States but on a basis of parity among these regions. Each region must make an overall commitment to world peace and back it up with financial commitment. They have to share in the costs now carried largely by the United States.

We have to insist on parity.

Total costs of the commitment by each nation to globalization cannot be determined. More statistics are needed.[9] Since 1945, the United States has made the major commitment to this progress. The total commitment by the United States to date is seventeen trillion dollars. That was part of the cost resulting in *Pax Americana*.

Looking back, the priceless part of our investment has included the loss of lives to maintain peace. That cost was borne largely by the United States and was unfair. There was no parity.

American lives committed to world peace with globalization can never be repaid.

There is no interest in pay-back for the dollars spent. We will never recover that investment. A quarter million dollars per American citizen is at best written off as our goodwill.

Change is needed for the future.

The current price we are paying is the damage to our national debt, to the balance of trade, to the value of the dollar and ultimately, as always, to our citizens as taxpayers. The deficits should not and cannot continue.

We need a cooling off period to make parity work, to equalize the flow of goods and services in the balance of trade, and to make needed adjustments between the ten regions.

For the United States we have sufficient economic statistics to measure what we provide as a global commitment to peace. The benefits, costs and fund sources include

1. defense
2. trade
3. foreign aid
4. international associations
5. charities and faith-based groups
6. non-governmental organizations
7. business by American corporations
8. other immeasurable funds[10]

We have some econofacts for these categories; however, they are only estimates. We do not have good statistics for the other regions.

Our total annual commitment is an estimated 1.6 trillion dollars.

The foundations for parity in global commitments to peace and economic progress are much more difficult to measure.[11] Several organizations are struggling to get meaningful results but answers are still missing.

One interesting result: the European Union, particularly as more nations are added in imperial fashion, spends more for armies than the United States. Add up the defense budget for each nation and see.[12]

Parity for all these costs of globalization is to balance the dollar commitment among all nations and regions.

The United States should not bear the burden of trade deficits, increasing national debt and a devalued dollar as well as leading the global commitment for peace.

By insisting on parity between regions and nations we will continue the commercial progress that is underway.

The annual cost to Americans would be eliminated. The slack

would be assumed, as it should be, by the new global community, the ten economic regions.

Timeout Needed

The United States provides a global example for all regions to follow, particularly in terms of doing business. At this time all regions are benefiting from the international commitment by the United States to peace and commerce and by the contribution of our businesses and by our citizens to world peace and progress. What is needed is that fundamental value of solid business ethics.

Our total leadership costs each American about $5,000 per year.

For globalization with parity, the United States has to slow down until the other regions are on a par, at parity, balanced with us.

The first step would be a moratorium on expanding existing trade agreements. We then need all regional groups to make a commitment to share the government costs of global commerce. The United States should insist on parity for the costs of foreign affairs including defense, full and fair disclosure, honest legal systems, charities and similar costs.

For a humorous footnote, tradition in Mexico requires "la mordida." This translates as "the bite." The charge is expected on transactions with foreigners in Mexico. A tip for service is one example. The system is not unlike what Zeke did to get some needed cash with slip-sliding cars at the creek.

As Bill Ybarra pointed out, there is corruption in too many nations. That corruption is far more difficult when there are laws in place and enforced. Requiring disclosure makes corruption much more difficult. We need the open book. We need the goldfish bowl.

Nations practice corruption through government officials

and individuals with direct access to government. To do business you have to pay "la mordida." There may be this slight difference allowable in parity. Equality is not required. A sense of balance is needed.

The cost is on a parity with what DC attorneys collect for lobbying the "big game." Studies might indicate how much parity there is between super-sized attorneys and the cost of "la mordida."

"La mordida" and its obvious equivalents need to be eliminated. Phase them out.

There are a few organizations looking at parity. The Council on Competitiveness works with Congress; Fair Trade Labeling and Certification procedures are in effect; and our Federal Trade Commission regulates what is "made in America."[13]

The International Competition Network is struggling to develop "best practices" for competition. ICN has no rule-making powers. The recommendations are to government authorities to develop laws for fair competition. May they find consensus among their working groups.[14]

How much more is needed? An excellent survey of two-thirds of the world's nations measures the readiness of the nations surveyed for competition on a complex foundation. The Global Competitiveness Report relies on a series of variables including "hard" statistics and "opinions" from a number of business leaders.[15]

The final report for each year since 1979 compiles the data and gives a rating of how well each nation performs. The key variable missing from the report is disclosure. There is no specific determination about how open each nation is to freedom of information. This may adversely impact all other data, including "hard" data from econofacts.

The main objective of parity is to provide benchmarks for each nation to improve its economy.[16]

Much more is needed for parity. The concept needed, the value to be enforced is basically fair trade.

Until we do better, the United States should quit bearing the costs of globalization. Think of the twenty-five thousand dollars per family per year. Remember the quarter million dollars since 1945, lost forever.[17]

Values Needed

American leadership has provided a new economic organization for the world, ten regions cooperating with one another to develop better ways for meeting basic human needs at the family level.

When we started economic reorganization, there was no master plan for Europe. The underlying plan was to promote world peace. We also knew we would pay. If not publicly and perhaps not even privately, we knew we had to make the commitment.

We have paid. Since 1945 the current total is a cost per person of $230,000. That is almost one million dollars per family. Our taxes and contributions have made *Pax Americana.* Peace and progress have been exceptionally expensive.

The unilateral contributions must end.

A level playing field and privatization work together, with the less government the better. As governments abandon ineffective, typically corrupt controls, the value to be promoted is competition.

Competition between businesses has required certain values. The United States developed these values:

- open access to markets
- absence of monopoly power (anti-trust)
- fair pricing—no price fixing
- disclosure of accounts (uniform accounting)
- reporting of corporate operations (securities)

The American system works. The values we developed are sound and ethical business values. Because they work, they are universal values. The globalized world would do well to adopt these laws for fair competition.

To return to Dogpatch, that "average stone-age community" was recognized to be "us" (as the **U**nited **S**tates). We have a long way to go but we will know when the "globe is in the very best of hands."

We are a long way from that shining city on the hill.

We will not get there with statism.

We will get there with economic progress.

For over sixty years, we have seen what works.

Stick with the proof. Accept the facts. Clear up corruption, level the playing field, and work through commerce and through the developing regions.

Always remember the "we" and the "us." In a democracy the citizens have to be involved. Be assured we "average voters" are to be trusted—unless we are ignored. To paraphrase: No government without representation.

To make this future workable follow our leaders.

Accept the facts of economic democracy.

Follow business rules.

Promote America.

See how Dogpatch in its stone-age lifestyles may have been America. The rest of the world is in no better position.

How do we proceed?

How do we do something about unfair trade?

SIX

LEADERS

In a globalizing world facing major changes, selection of leaders is a vital task.

Ross Perot centered on the issue during the first presidential debates in 1992. Onstage with George Bush Sr. and Bill Clinton, Ross asked how we the voters should choose between the three and suggested that an important consideration was who you would trust to manage your estate.[1]

Who should you trust?

Who could best manage the economy?

Good questions. Of course, anyone observing American democracy at work sees nothing but problems, accusations and chaos. Commentators find nothing but errors and the media show nothing but disasters. Fact-based questions are not asked or pursued. Good news does not exist. The long-term question Perot suggested is ignored along with many others.

How is anyone going to know who to choose?

What is not seen in all the debates is how our democracy works.

Fundamentals

Great leaders in democracies have agreed on one thing: democracy is not a very good way to run a government. Churchill said it best:

> Democracy is the worst form of government except for all other forms that have been tried from time to time.[2]

Some current critics of America suggest democracy will not work in all nations. Churchill might have agreed. He said:

> The best argument against democracy is a five-minute conversation with the average voter.[3]

The key international charters we have signed with the rest of the world declare democracy is the way to go. The problems some nations have setting up democracy have not been carefully considered and may relate to a person getting elected and then abusing the power of the system that made the candidate the leader.[4]

Since 1945, we have several solid examples of democracy working. We have seen Japan after 1945; with no prior tradition for democracy, it is currently flourishing. The same is true in Germany. Doing well, thank you. In Iraq the big election there resulted in 70 percent participation and approval.

Democracy works. Churchill had it right the first time. How does it work? The critics have always been with us. They will say anything, and often do, about our system failing. Elections will not work. Free speech is a failure. History proves the naysayers are wrong.

In America we have the answer. Every citizen is a potential voter. We have the same freedom of speech the critics have. We exercise that freedom easily and well. Freedom does not mean a total understanding of all issues so that we can make the best decision. Until we get much better disclosure of facts from the government and from the media, we will not know all we need to know. The key is that we need to know the competing issues. For that, we need the facts.

We correctly assume there are conspiracies at work in specific situations. The hidden facts are too well protected for us to know what is really going on. We need the goldfish bowl. Newspapers have always and wisely attacked politicians and candidates in an effort to force disclosures. This practice started with the first national election and will not go away in a nation dedicated to free speech.[5]

We do not know everything we should. We vote for reasons not necessarily based on important facts. In our lack of information and in our freedom, we vote according to what many consider a "sacred right" to vote in the privacy of the voting booth for whomever and for whatever reason we choose.

The experts then tell us that democracy works because the aggregate vote is close to accurate; that is, the total voting by all citizens is effective in producing a rational final decision.[6] In other words we somehow muddle through and do what is best.

The United States has been fortunate. On hindsight, we have somehow made the better selection most of the time. Perhaps our success is because our elected leaders have risen to the occasion.

Experience shows American voters are solid citizens who know what they are doing. The fourteen greatest citizens profiled in chapter 1 show this fact. We pay attention to the news, we discuss issues with friends and we make the best choice based on what we know.

After all, America has been a democracy for over two hundred years. We have learned how to talk about elections, candidates and public issues. We have a keen instinct to make the best decisions.

If we fail to do so, we somehow survive. A dictator has yet to take over. The founders wisely divided power among many leaders. We are well served by our democracy.

In the privacy of the voting booth, we have full freedom to choose who we want.

We dutifully exercise that right.

Candidates

What should a candidate understand in filing for election?

There is no job application to be president or for most other elected positions. No formal resume is required. Experience and statements of positions are prepared. We rely on public appearances, competition between the candidates and the freedom of the press to bring out the issues and develop the facts we need to make our decision.

We are inundated by advertising. We know how to separate the wheat from the chaff.

Debates are the way to present candidates. How do we sell this candidate? We will get to know the candidates. In effect, we have job interviews.

Polling is standard. One leading example is that we routinely check on how the president is doing. Gallup reports this question is the most frequently asked in its history.[7]

We are interested in how our hiring works out. We have job performance reviews, constantly.

The qualities good leaders need have been discussed by many experts. Eisenhower listed six:

- self-restraint
- understand the qualities making America great
- calmness making decisions after mature reflection
- strength of decision based on sound advice from strong advisors
- experience to prepare fully for the job
- strong character, leading by principle, not expediency[8]

Several psychologists interviewed historians and came up with their own list:

- outgoing and highly sociable
- high aspirations, seeking achievements for the nation
- hard-working and persistent
- open-minded and imaginative
- tolerates adversity
- assertive
- stubborn
- disagreeable[9]

A *Time* magazine editor studied presidents and concluded there are thirty-one qualities. Eight are basic:

- look like a president with a "normal" personality
- including integrity in private life
- intelligence with a sense of history and of vision
- religious affiliation
- good communication skills
- a sense of humor
- an optimist
- an ability to compromise[10]

The most recent list is straight from the West Wing, by Karl Rove. He asks what makes a president effective and able to rise to the occasion in one of the world's toughest jobs? He lists the following:

- clarity of vision
- clarity about the goal, the overall strategy
- familiarity with legacies from past presidents
- emotional intelligence with internal self-confidence
- respect for the polls but not dictated by them
- a strong team giving solid and straightforward advice[11]

These lists are helpful for the candidate, once elected. Vital considerations for the candidate prior to election day include:

Appearance—looks like “a leader” so we decide to like the candidate—or not, as we do with everyone.

> Appearance is everything. One scene makes the case[12]—two women watching a debate remark about the candidate’s hairdo as if that had anything to do with issues. Some of us recall how Nixon melted during the debate with JFK—the studio lights had enough heat to bring sweat through the makeup.
>
> We routinely make judgments strictly on appearance, first impressions count for everything and, in any election, we will judge on appearance.

Integrity—straight talk is best because we must have accurate facts to make a personal evaluation to trust—or not to trust.

> Honest answers are vital. There is slack for equivocation but candidate statements have to be basically honest. The measure of truth-telling and accurate factual statements is essential to government.[13] We should decide accordingly.

Disclosure—an open personality with full disclosure, to show sources of wealth and key supporters.

> Accept life in the goldfish bowl. Open interviews provide disclosure. Does the candidate answer the question? Does the candidate entertain questions? Tom Brokaw has an interesting test—does the candidate answer with a yes or no or do we get a long explanation?

Experience—business knowledge is helpful; we elect governors over senators because governors manage statewide operations; senators just vote (we tend to presume).

> Part of the test is how strong is the candidate? Any campaign is grueling. Primaries bring out the best and the worst in any person. This is an interesting test of how the candidate will handle

a national emergency, a 9-11, a Katrina or a Cuba missile crisis. We get an idea from the campaigning.

Experience in management is also important. Presidents have been elected from governors, not senators. Governors have fewer of the issues DC critics apply daily. Governors understand business. It is the economy.

Values—understand America and the values we have for our way of life.

Of these many considerations, the key seems to be appearance. How does the candidate conduct himself or herself? Is the person a decent human being? Does the candidate speak to me so I understand? What do my instincts tell me about the candidate's body language?

Candidates beware. An election is very demanding. Be prepared for the questions voters have. Work hard. We are talking about working 24/7. Hang in there. Anything can happen and nothing counts until election day after the counting is done and the winner is certified.

The process is worth the effort.

Voters

Part of our commitment to our extraordinary democracy is to vote. The characteristics of the candidates are useless if citizens do not vote.

What should we consider?

- a sense of public service, not running for office for personal enrichment.
- patriotism to our ideals including the democracy itself; do not assume patriotism; look for it.
- understanding that all citizens need to be part of the process—as in get out the vote, or at least get out and vote.

Questions voters should have for any candidate:

- Does the candidate answer questions directly as possible?
- Is the candidate willing to disclose personal income and assets?
- Is the candidate reasonably familiar with America business?
- Did the candidate's personal wealth come from government?

A person does not have to be a candidate to participate in our democracy. Because we are a democracy, we exercise our duties by participating in the election process at all levels of government. Elections are necessary for public office statewide, in the county, citywide, for school board positions and to run special districts.

We have to participate to make democracy work.

In the greater scheme of things, we are the voters and we have the final say. We hear the first word but we have the last word. In the privacy of the voting booth, each citizen makes the preferred choice.

One final, very personal consideration at that moment of choice: we are hiring our leaders so do the right thing in casting the ballot or punching the hole or throwing the switch. Vote for the person you know is best.

Remember, once leaders are elected, they are virtually impossible to fire.

The last word is not when we leave the voting booth. In between elections, our duty includes letters, telephone calls, emails, appearances and other networking in a free country. We need to participate.

We have the duty to exercise that vigilance essential to our freedoms and to our future.

Issues

As may have been noticed, these lists for candidates and voters ignored issues. Appearance is so important that issues do not appear to be a major concern for voters. In fact, many voters will ask what the candidates stand for.

The issues are far more important than the appearances.

There are issues of vital importance to some of us:

- healthcare (getting everyone to pay)
- education (getting costs down and quality up)
- immigration (do nothing or insist on getting legal)
- no taxes (stay out of my pocket)
- union rights (for unions and employees)
- privacy (stay out of my bedroom)
- terrorism (be nice or be strong or both) and
- world peace (maintain a strong military)

On these policy issues the candidates will waffle around because the facts will change. Flip-flopping is a valid issue and is important. Someone, as they say, who gets bought should stay bought; that is, they should stick by their guns, say what they believe and believe what they say. But give the candidates a little slack, and bring a little sense of humor to the race.

The candidate's plans have to be considered. An activist with many plans for new programs must face the cost of the programs. No program is without cost. And that means taxes. Americans pay 40% plus of their annual income to government, including federal, state and local taxes. Any increase should be carefully justified and fully disclosed.

Several Internet sites have issues listed with visitors able to select how they feel about those issues. A total score is developed with a recommendation of the candidate who most closely agrees with the issues you support.

In the final analysis, your personal assessment becomes the final decision. What will this candidate mean to the future of the country? What will this candidate mean for me?

Spend a little time making your decision and then good luck in your choice. And good luck to America.

One further consideration: of all the issues facing a president, the two most important are the economy and foreign affairs.[14] Between the two, foreign affairs concerning national defense remains the most important.

We expect prosperity and we expect safety. Both relate to globalization.

Global "Governance"

There are major changes underway on the global scene. One is reform or replacement of the United Nations. The United Nations is corrupt to the core. Major changes are needed.

The heart of this long-term issue is the type of world government needed for globalization. In 1945 there were two approaches:

1. political union with the United Nations and
2. economic progress with regional economies.

The political approach was and still is a complete failure. Between the two approaches, economic progress is far ahead of completing any United Nations goals. Globalization is proven to be the most effective means for bringing regions together. The ten economic regions are united or are moving toward political unions.

The basic alternatives in 1945 were more government control or democracy and commercial progress. The statists lost. The fall of their dictators proved state control does not work. The success of commerce with democratic freedoms proves global trade works.

In the twenty-first century, the key issue for the globe is political union. Should we have a world political union based on the United Nations or one based on the regional unions still developing and uniting?

The United Nations is working hard and mostly in secret to set up a new world order. The major plan is for a "global neighborhood" developed by an "informal" Commission on Global Governance.[15]

The "governance" proposal is fundamental and far-reaching. Democracy is abandoned. Global taxation is adopted. The United Nations would control the world's "commons," which means the skies, the oceans, the land (and its resources), and outer space. A small and likely ineffective standing army would be in place, 10,000 soldiers to go wherever needed. No vetoes would be allowed. Decisions would be by an undefined, nonrepresentative "consensus."[16] The United Nations would gain control of the economic system, the World Trade Organization that is working so well for the regional political unions.

The extensive plans for the United Nations' "core values" have no protections for our values such as those protected by our Bill of Rights against government. Many of our rights would be replaced or denied. Taxes would be widespread and would include

- An added charge per barrel of oil of ten dollars.[17]
- All banking transactions would be taxed.
- Land use would be controlled down to the local park.
- Mining and oil drilling would be controlled.
- There would be many more.

In short the "governance" proposal would reach everywhere. Political globalization would be complete in the hands of a corrupt United Nations.

"Governance" has been under development for at least ten

years. The recommendations were to be implemented by 2000. Any dissent was prohibited. A group of like-minded nonrepresentative people would agree with a "consensus" and control would result. Open and honest debate was not acceptable. A member of a "governance" committee might be "upset" by a proposal and that would prevent further debate. The fact that the proponent of the proposal would be "upset" by not being heard would not matter. For example, John Bolton was criticized and silenced for even raising questions about "governance."

This far more powerful United Nations proposal was written by appointed, not elected representatives, some from nations listed as corrupt. The advice should not be from them. The advice to them would be, "Clean up your own nation's corruption before trying to take over the world." In terms we understand, "Clean up your own backyard before worrying about mine."

The alternative course is far better. The economic areas now developing into regional unions—such as the European Empire—need to complete their unification before turning to a new global order. The regions could then consider a new world organization based on what works.

The United Nations should remain a harmless debating society. The "governance" plans were developed by such "debates." Essentially they are like tea parties.

In the real world of honest debate on important issues, there must be vigorous and robust discussion followed by open elections. The process is called democracy.

Not so at the United Nations.

The challenge is made here and now: supporters of "world governance" should agree to open debate on the fundamental changes proposed. This would include taxation, currency, armed forces and personal rights.

The hypocrisy is complete when the "world governance" proponents declare support for democracy but carefully plot secret approval by carefully selected friends with the same "core values."[18] This is political conspiracy at its worst.

This approach of avoiding democracy is typical of the statists. The European Union was supposedly committed to democracy; however, when unification proposals were submitted to voters in several nations, the proposals were rejected. The election was a disaster for the Empire.

True to form, the leaders decided they did not need approval by voters, that there was enough ambiguity in the original plans to go forward as a treaty, not a new constitution.[19]

So much for democracy.

Our founders developed a constitution that handles all issues. If some statute passed by Congress is unacceptable to the citizens, we elect new representatives and change the law. If the Constitution itself needs change, we propose amendments to correct the problem.

If change fails, those wanting the change did not do a good job convincing a majority. They have every right to keep trying. The suffragettes did. The temperance backers did. Interestingly, they lost and then won within a decade.

Such working democracy is not for statists. They try more devious ways: get friendly judges, go ahead and unite anyway, or resort to violence. Forget the written words of our Constitution. Change as you see fit.

These alternatives are not democracy. There is absolutely no excuse for going ahead with "governance" in the absence of democratic procedures for review and approval.

Unfortunately, the "world governance" group does not understand "No!" There is no respect for our democracy or any democracy. The approach taken by the meritocrats, the elitists,[20] is secret and unilateral.

The best advice for "world governance" plotters:

> Submit your plans to the electorate.

For the United States, several steps should be required to protect our Constitution and our values:

1. First, treat the proposals as a treaty requiring a new constitution
   —two-thirds Senate approval required.
2. Then, consider the proposals as costing more money
   —House approval needed by a majority with Senate concurrence by a majority.
3. Treat the proposals as requiring a national referendum
   —send the proposals to the states and to American voters as an amendment to the Constitution.
4. Take each step, one at a time. There is no emergency.

Sovereignty is involved. We defined sovereignty under the Constitution. We have the right to decide to keep or change that sovereignty.

If change is needed for a new world order, approval should be obtained from the voters. If we are going to be asked to give up the United States, we have to be given the right to vote.

Leaders need to take a strong position on the issue of global governance. In the opinion of each candidate, will the voters get to review the "governance" proposals?

The basic problem is practical reality. Leaders at the United Nations have no concept of the real world. Corruption and protecting its cash flow to individuals has made you jaded. You decide to be involved only for personal profit. Avoid the corruption.

Democracy is the way to govern. Business leaders learn how to campaign, how to make sales. The United Nations needs to learn how to sell the "governance" proposals. Allegedly part of a democracy, the leaders at the United Nations should encourage voting.

They do not.

For money matters the United Nations needs to learn about

business. To do anything a payroll is required. This means hiring employees and paying them in a timely manner. To meet the payroll, money is required. This means taxes.

The means to pay for "world governance" must be debated.

As a reminder memo to the United Nations, the United States went to war for freedom on a key issue—no taxation without representation. We opposed taxes not for the reasons Galbreath suggested, that we were selfish. We knew greed and corruption would compromise any government leaders so the fewer the better.

Get with the real world, United Nations. Develop your proposals out in the open and sell what you believe works.

Just good business.

"World governance" will not work any other way.

Listen to our business leaders.

Again, to paraphrase, no government without representation.

Leaders for America

To respect our democracy and our values our recognized leaders should be consulted, if not by the United Nations, then by the United States.

On the diplomatic scene, John Bolton is willing to speak up for America, to challenge the United Nations on issues important to us. World politics are very real politics and power. John understands our power to protect our values.

Bill Gates is another success, and his speech to the World Economic Forum is far-reaching and profound.[21] What he emphasizes should be considered in plans for the political reorganizations that are underway.

"The Donald" Trump would be a vital addition. Results are needed. He will bring the solid business values needed. If not, you're fired. We will not be "had," not any longer.

Keeping an eye on these three leaders is the man most qualified to work with key executives, making sure they work effectively. Warren Buffett would be a vital member of a team to improve globalization.

Assuring cooperation among the strong-willed and highly diverse would be Mike Bloomberg.

Finally, to bring a little muscle and assure the job gets done, bring in Arnold Schwarzenneger.

Put these leaders in a room and see what they say.

Then listen to them.

Values for Voting

America is committed to democracy. We have made it work. One reason is our well-developed voting systems to assure honest and accurate voting and results down to the local neighborhoods.

Election improvements are underway to assure as many citizens vote as possible:

- Information is available on most issues and candidates.
- Local officials conduct elections and count ballots.
- Local officials verify all voters as lawful.
- Voting on issues and making laws with referenda.
- Voting made as easy and convenient as possible—not yet like Congress with a button on your desk.
- Internet voting has not yet arrived—attraction for hackers is probably too dangerous.
- Voting absentee allows for a full count from citizens.
- Thirty-day voting period.
- Mail-in ballots encouraged.

Our democratic values include a determination to hear from the voters, to get as many to vote as possible.

Once an election is over, the interests change. The candidate becomes the elected official and we have protections against the elected officials. Once in office greed takes over. Leaders have been known to go too far, to become arrogant.

Contrary to statists ideas, we have "core values" to protect us from government.

Our Bill of Rights provides protections against government leaders.

- We have free speech and religion, in effect assuring freedom of thought, that an open mind is important.
- Freedom of press.
- We honor the right to protect ourselves and our home, including having weapons.
- We respect the personal self and personal property.
- Open courts and due process are guaranteed.
- We have the right to a jury.
- Property is yours unless government pays for it.
- Local government is protected from the national government.
- Privacy is protected.
- Equal protection of the laws is granted.

We protect our citizens with these universal values.

As might be expected, the current drive for statism by "governance" proposals ignores these values.

The United States is the leader in globalization, and change is the most important given on the global scene. We need change to improve the American economy and to promote stable economic regions. We do not need change to a powerful United Nations with full governing authority. We do not need more state control.

Ronald Reagan zeroed in on the issue of change when, during the presidential debates in 1990, he mentioned Jimmy Carter's ongoing promises of more government spending and said, "There you go again."[22] Those four words hit the nail on the head. Carter was promoting the same old government programs to handle change. Reagan said those old solutions of more and more government had not worked, do not work and would not work.

What we need, Reagan was suggesting, is change to what we know works. American values work. Statism does not work. A commercial economy works. Government giveaways do not.

The globe has moved too far from those proven values.

In a time of great change we need renewal of those values. We do not need something new, unproven, theoretical, very expensive and destructive of our values.

Change is a given. We always have change.

But change to what?

There are values we must promote and protect.

SEVEN

VALUES

Behavior experts say that when seeing something approaching in the distance, the mind first determines if it is an animal or a human and then determines whether it is friend or danger.

Those first meetings are so important.

One proven way to make a peaceful first meeting, that all-important first impression, is to bring a little humor to the meeting. Like giving a speech or just talking to a group, start with humor. It's a very friendly, winning way to express peaceful intentions.

Because of the vast cultural experiences being brought together by globalization and because of a notable lack of respect for freedom of speech, this friendly way to meet and visit is virtually impossible.

We should at least take a closer look at people we meet and try to begin a friendly dialogue. As change continues, reassessment of our values is needed, for more friendly first impressions.

Start with the most obvious.

Humor

As an example of "politically correct" humor, my sister calls or emails to remind me, "You never write." What is my response? If not talking, writing is virtually all I do. "My dear sister, I always write." Do I send her all the pages for the day? As an in-joke, there is humor. Others might need an explanation. Or did you get it?

But the ultra-critical, politically correct person, that far too attentive-retentive character will point out something is not "right." Like, why is the sister doing the calling? Why not the male? Why did you omit the mails? Something against unions? Isn't that punch line too vague, even between brother and sister?

There is no room for the best approach for a friendly meeting with a new acquaintance. There is no warming up a crowd. We are far too humorless.

In a day where we have to assure everyone that we respect them, even though that should be a given, the only truly permissible humor has to be self-effacing. Humor requires a mutually shared friendship with a common background of knowledge and values. Humor at the global level presents a huge challenge.

There is an effort underway to globalize humor.[1] Studies have only begun, but the first steps are being taken. My experience, limited and anecdotal, shows some consideration of the subject.

Americans are good at humor; thank you, Jay Leno and your gang of fiercely funny competitors. Our humor has been around a long time and basically involves men making fun of problems they encounter, laughing at themselves. Situation comedies followed, with the man in the show never getting it right. The jokester writers missed the point that their comedy was laughing at someone else's expense. Humor is humor when we laugh together. Of course, there is no sympathy for men.

We have black comedians who are among the very best; thank you, The Entertainer and all. We have twenty-something humor which is one stupid mistake after another, centered mostly on bodily functions. Must be something kids did not learn to leave at home.

Latin Americans, and especially Mexicans, have a quick grasp of humor. A singing population anyway, they love the chiste, the quick joke. Longer stories with a punch line are a little harder. They want to laugh right now.

The English, as in Brits, are humorous in a droll sort of way. Humor has to be externally directed and be something impossible or too obvious. They are a very clever lot but there's too much "in-joking."

French humor is missing, an unknown quantity and quality.

Other Europeans have a solid sense of humor, not unlike Hispanics, that may result from long years of oppression. Even a friendly greeting is reason for humor.

Japanese are always quick to grin and laugh. We should work with them more closely.

Chinese are very pleasant and quick to grin. We need to know them better.

Muslims have a serious problem with humor. Well they might since some jokes carry the death penalty. The Muslim book of humor must be a small item, with blank pages. No comedy clubs—it's way too dangerous to laugh.

Where is Zeke, the certified Jokemaster, when we need him?

When core values are addressed, communications are even more difficult. Anger and violence have been known to occur.

With this weak, strictly anecdotal opening limited to writers never writing and humor needing globalization, values have to be considered.

More humor is needed. Efforts are underway to globalize humor but barely a start has been made.

One positive sign is that American humor may be taking over our politics. Candidates routinely appear on comedy shows. Perhaps we have a comment on the humor that elections are becoming.

Candidates, lighten up.

Globalization of Values

Globalization is making more and more people aware of global events more and more quickly. Future shock is everywhere, instantly. When high drama occurs, we know about the events immediately; sometimes they unfold as we watch. The horrific events on 9-11 created global shock.

In our vast instant communication systems the question is, what can be done to promote globalization of values in a peaceful way?

Consider this, that the values that are "made in the USA" are not just for Americans. Many developed through Christianity in the broadest sense, reaching back before Abraham and moving forward to embrace most religions.

Our founders in that creative era from 1776 to 1789 were inspired by open and honest discussions between citizens struggling to define their new freedom. They chose democracy. The founders and their values were inspirations of Thomas Paine, who proposed the democratic values that our founders then put to the test in the real world, to what would as a practical matter work best.

All values of any worth are universal. This is particularly true of democracy, enshrined as it is in most international agreements.

In addition to democracy, what are our values as Americans? Our values as human beings?

Some have been outlined already—personal values, business values, economic values, law and order values, values for and against the government, fair competition for fair trade, political values and more.

A basic value debated worldwide during the period 1929 through 1992, through the Depression and the Second World War and then through the cold war was whether to have democracy or dictatorship. The dictator would control every value of his citizens. On the other hand, we promoted freedom through democracy and business, of individuals responsible for themselves and their values, all of them.

By 1992, after we decisively won the cold war, the value question of government by socialism or by individuals acting through a democracy was settled. The end of history had arrived.[2] There was no further debate about political organization. Democracy prevailed.

As early as 1947 but clearly by 2000 the American economic system had proven its value. We started with our experience in successfully uniting the thirteen states. Before our Constitution was effective, we were thirteen semi-independent nations, much like the global system today. By 2000, our basic system of a free economy and regional unification was working in Europe. Most regional groups have started their own planning for union. Growth has accelerated with another compelling result: more people are above the minimum accepted poverty level than ever before.

Like democracies where election and debate are not perfect, our business economy is not perfect; however, to paraphrase Churchill, like democracy, commercial freedom works better than any other system. Democratic business has done far better than the United Nations or any its governance plans.

The socialists had their chance to prove their system worked. They failed utterly and completely. None of the dictators survived except a few still struggling, with their citizens excluded from the economic progress of commercial democracy.

Unfortunately, the socialists or statists or "government control people" refuse to admit failure. They continue to promote control wherever possible, bypassing democracy, refusing disclosure and avoiding debate that is full, fair and honest. They seek to impose their humorless misery on the rest of the globe in their statist way, by unilateral fiat.[3]

In short, the cold war is not truly over. The socialists and statists still see government as having every answer. The cold war continues. The peculiar values for the all-powerful dictator and a ruling junta are still the goal of statists. History has not ended.

The new cold war does not involve the military but to some alpha-psychotics, violence is okay. Basically, we have a continuing war of words.

Because we believe in free speech and democracy, we listen to the statists but they refuse to concede. Pride moves them forward. They have no shame. They claim relativity to any values and struggle on, suppressing dissent in their hypocritical ways.

Leaders of democracy believe in free and open discussion based on fairness for all interests and with ethics governing the issues in dispute.

The fight is specially directed against America. We have been the leaders. We provided *Pax Americana*. We overpowered the Depression and the dictators of the left and right, the socialists and the fascists. The statists had every opportunity to prevail. They are losers.

They remain noisy street fighters. We remain in a war of words where the statists, with the facts set against them, have no ethics about facts and reality, about solutions proven to work. They invent econofacts. When all else fails, they willingly resort to violence. They are hypocrites.

The values most people follow are branded American values, and they are. The statists then attack the universal values, not for their central values, their "core" values. They attack our values as "Christian" or "American."[4] Any fair-minded observer knows those values are universal values. Most people accept them and follow them or continue to struggle to achieve them.

The globalization of the values reviewed in the preceding chapters are compromised by the foolishly defiant and too-often vicious statists.

An effective response to the word warriors is necessary.

Promotions

Our American values have been covered. Our greatest

Americans have made them work, our business success makes them obvious, our problems with greed lead to charity and our way of life shows them in action. We do not preach; we show.

What we need is one other value, that of standing up for our values. As Americans, we need positive action for our values. They work, they are proven, and they are gaining universal acceptance. All peoples want the secure family lives and values we have.

Note that our positive value of standing up is clearly unlike the United Nations staff members who know of corruption in their organization and in their homelands but do nothing. They have the gall or the "emperor syndrome" to try to improve globalization by imposing state control. Clean up your own homeland; then worry about the rest of us.

We are doing something.

Our values are "made in the USA." Our goods and services need to be "made in the USA." Our values were made with robust, sometimes harsh debate, too often with individual sacrifice, and always with determination. We have not added to our boundaries. We forgive and work with former enemies. We learned how democracy and business work together and then showed the globe how to do it.

We even remain gracious while confronting corruption.[5]

We need to stand up for America. We have to promote our values. One small but vital way is to participate in our democratic process, to vote.

How else do we get rid of the rascals? Is there a better way to promote our democracy?

The value added to the many values mentioned before is *to do something.*

Open and Honest Debate

To promote our positive values, we need free and open discussion of the issues of globalization.

Radio and TV talk shows are a key source for debate. On radio and television, we listen to the problems of the day, the missing child, the airplane delayed, the resignation of a leader, the failure to control our borders, the problems with other nations, and all the other "breaking news."

The talk shows then turn to discussions, what some might consider debates, a comparison of our values.

The talk-show hosts, what some call Radio Free America and TV America, get the participants, victims, activists and experts on the air or onto the ever-larger small screen. Concerned audiences tune in.

Some media present all sides of issues and particularly of the individual interests directly involved. The major media fail. Like the United Nations "tea parties," disagreement is not acceptable. Like college peer reviews, do not "upset and stress" with facts. Agree or remain silenced.

There is a better format.

In court, final argument is controlled by a judge, who typically keeps a low profile.[6] There are at least two attorneys presenting the different interests. Both sides are skilled and experienced. An excellent review of the issues and related values on trial are fairly and honestly debated for a final decision.

Media hosts should do what any judge would do. Do not allow interruptions of one side by the other. So many discussions become "everybody talking, no one listening." The audience cannot hear what is said. The discussion becomes nonsense.

The host needs to turn off the mikes with the exception of the guest addressing the question.

Too often, the host goes into a long-winded question that is little more than a statement of what the host believes. A good judge lets the debaters make the case. The host, of course, is trying to pin the guest down but the audience needs to hear the guest. Too often, the guest will do what lawyers fear, that they will "shoot themselves in the foot." The guest (the attorney) makes such a foolish remark that the audience (the jury) easily adjudges the person and his or her values.

Judges maintain control with the gavel and the bailiff. The hosts have similar controls. If a guest refuses to answer a question, turn the guest off and go to another guest. Or let the guest speak freely and possibly ruin his or her own case.

A good judge will control the lawyers. Give them their time but make them stay on point. Do not allow statements irrelevant to the case. Meet the time schedule allotted to each side. Be fair. Make an effort to present all sides. Do not leave "propaganda," the omission of key facts.[7]

The host should do everything possible to assure a fair and balanced discussion of the issues. With a format working in good faith to get information to the audience, key issues can be aired and "ventilated." This means the various interests get a fair chance to shoot holes in the opposing side's case. For any measure of ethics and fairness, a full presentation is needed.

Let the voters decide. Communicate a fair, balanced, unafraid and complete picture to the audience.

A quick note on real cases before juries. Trials are very much like dramatic plays. There are three significant differences. In a trial you are never sure what the witness will say. Also, you get only one trial. And the attorney presenting the case has to contend with another attorney who is presenting the same facts with the same witness but with an entirely different ending.

This judge/jury format is recommended for radio and TV talk shows. Comedy shows could add humor by presenting guests in the same format.

There is a greater possibility here. In the past, wars were sometimes decided by a champion of each side taking on the other in hand-to-hand combat. One example is David against

Goliath. In the Trojan Wars, Menelaus and Paris made a stab at it but the rules for one-on-one did not hold.

The major globalization proponents should debate the issues. Strict rules should apply, like the rules for final arguments to jury. People can be selected to assure a balanced decision. After the debate, a vote should be taken by those involved. The majority vote decides the issue. Real results follow, such as money paid or programs started or territory lost.

An example: sanctions on Cuba. Both sides are ready. Full debate ensues. Cuba's citizens vote on dropping sanctions for economic freedom. Sanctions continue or end. There are many more similar examples.

Our democratic traditions and values show that debate is one good way to lay values on the line and work toward a resolution.

The challenge is for the statists to select their proponents and appear for an open and honest debate on the talk shows. Unfortunately, the statists do not believe in debate.[8]

An interesting alternative to open-ended talk and to the need for humor is already developing. The comedy shows are taking over the discussions. We may get some humor about globalization. We may just globalize humor. The political scene may be changed for the better.

Global Union

Values, cultures and conflict will continue to be debated. Without humor, serious confrontations may result. Hopefully, with America's military peacekeepers and peacemakers in firm control, war will not result.

When will these values be resolved sufficiently to assure a world at peace, a world united?

We have a long way to go.

The United States was once a divided nation. We had southern states committed to agriculture and slavery. The northern states were expanding their economies into manufacturing. For several decades the underlying issue of slavery was avoided. There were debates, some violent. One member of Congress was assaulted within an inch of his life by a southerner. The attack occurred in the Congress. Violence in the form of war broke out when the North finally decided the time had come to end slavery.

In our United States we had competing value systems. For seventy years debate and compromise were tried. When the majority insisted on freedom, the lines were drawn. War followed.

In the end, we remained a union, scarred but stronger than before.

Similarly, in the world today, the values at stake will take a long time to accommodate. We will have a united world, one less likely to go to war, when we have the following:[9]

- agreement on goals and values
- a single military command paid by all members
- open borders for trade and for people
- a single money system
- an agreed-upon single language
- agreed-upon fair taxation
- free and equal voting rights for all citizens
- freedom of speech

Some progress has been made. Regional unions are moving ahead with these ultimate goals in mind.

Until globalization worsened our national position, we had the globe's means of commercial exchange, the dollar. The euro and the yen have gained considerably in the last few years.

We remain a long way from a single language. The schools try to teach English but too many experiment rather than relying on proven systems. Teaching students a second language is a start but much more is needed. Airline pilots have finally agreed to English. Thanks to the Internet and to Bill Gates, English is favored for the World Wide Web. Thanks to the Brits, the commercial world is largely in English. The main feature of globalization—instant and understandable communication with most people—is available.

Open borders is an excellent idea along with free trade; however, no nation practices open borders and the powerful demand for free entry into the United States makes this highly unlikely.

The United Nations charter provides for a unified military command.[10] Never used, the provision is still there. Instead, America's military provides the necessary peacekeepers.

Too many values are not settled. The main one remains statism versus democracy. Planners for government control sit in their ivory towers or attend their tea parties with salaries paid by the United Nations. They are trying to demand and command global control quickly. Like dictators, they have failed, so far.

The way to unified values is with open debate and free elections. Union mandated from above will not work. The globalization of values has to occur in actual practice with a practical evolution, not a "big brother" command from above.

We have a long way to go.

There is no rush.

A new development offers another alternative. A group in Canada has organized to seek union with the United States. These Canadians want to be part of America.[11] Instead of a new world union with the United Nations or a new world union by alliances among the ten economic regions, they unite into America.

There is discussion of a North American Union by the United States with Canada and Mexico.[12] Information on the proposal reveals that a very deliberate joining of specific governmental functions is underway. The details need to be presented to the Congress and an advisory vote should be taken by the

Senate and House to continue the debate on all the terms of union needed for any United States/Canada/Mexico merger.

Whatever is happening with the ongoing discussions must be presented in the open with full disclosure and fair debate. The North American Union and all such unions will fail unless fully discussed and then voted for approval or rejection by the citizens. Procedures for voter approval of any "governance" should be required.

When independence was declared and when the Constitution was approved, all thirteen colonies had to join. Unanimity was necessary. The final approvals came after long debate. For independence, a year was needed to consider the issues. For union under the Constitution, there was extended debate in the Federalist over several years.

We should proceed the same way on any new union.

Celebration

There is more to be done. With all this activity occurring globally, the missing element is America. Our silence may say we agree. As usual, we are gracious to a fault to our enemies.

The missing value from our list of universal values is that all-important value of taking action.

Celebration is one way to take action.

Boston is a major center for July the Fourth celebrations. The New Englanders believe they earned the right to an extended celebration. They did. During the Revolutionary War, New Englanders resisted the British, drove them back into Boston and then scared them away with cannon without gunpowder. During most of the war Boston was American territory, the only major area that drove the British out and kept them out.

Rightfully, July the Fourth is a powerful, moving celebration with bands, parades, speeches, patriotic music and fireworks. Once celebrated, Boston takes off for a month or so. The immediate excuse is the summer heat. The subtle rationalization is that they were better at defeating the British than the rest of the colonies so they get a longer break.

Note the touches of humor: cannon without gunpowder, a well-earned extended celebration and more.

We in the rest of the nation also need a longer holiday, to celebrate America for Americans. The beauty of our celebration will let the rest of the globe know what works. We do not just talk about freedom; we celebrate freedom.

The principles we established on July 4, 1776, need to be renewed. We may not be able to take off the rest of the summer in the fashion of the New Englanders but a weeklong holiday would be appropriate.

There are other uniquely American holidays. One is Presidents' Day. Again, the values of our nation and its leaders in times of crisis should be remembered and celebrated.

Memorial Day honors the sacrifices we made for the current *Pax Americana*. With Veterans Day, key remembrances should be honored.

Labor Day ends the long, hot summer and the vacationing. We are rested and refreshed, ready to return to work. The workforce deserves the summer break; we all deserve the break.

Thanksgiving is uniquely American. The entire concept of giving thanks for a year of unusual hardship is beautiful. We take the time to appreciate what we have done and what we have received. Even in bad years, the day reminds us what we need to do. The global community would benefit from the values reflected in this holiday, not as an American holiday, but as a time to pause, give thanks, and renew faith while taking the all-important time with family and friends.

The holiday season also celebrates the past year and the coming year. Started as a Christian celebration, we now have the time to celebrate several faiths. Again, an American value is shared with others and becomes universal.

Even those who recognize no faith higher than themselves should take time to relax and enjoy the end of one year and the beginning of another.

Buy America

"Made in the USA" covers many things. In a period of rapid globalization, we have to emphasize America. We are losing huge sums of money in the overall battle of the regional economies. We are hurting because of our dedication to world trade.

We need to correct the balance and buy America. A preference is recommended to help the process.

We have purchasing power, more than any other nation or region. Use our consumer power to favor America. We cannot impose tariffs and quotas. We have the option to favor America. As individuals we can exercise the 10 percent preference.

Buying America is difficult.

In a trial against Chrysler, one member of the jury panel raised his hand and approached the judge. With his face growing ever redder, he could barely keep his voice down. "I had a Chrysler once. Worst lemon ever. Cost me tons. Never ran right. And those . . ," he sputtered, "those crooks over there never, never ever got it right."

The judge did not hesitate. "No way to give them a fair trial?"

The man shook his head vigorously. "Never bought another American car," he angrily added, "and never will."

Glancing at the attorneys, the court shrugged as he asked, "Any objections?"

The man was excused.

Here is the problem. The easiest way to buy America is to

buy your vehicle here. For many with long memories, that is the hardest step to take.

Over the years since the owner of the Chrysler lemon expressed his utter and total rejection of all American autos, much progress has been made. American cars are manufactured everywhere in this globalized economy. My experience is that our automakers have excellent products. Even though assembled with parts from abroad, the ownership is here. When buying America when so many products are assembled from overseas, the owner is the key.

Buy products from American-owned companies. Understand that the owner may be Ford or Exxon or our other corporate giants. For local purchasers, however, the person helped will be local such as dealers, shop owners and other businesses we visit anyway.

There are other ways. Do not buy prescription drugs from abroad. Not only will your money stay in America; you will also avoid potentially dangerous prescriptions. This will be tough because Internet medicine is inexpensive and easy. At least consider the 10 percent preference.

Internet purchases are growing. Stick with American companies. Use the ever-popular E-Bay. Those sellers are not huge auto companies. Typically, they are Americans doing what we do best, we go into business on our own.

Make your purchases at local stores. Recall that Wal-Mart is localized. Stay with your neighborhood stores. Even with vehicles, foreign autos are usually sold by American dealers.

The Appendix lists some additional sources. The Net has many more sources. Look for "buy USA."

To ease the cost of buying more expensive made-in-America products, there are limits. For many families, paying more or even having the time to shop around is too expensive in terms of both money and time.

There is a small way to support America. Use the 10 percent preference. When buying America, find the product, compare it to the foreign product and give America a 10 percent break.[13]

This preference can apply to vehicles as well. Buy America unless the alternative foreign-owned vehicle model is over 10 percent less.

This same measure can apply to all government purchases. New York City sometimes promotes the preference although at only 5 percent. Your city, county or school district could do the same. There may be problems because of free trade agreements. Dependent on legal advice, competitive bidding should include a 10 percent advantage to American companies.

If governments are barred, private citizens are not. We should favor America by 10 percent. Private American companies should favor American products by 10 percent.

This favored status should be maintained until we have a level playing field in world trade. The obvious economics tests are: the value of the dollar, the balance of trade and the budget deficit. We will know when globalization is level; foreign products costing more than 10 percent will not be available on the global market.

Sell America

Celebrating America is good promotion, creating good feelings or at least empathy for us around the globe. We are selling what is made in America—our values.

We also celebrate America by showing the colors. Some view this as arrogance or they shrug and say it is unnecessary, that "I am a good American." There is no doubt that almost every citizen in the United States is a good American. The need to celebrate and show the colors is to sell our values. We are behind in the globalization wars. We have to promote America, to sell what has been made in the USA.

Wearing a flag pin is one example. Men and women can do it. Flying the flag is excellent. Leave one posted on the outside wall, with a light on. A flag decal on the car is routine. Just as the flag was flown on Iwo Jima, on the moon and at the World Trade Center site, display our symbol proudly. Any red-white-blue color scheme speaks for America.

The colors are beautiful in their own right. They are fashionably correct.

At the very least, buy your red-white-blue from America. Standing up for America is just that type of purchasing.

American companies should display the colors as a sign of support and to let the buying public know of their commitment. A company flying the red-white-blue is a sign to Buy America.

There are a few more considerations to promote America.

We have to speak English, which can be taught in schools or in places of employment. At the very least, employers should encourage workers to learn and use what is in fact our national language. Incentives can be provided to get those workers to classes.

Remember language is free speech. We cannot force the language on anyone. It makes good sense to encourage English. It also makes good sense to learn English.

Whatever happens with our immigration policies, we have to close the borders, to control our in-sourcing. Cuba has the wet foot, dry foot rule. If the refugee from Cuba is on American land, we recognize that person. Rights follow with registration and citizenship.

Anyone who has worked with an immigrant will see one key point—that person wants a job and wants to stay in America. If that is the case, register and seek citizenship. If not, the decision is theirs to live the risk.

We need to expand guest workers. Illegal immigrants reportedly pay large sums to make a dangerous voyage and live here under a cloud. Set the guest worker program high enough, charge enough to cover our cost, and let them in. The cost should be significantly less than the brokers charge to sneak them in. The trip would be much safer. At least they will be registered and paying.

The main step we have to take is to lend our support to our values.

- Show the colors.
- Buy America.
- Promote America.
- Attend political and government meetings.
- Make talk shows respect America (don't tune in if they don't show respect).
- Remind our leaders to advance America.

Our political leaders at every level, from city, county and school district to statehouse and capitol, are free traders; they support globalization. Fair trade should be their policy.

There are other ways to advance America. Enjoy life here. Follow the American Way. Earn the old-fashioned way—work for it. Celebrate American values. Most Americans will not even notice a change.

Socialists will. The government control people do not have a sense of humor. When the Berlin Wall fell, statists lost the battle for the minds of men and women. Statists remain unhappy, even bitter. They dislike our celebrating and enjoying America every day.

Maybe the statists will get over it. Maybe they will learn. I doubt it.

We help them learn by celebrating America.

What to do?

Globalization is with us to stay.

Globalization of values is difficult and will take a long time.

Democracy in America recognizes and requires voter participation in globalization. We have to agree to any changes to our values or our government.

Right now, no fundamental changes are needed.

We made America the most powerful nation, *Pax Americana* is global peace, and American democratic business made the current and foreseeable economic progress.

We should keep doing what we have done so well.

Always remember that old-fashioned value of our history—stand up for America.

EIGHT

RESULTS

Of vital importance to any activity is the result.[1] The real measure of the economy is not with the politicians or economists saying we are making progress or not. The real measure of results is with businesses.

Profits Mean Productivity

Business owners turn to accountants to see the results. What does the bottom line look like? Is my company making money? Do I have a profit? If your accountant follows the generally accepted accounting principles (GAAP), you will have a reliable answer.[2]

The questions are relatively simple and direct. The answers tell the owner the results. In the aggregate of all businesses, the answers tell the politicians and the economists whether the nation has progress or not, whether we have a profit.

Recall that the one basic rule for politics is to assure good economic results.[3] Politicians have to know the real results so they can take action to assure economic progress. You may rest assured they will speak up.

America was not making money in 2008 or 2009.

The economy was not okay in 2008 or 2009.

American Leadership

Based on real results in business, America has been a remarkable success since 1945—until 2008. We have been and remain the most productive nation in the world.[4] Under our economics, our business leadership:

- we became the economic number one in 1920;
- since 1920, we achieved and maintained the highest gross national product among all nations;
- since 1947 we have promoted globalization as a national doctrine; and
- we have seen most nations adopt our model and succeed.

Our leadership included a commitment to helping others. Starting with the Marshall Plan, we have given much. Over the decades since 1945, we have also routinely promoted the concept of multinational economies. Our doctrines for "globalization" and for "regionalization" worked and are still working.[5] In the process we have seen real results worldwide in bringing millions out of poverty with jobs, not empty, one-time gifts.

We made global economic progress and history, bringing *Pax Americana* to the world.

Unfree Trade

The major problem has been the balance of trade. We have borne the burden of globalization at a huge national cost. The cost per taxpayer has been $250,000, an overwhelming personal expense.[6] The cost to America has been one trillion dollars in foreign aid and other assistance. This total does not include the cost of "free" trade, only free aid.

Over the years, we have not correctly evaluated our success. The world economy has changed since World War II ended and since the end of the Cold War. We now have a world where there are several very successful and productive economies. Change in our policies is necessary.

For the past five years, we have been at the very bottom of

the charts for the balance of trade among nations.[7] Our support for capitalist economies worldwide has been and remains very high. As the 2008 economic downturn shows the cost to us of "free" trade is too high.

For the past ten years, several regional economies have exceeded or equaled our gross national product. We welcomed this competition; now, however, the new economic groups must help bear the load.

On the international trade balance sheet, we are down almost one trillion dollars.[8] This cost of free trade is in addition to the foreign aid and other contributions we have provided. Our trade balance is an imbalance of trade. Our dedication to "free trade" has not been free at all. We have "unfree trade." To the backers of so-called free trade—unrestricted global trade—look at the results; free trade has not been fair and balanced.

In the process of globalization, free trade has become too great a burden for America alone.

Changes are necessary.

The Problem of Trade Deficits

For many years, the assumption has been that our trade losses were offset by investment from abroad, that our debt deficit covered our trade deficit. Deficit plus deficit is more deficits, not less. The contradiction in terms is obvious; however, that so-called virtuous circle was the accepted wisdom among free traders, those politicians who would not accept any changes.

The subject of the huge trade deficit was reviewed by a bipartisan commission in 2000.[9] How bad is the trade deficit to America? Despite very optimistic conclusions on all issues, the Trade Deficit Review Commission admitted the two deficits of trade and of the budget meant the economy could tank.

Issued on November 14, 2000, the report stated:

> Large and growing trade and current account deficits may pose risks to the U.S. economy, at least in the long term.

Optimistically predicting that necessary adjustments would occur and that the deficits risk would never happen, the commission warned:

> The consequences could be severe if it were to occur.

They strongly recommended

> (1) fiscal and monetary policies to take care of a deficit downturn and
> (2) improving competitiveness.

Nothing was done in the years that followed.

In September 2008, the forecasts of doom came true.

The "severe consequences" that could not happen?

They happened.

The time has come to end that imbalance. There were many warnings about the trade deficit, the loss of jobs and related decline in family income, the threat of mortgages going under, and the need to keep energy prices low.[10] The warnings were ignored, all in the name of free trade.

By September 2009, we remained in the troughs of the downturn.

We have an excellent opportunity to bring balance to the imbalance of trade, to improve globalization, and to right the economy.

Parity for Global Trade

To restore balance, we need parity among nations.[11]

A key first step to a "fair trade balance" would be openness and transparency in the economies of our trading partners. We need open trade.

Transparency in national accounts and transactions is essential to fair competition. Disclosure eliminates the hidden corruption that costs America so much. The estimates vary but the cost of unfree trade to America—in most cases—exceeds 20 percent.[12] The more seriously corrupt trading partners exceed a 50 percent perception of corruption. The measure of corruption does not easily translate into dollars. Using the percentage of corruption as a direct measure of the dollar deficit, the total cost to the United States should be evaluated and balanced.

The "ethics of fairness" on a global scale may appear impossible to implement. The imbalances are huge, are very expensive to the United States and very favorable for the corrupt nations. Changing that advantage may be totally unacceptable to some nations.

At this time of adverse economic results globally, there is no better time for new, open, and fair rules and accountings. Some nations are acknowledging the need for parity. Peter Mandelson, the British business secretary, made the first such recommendation to improve trade balances.[13] The G20 nations endorsed a limited parity in late September.[14]

Consequences of Unfree Trade

Looking at the long-term trends, taking an overview of global trade since 1945, the imbalance of trade is the primary reason for the economic downturn of 2008.

The reason for the economic collapse is reasonably clear. The trade imbalance was draining needed progress from America. A fundamental assumption was the American economy would always grow. This did not happen in one critical sector. Family income was not increasing. This critical economic index was actually declining. Jobs were lost and were not being replaced.

Our trade imbalance meant a loss over the past thirty years

exceeding 700 billion dollars. Converted to real costs to American consumers, this meant[15]

- the loss of over 20,000 jobs per billion dollars of deficit;
- corruption perception for our major trading partners of China, Mexico, India, and Brazil placed them in the bottom 50 percent of corrupt nations;
- many more major trading partners were in the corrupt list; and
- noncompetitive (inaccurate) accounting is accepted even among European Empire members.

Because of America's dedication to "free" trade, we have carried the burden of the corruption practiced by too many trading partners.

Corruption must be reduced and disclosure is the first step. The related step would be accurate accounting based on the agreed principles, like GAAP.

Economic Growth Reversed

There is the belief that growth would be maintained with adjustments to monetary policy as needed.[16] By adjusting interest rates up or down, we could slow down or speed up the economy. Over the long term, we would maintain a stable economy.

The reasoning was based on results. Businesses need credit for monthly expenses and for expansion. The federal government would make money easy to get or hard to get based on overall economic progress, on the results businesses were having nationwide, in the aggregate.

The ever-worsening trade imbalance and resulting loss of jobs made progress ever more difficult. Businesses did not just go overseas; many hired overseas. As the economy worsened, only interest rates were adjusted.[17]

In September 2008, the economy collapsed.

At the end of 2009, we were still rebuilding from ground zero, mainly with government spending. Apart from record-low interest rates, nothing has been done to promote business spending, to allow for expansion and hiring. Stimulus money has gone to individuals who do not hire; they use the money to pay debt and other expenses. Companies do the hiring but they are not encouraged to hire.

Equity in America and the American Dream

As the economy worsened late in 2008, America met Joe Wurzelbacher. During the election campaigning "Joe the Plumber" asked then candidate Obama about going into business.[18] Rather than encouraging the man to pursue an important part of the "American dream," the recommended course of action was "sharing the wealth." Joe was then routinely "palinized" and so too was the idea of private individuals going into business to hire people, make a profit, and pursue economic progress (profit).

This idea of equity for citizens had been one of the "politicized" turning points for the downturn. The policy had been in effect since the mid-1990s. The goal was to allow as many citizens to become homeowners as possible.[19] Homeownership would encourage people to protect their property and its value with conservative government policies. Others embraced the policy because people would have a key reward of the American Dream. As a homeowner, they could participate more fully and with more confidence in our way of life. Homeowners would have "equity in America."

The "homeowner now" policy took on a life of its own. Mortgages were granted to many who could not afford the payments. Bank policies based on sound business rules that forecast good results—the repayment of the mortgage—were ignored.

Bankers would sell the mortgages and, realizing good results, added sales forces to the mortgage programs, resulting in a further wandering from sound banking practices.

Some applicants were clearly not qualified. Submarginal loans were justified to the lender because low interest in the early years would be paid back with higher interest in later years. Monthly payments would go up in later years to cover lower early rates. In a growing economy, mortgagors would make more money and could afford the later increases.

Federal mortgage agencies helped underwrite the loans. Fannie Mae and Freddie Mac added millions to the homeowner lists.

A fundamental business rule was violated.[20] You do not make loans that do not repay. Facing heavy-duty political pressures, the agencies went ahead and the banks complied. Loans were politicized.

Because of the imbalance of trade, the economy did not grow. Jobs were lost. Personal income was stagnant, even declining. Collapse was inescapable. Some analysts saw the accounting problems and sounded warnings. Government agencies charged with enforcing accurate accounting did nothing. With ostrich eyes, politicians were ignoring the problem.

The bad economic results were apparent. Our leading ports became tall stacks of empty trailer containers awaiting nonexistent export cargoes. Factories closed, companies went overseas, and jobs disappeared. One dramatic instance was the closing of the huge Bethlehem Steel plant in Pennsylvania, recently reopened as a casino.

The greatest tragedy played out in too many homes across America. Families suffered job losses. Mortgages could not be paid. The result was widespread, a huge shock to many financing institutions where mortgages were encouraged by sales forces intent on selling the paper. Banks collapsed.

Still More Shock

There was another shock to the economy.

The American model for business success included low fuel costs. Success meant more energy was needed.[21] This meant more oil. People, goods, and services have to have gasoline. World demand rose dramatically in the early 2000s. As demand rose, another well-established business rule went to work, the price of oil went up.

Consider the results.

The latest series of "shock" increases started in early 2005. Oil went from $68 to $147.50 a barrel, an unprecedented high. The price of gasoline at the pump would increase 400 percent through July 2008, from 90¢ to $4.00 a gallon.[22]

Soon after the increase at the pump, mortgage foreclosures—already increasing—rose higher.[23] The "shock" was clear by April 2008. Every year, another million homes were in foreclosure.

Bailouts were attempted. Some mortgages on the edge were helped. For far too many, salaries stayed the same. Foreclosures continued.

Consumers most dependent on cars and trucks were at the point of the hurt. Public transportation is not feasible in too many "Walmart" areas.

The result? Low-income families carried the burden of the twin shocks of loss of jobs to overseas companies and the dramatic increase in gasoline prices. They could not afford the mortgage and the gasoline. Many had no choice. They just "walked away." They gave up their equity in America.

Economists debate whether oil increases have much impact on the economy.[24] The disagreement among the economists is all too typical of the "politization" of economics. Look at the results—the trade imbalance worsened, jobs were lost, family income declined, there was the rise in foreclosures, gasoline prices went up and foreclosures increased. The twin "shocks" resulted from ever-worsening trade imbalances.

Avoid the politics imbedded in economics. Look at the results. Economists need to adopt general principles for their calling. During most of 2008, they could not even agree on whether there was a recession. But try to get economists to agree.

The problems were not only with family mortgages and the price of gasoline at the pump. Business depends on oil. As the price increased, so did the price of everything. Government statistics showed little inflation; however, politics is again involved. The index is deliberately skewed to ignore many key products and services.[25] Once again, look at the results. Most Americans knew prices went up when they booked airline flights.

The notion that the economy would keep growing came to an end. Monetary policy responded with lower and lower interest rates. The impact was too much.

Collapse

The economy began its collapse in April 2008.[26]

The drama started when Bear Starnes had to be saved. With substantial help from the government, JP Morgan made the acquisition.

Not enough. The economy tanked in September 2008. The Fed took over Fannie Mae and Freddie Mac.[27] Then the Bank of America acquired Merrill Lynch. Then AIG received help. In October, bailout legislation passed Congress.

For many, confidence in the economy, in America, and in the future plummeted.

With the presidential race running strong, the drama moved to the campaigns. The incumbent party was out of office.

The final drama in 2008 played out when the major automakers asked for help.[28]

The drama continues a year later. Throughout 2009, more and more jobs were lost. The economy was not responding to huge infusions of federal money and federal ownership. Our political leaders are unable to find a government solution.

The most productive, hard-working, competitive, and generous people on the globe cannot find work. There rests the high drama—no jobs.

The outcome was political. The usual division between "tax and spend more" or "tax less and spend less" was at work. Some believed the government would save everyone by running everything—even though government does not understand results and profits. There was little bipartisan analysis.

For most Americans, the reasons for the downturn were irrelevant. We had an economy in trouble. Americans were hurting and all saw more hurt on the way. As usual, voters cast their ballots based on economic progress because there was no progress.

In addition, too many stayed home, totally turned off by politics. This was a mistake with correction already promised for the next election. Two million "Tea-Partiers" showed up in Washington to protest current, ongoing failures.[29] Even NASCAR should be concerned. If oil prices increase, future races will be with bumper cars using C batteries. Americans like Joe the Plumber see a way out; get business going. Americans know how bad government has been and know something must be done. Government must let us do it.

Chapter 7 suggests participating in politics by at least voting. Buying America helps. As the most powerful consumer market on the globe, avoid overseas purchases. Buy America.

An End Results

With the collapse in September 2008, the McCain lead vanished. Obama became president.

America is to be congratulated for another peaceful transfer of power.

A year later, however, the big issue remains.

How do we correct the economy?

How do we get America back on its feet?

As global leaders, how do we get the world back up?

To repeat, the American people are the most productive, hardest working, competitive, and generous in the world.

How do we get productivity going again?

NINE

FREE AMERICA

New York City has a fascinating way of naming streets. Political and vocal as the city is, everyone and anyone may be heard on any issue. This includes naming streets. Perhaps wisely, the process is often compromised by accepting all names.

The federal courthouse is officially located at 500 Pearl Street but that street is closed for security reasons. The main entrance is on Worth Street so that barely two-lane street has both names plus Avenue of the Strongest, the title adopted by the city's sanitation services.

On March 10, 2009, with confusion expected for the big case, the public arrived at the federal courthouse at Pearl on Worth making expanded sanitation services necessary. Worth is only two lanes, but New York City drivers are able to make four lanes, mirror-to-mirror. That day, the crowds took the rest of the space with broadcast trucks, interview areas, lines waiting for security check, and more.

Bernie Madoff, the great pyramidist, made off with almost 65 billion dollars.[1] He was appearing in court that day to answer to his investors, to the government, and to the courts.

The case is an excellent example of government not doing the job. To steal that much money, Madoff had to have a cooperating accountant, SEC investigators unwilling to work, and the climate of greed that prevailed.

Madoff received 150 years in prison. The trustee of his investment company is going after all sources of funds held by family, associates, and others. His auditor has been indicted.

The case stands as an example of how business goes bad when government fails. The same government failure to act characterizes foreign trade and the imbalances, poor bank loans, banks allowed to make loans and then promote the investment, moratoria on oil drilling, failure to seek parity with foreign trade partners, and inability to enforce disclosure.

Since Congress accepts the same loose standards for accounting and reporting, perhaps the results of the down economy are understandable.[2] They are not excusable. Unfortunately, Congress compromises the economy like New York City complicates streets. Unlike New York City taxis, Congress does not know how to drive the straight and narrow.

Getting Productive Again

1. LAFFER TAX CUTS

Some politicians recommend tax cuts to put money in the hands of business. Productivity would increase. This has been the result on three occasions in the past.[3] When taxes are cut, the Laffler curve goes to work. Investments go up. Business has money to invest. Since business does the hiring, there are more jobs. Productivity increases. The economy gets moving. Tax income increases.

The 2009–2010 Congress is not likely to lower taxes for business.

2. GOVERNMENT FAILURES

There are other alternatives, and the situation remains so bad that many attempts at solutions should be undertaken. We need more than "government investments" (AKA taxes). Money for government ownership and administration is not needed. We tried "government work" and got the results to be expected.[4]

Such government control, also known as socialism, has routinely failed. Even the United Nations acknowledges the private economy, those businesses seeking a profit, do better than government giveaways.[5] Even Obama admits to government failures such as the U.S. Postal Service.[6]

There are too many more examples. Of some 550 federal government agencies listed in the Code of Federal Regulations, how many are a success?

AMTRAK has yet to stand by itself. The CIA is widely excoriated for not finding weapons of mass destruction and now for predicting Iran was not interested in going nuclear. The Census Bureau wants to estimate voters rather than count them. Drug enforcement is not up to the task. We have an immigration agency but our borders are wide open. The Defense Department routinely spends too much money. Education remains a crisis.

The government efforts over the past year have been band-aids. Treasury, the Comptroller of Banks, and the Securities and Exchange Commission did not do their jobs.[7] Fish and Wildlife has been far too effective, protecting fish over human beings. Forget the office of government ethics. Child support could do a far better job. The Bureau of Indian Affairs still owes billions stolen from tribal councils. The Internal Revenue Service commands no respect. The audit becomes a lottery, with attention centered on a few taxpayers to the exclusion of most others.

Some do a very good job such as Social Security and Medicare.[8] There are far too few examples of excellence.

Then we look at Congress and accept their mistakes and misbehavior only because most Americans have a good sense of humor. Not having a job is not funny. Many of the problems with federal agencies rest with the Congress. The White House remains incapable of full disclosure.[9] At least the Supreme Court remains above the fray and its decisions are accepted despite great debates.

This appreciation for the courts is not to endorse the lawyers who need far better ethics and controls.

Why consider government for any solution?[10]

3. DOING BUSINESS BY THE BOOKS

There are many solutions not requiring government money and government control of the economy.

First, the proposed government spending should require tax increases. An old business rule is you should not have a budget deficit.[11] To spend, tax increases are needed. Not happening. Tax collections are down as more money is "invested." Print more money. Let the national debt go up. Do not tax, at least not for now. Goodbye dollar.

The deficits in trade and in the budget are not acceptable.

There are solutions in addition to printing money and pumping it into the hands of consumers. The "pump and print" solution will prove useless. The millions to consumers will not be invested and no one will get a job. Debt will be paid. Investors will get their money and wait, looking for favorable policies from Washington.

Productive America needs the reassurances and the opportunities. Business needs to know there will be a reasonable opportunity to make money. Instead, investors foresee higher taxes and then even more taxes. Health-care costs alone promise to add a heavy burden. There are no assurances of improved costs of energy. Investors have seen businesses taken over with no sign of release from government control.

There is no promise of good results, of profitability.

To repeat, we are the most productive, hard-working, competitive, and generous nation ever. We need the traditional solutions, the business solutions that work. Solutions being tried are based on government ownership and control, a garden variety of socialism that failed in the Soviet Union and many more nations. Those solutions are gone—for good reasons: they do not work.

Doing business by business works.

What are some key steps?

Basic Initiatives

There are five basic initiatives, all addressed to increased productivity. None costs the government money. They will make money and pay taxes to the government. They will not cost the government any money and they will not increase the deficit.

Business programs are never universally acceptable. Different groups will have to give and take to get a final, massive program underway.

All programs will be uncertain in their success. Still, productivity by business remains the key to improve the economy. We need to use all economic views.

Two productivity initiatives relate to the imbalance of trade. One of the two requires openness and the fair trade that results. The other makes America more competitive and more productive. Both mean more business into the United States.

The third seeks prompt recovery of funds wrongfully taken. The lesson will be for business leaders, accountants, and attorneys to follow the rules.

Another ensures more pollution-free electricity.

Still another puts a huge asset back to work.

These initiatives would be in addition to pending proposals to spend. The productivity initiatives would increase productivity and add taxable income. Unlike one-way spending proposals, productivity initiatives address more jobs, open trade, and the deficit.

1. THE IMBALANCE OF TRADE

Require Open Trade

The trade imbalance has to be corrected. Trade has to be balanced. Major adjustments to our doctrine of globalization are necessary. The huge disadvantages we have carried since 1945 should end.

First, our trading partners have to clean up their corruption.

Transparency reduces corruption and will improve fair trade. Transparency means disclosure of the rules and procedures for companies in America and for companies as the trade partners. Competition terms will be disclosed and fairness will be uncovered and better enforced. We will know what our trading partner does with its terms and conditions for trade.[12]

If the corrupt nations go transparent, major improvements result. Several research organizations provide these important lists:

(1) corrupt nations
(2) nations without disclosure
(3) nations condoning unfair competition.

Those nations must open up and clean up or face sanctions and cutbacks in trade. For the last step, if a nation does not comply, we favor America and we buy America. If our government remains dedicated to "free" trade, private citizens need to buy America.

America's global business has not been painful to foreign countries. Many have seen the benefits of open competition and have welcomed American companies. At the same time those nations have improved conditions for their employees. Many overseas nations have started social support services more comparable to those in America. Wages are higher; low payroll costs are no longer the big benefit for American companies.[13]

Regionalization of trade has also developed with results similar to the experiences America had building its "common market." We need to continue regionalization to improve competition and reduce the trade deficit.

We will not quickly obtain a corruption-free system of trade.

Major progress results if corruption is reduced to a measureable 10 percent or less.

The sooner we have an international system for full disclosure with enforceable rules, the better the foundations for coming out of the downturn and returning to stable world trade.

Powerful incentives are in place for most nations to join in adopting uniform accounting standards. There is no need to endure another global collapse.

Empower Business in the United States

America is an aggressive competitor on the global scene, but the competition is not fair and we have paid with a disastrous deficit. Other nations will not quickly clean up their acts.

Action within America is needed.

Business rules in America should be on parity with the competitive advantages granted by other nations to their companies. Whatever advantage one nation grants its businesses, we should consider adopting here.

We need open trade, with American business as free of government burdens as possible.

The changes offset unfair advantages by any trading partner. If we have to reduce taxes on business here because an overseas nation has low taxes, so be it. The same review should apply to the many areas of business competition. We do what is needed to compete fairly. Call it open competition. We are all on the same playing field.

Adopt procedures to welcome companies here and to keep companies here. Make "dollar flight" an unattractive option for companies. Keep our dollars here by keeping our companies here, by having the same rules they would have abroad. Do not sit back and let other nations adopt more favorable business rules. Amend our rules to maintain parity with the rules of other nations.

Give our companies the same lowest burden any nation imposes on its businesses.

Again, an improvement in our competitive position would increase national productivity. The imbalance of trade should be reduced even more. There would be jobs.

We will end the huge deficit that collapsed our economy, and the global economy.

Free trade has never been free trade in the intended sense. There have always been restrictions, usually harmful to America.

We need fair and open trade.

Drop "free trade."

Go to open trade.

2. IMPROVING COMPETITION WITH OPEN TRADE

The State Department conducts an annual review of trade conditions, of the terms and conditions for global trade.[14] The review looks at 272 nations recognized by the CIA. The major trade partners are analyzed. There is room for improvement in almost every nation and in almost every area of business.

The following are key areas of competition needing full disclosure and change because we do not have parity:

- unrealistic trade policies for imports overseas, forcing America to pay more than other companies.
- unnecessarily restrictive standards for certification, testing and labeling of goods from America.
- foreign companies bid on projects in America but their procurement policies keep America out.
- intellectual property protections for our copyrights, patents, and trademarks (our ideas should not be stolen).
- export subsidies favor foreign businesses, keeping America at a disadvantage.
- anticompetitive practices by some nations maintaining

restrictions on American goods and services.

- corruption and bribery favoring foreign companies over American companies.
- investment barriers to protect local businesses at the expense of American companies.

Many of these illegal or unethical practices are difficult to prove. Some rest on solid perceptions but do not have courtroom proof. Statistics are simply too unreliable. Once again, we turn to results.

Where the trade imbalance is way out of line, again with a 10 percent minimum allowable spread, America must take steps for fair and balanced trade. Steps against a corrupt nation include publicity, effective protest by our diplomats, direct intervention by the State Department, and sanctions. Do something effective.

Enforcement efforts with heavy consequences offer many more options. Reduce trade, block foreign companies, impose banking sanctions, set temporary freezes on trade, adopt embargoes, and more. Get tough.

Finally, Americans should buy America. As the strongest consumer market in the world, we would have a powerful impact—and an enforcement tool for open trade.

There are administrative and judicial procedures in place to consider claims. The World Trade Organization is making progress. Get it to expedite.

Action is needed now to take global trade out of the current downturn. We need positive action with real results to get trade imbalances back in balance. Too many agonize over a Gordian knot. We need to cut through the red tape and get the nation and the world out of the red ink. The objective would be trade parity, not more trade and debt deficits for the United States.

In the greater sense, an international policy review with representatives from the major economic regions should provide a restatement of the laws to achieve parity.

We need to be ready and unafraid to act unilaterally to prevent further imbalances in our international trade accounts. Get moving to get jobs.

3. ENFORCE BUSINESS RULES AND REGULATIONS

Another major area for improvement is aggressive enforcement of our business rules. These rules are the accounting principles business must follow. Vigorous enforcement of honest accounting will return to investors the ill-gotten gains taken by dishonest or negligent business leaders. More laws are not needed. Strong enforcement of existing laws is needed, right away. Ask Madoff.

The objective should not be only criminal indictments and prison terms. Civil penalties with strong enforcement will produce a measure of justice much more quickly. We know where the money was misdirected. Go after those unjustly enriched with a prompt receivership or other lock on their assets, all their assets. This includes not only the executives and their associates; the boards of directors are also responsible.[15] And the accountants who said the bad reports were good should pay up. Any advisers—including lawyers—should be accountable.

Make prompt demand on these leaders with the suggestion of prompt refund of the missing money. Obtain settlement of all issues with acceptance of the offer and prompt payment of refunds. The clear implication is to pay up now or face far more serious penalties. Hire lawyers to move forward.

4. SUPPORT AND PROMOTE NUCLEAR ENERGY

Another initiative for productivity deals directly with energy.

For the long-term future of America, electric power is essential, an absolute necessity. America needs electric energy in large quantities and as pollution free as possible.

There is no alternative to electric energy. The demand is huge.

Electric energy is necessary for businesses and homes as never before. The demands of the Net are huge and growing. Light is vital to safety and travel. Electricity is absolutely necessary for health care.

By definition, the electric car requires electricity.

One answer for the energy mix is nuclear power, a widely used and very safe source for electricity.[16] The technology is well established. Pollution is zero. The initial expense is heavy but the long-term fuel costs are negligible.

Nuclear power is in use in every major country and is a vital element of the long-term electric needs for most power grids. There are 439 units in service worldwide. Of 37 under construction, only one is in the United States.

Some activists oppose all electricity. They have a nonnegotiable policy for the reduction of electricity. They do not want more productivity; they oppose more power; their preference is not progress but a near pastoral life for everyone. They are a small but vocal minority.

Some rely on experimental sources that are less than reliable and more expensive. The renewable sources require large areas of land and have more down times. They are not proven. Try them and build nuclear.

The major problem is the ease for some to oppose new construction. We need procedures to expedite review, approval, and construction. These procedures are essential for nuclear power. The same procedures should be in place to avoid undue delay of any new sources. Expedited procedures include deadlines for review and presumptive approval plus accelerated judicial review and presumptive approval.

At the end of 2008 electric utilities had announced plans for many more nuclear plants.[17] These twenty-four applications should be welcomed and expedited. New plants must be encouraged.

5. PROVIDE MORE FUEL FOR ENERGY

Another important addition to our productivity inventory, one that does not require government spending and higher taxes, is to use a basic source for fuel.

FDR was plain spoken when he proposed lend-lease of destroyers to Britain. He said if a neighbor's home is on fire and we have a hose, we lend help.

To be plain spoken, when a home has a treasure chest filled with money and the debt collector is banging on the door, pay up with the hoarded asset. If we face a rainy day, we cash in savings. We are now in the midst of a hurricane and have no choice but to cash our assets, to pay the creditors and get back to work.

We have a huge treasure chest of black gold, ready for development. Examples include those hidden in the far north, in the badlands and in offshore sites. One asset is valued at four trillion dollars.[18] The income to our government would approach one trillion dollars. That money would substantially reduce the projected deficits for recovery from the 2008 downturn.

The best solution for American productivity is to produce the oil reserves we have. The recoverable reserves are relatively inexpensive to produce and are ready to go. And get more jobs.

For the short term we have to have more oil. That oil is available within the United States, and should not be purchased from our enemies. That oil is absolutely essential to low-income families who must have an auto and inexpensive gasoline. We have to have inexpensive gasoline. Low-cost fuel for vehicles has always been a critical part of our economic expansion. Get that progress underway again.

Some say ten years are needed. In fact, the North Slope was expedited in 1972 and began producing in two years. We eased out of the Arab oil embargo. Hire some Houston roughnecks and turn them loose. We need to cut out the red tape and expedite decision on protests.

Some say America's reserves are only 3 percent of the total world reserves. This is irrelevant. We need oil for America, not for world needs for the next fifty years. Our undeveloped reserves are 20 percent of America's foreseeable needs into the next decade.

To prevent future oil price shock we need reserves under our control. Owning an asset better assures supply at reasonable rates. Added reserves are an important addition to the negotiating power necessary to keep prices down.

Some have a knee-jerk reaction, saying, "We want to get rid of cars, don't we?"[19]

We must have autos. Inexpensive gasoline means our economic progress is much easier. Many electric cars are hybrids, requiring gasoline. We cannot abandon cars; afterall, Detroit needs jobs.

The prospect of inexpensive gasoline should bring pleasure to the tax and spend advocates. If we need to control auto use, do so honestly. Raise the gasoline tax. Let that tax fluctuate with the market price. The market price cannot be controlled. Set the desired ceiling and tax away. Develop a floating tax on gasoline.

Full Service Recovery

There are five initiatives for improved productivity. There are many more to jumpstart productivity. If reduced taxes on investors are unacceptable, free the sources for productivity from regulation and delay. Energize the American spirit and renew faith in the American way. And we get more jobs.

Recognize that the problems we now face are a result of government control, promoting exports on unfair terms, preventing oil exploration and production, slowing nuclear plants, condoning bad banking practices, failing to enforce securities regulations, and more.

We need a full-service recovery program:

- *demand* parity to reduce the trade deficit.
- *pursue* support for globalization from other nations.
- *change* laws hampering global competition.
- *demand* maximum competitive parity with other nations.
- *produce* our own oil.
- *promote* nuclear energy.
- *recover* misappropriated money.

Turn America Loose

As we saw in chapter 2, we are more productive than any other nation.

Eliminate guesswork from econostats and from the political economics outlined in chapter 3.

Take control of the human incentive called greed disclosed in chapter 4.

Insist on parity by at least approximating fairness, the approach outlined in chapter 5.

A unified program to increase our competitiveness and to use our available resources will be the words of assurance many American investors need to hear. Leaders reflecting the qualities in chapter 6 will do the job.

American values reviewed in chapter 7 are at the heart of the initiatives. If solid business values are not acceptable, then turn to what is made in the USA, buy America, and promote our values.

Policies dedicated to productivity will also improve the economy and add jobs. We increase American confidence. We get results.

In the final analysis, we know some guidelines work. Reduced taxes work. Reducing government regulation of business works. America has the productive power to get back to work and do the job. Promote jobs for Americans.

We do not need to experiment with unproven initiatives.

We need to do what we did not do in that period from 1992 through 2008; we need to follow the rules of business.[20] The rules have been developed over many centuries. Respect them. A few relevant to the 2008 downturn include:

Honor uniform accounting and disclosure; abide the rules.

Avoid loans that do not repay; include growth costs.

Get assets to work; do not let them lie fallow.

Encourage productivity and competition; that's business.

Get investors back in business, develop the unlimited opportunities in the free market, and watch American business go back to work.

In our democracy, participation is necessary. If nothing else, we have to vote.

Too many voters stayed home last election.

More than enough to assure results in elections were seen in Washington on September 12.

Voter participation is essential.

One big step is Open Trade to restore America's economy.

Until then, buy what is made in the USA.

There are many more.

To summarize, turn the world's most competitive, hardest working, productive, and generous people loose.

And stand back.

CONCLUSION

Hope and Plans, Change and Renewal

Bald eagles over Central Park in New York City? No way. Too much pollution, too many people, too globalized, too different, no agreed values, etc.

The event happened. An intrepid photographer watching an endangered hawk's nest, noticed the hawk looking up. The photographer followed the sight line and saw the eagle, complete with a fresh fish in its talons. He got the photo. There are many more of the magnificent birds nesting along the Hudson River, not too far away.

The eagle was a profound demonstration of a world of nature above the most globalized city in the world. Aside from being a vivid comment on the state of protection and promotion for the environment, there was an additional meaning almost too easy to understand.

Bald eagles are the American symbol and the American Way. They stand for America and our successful efforts to promote our American Way. Our eagles are another measure of accomplishment for our greatest generations, our globalizing generation.

Once nearly extinct, our conservation efforts have witnessed the eagles' return. Our eagles are nationwide.

There is much more. As a symbol for America, bald eagles represent important values about who we are. The eagle represents family and fits with the learning provided by our greatest, of giving our children their nest and of giving them their wings.

News of that one eagle over Central Park was a pleasant surprise, validating what we have done.

We always have our hopes, our dreams. Those future-looking ideas need to come out of the imagination. Our hopes and dreams also need specific plans. The process is not difficult to reduce to specifics. We want a business. Draw up a plan.

Then the tough part starts.

We had the hope for peace in 1945. We drew up plans for political and economic solutions. The political solution failed. The economic plans worked. We had some failures but we persevered and succeeded.

For the future we need specifics for our hopes. One basic hope is for world peace. We are getting there, with the ongoing economic progress bringing the peoples of the globe ever closer together.

We will not get world peace by political planning that imposes more government on us. We need political planning that grows with globalization. That planning must include democratic participation and approval.

That planning is not yet happening.

We also need change. We have seen monumental change since 1945, of keeping the peace, of ending the cold war, of avoiding nukes, of bringing economic improvements to families on a global scale, of reducing global poverty through a very practical, ongoing plan.

Change happens all the time. The change brought about by the greatest generations, the global generations, has been positive and progressive. That change continues.

We embrace change and we make improvements. We make the changes with all due respect for our values. We have to continue changes for the better by renewing those values and systems, by keeping the peace to allow globalization to flourish and by insisting on parity for the expanding, changing global economy.

The problems are clear. We have carried the laboring oar. We have committed our young men and women to the task. We have committed our fortunes to the task.

The cost has been huge. The balance of trade continues against us. Our deficits continue to grow. We have a seriously devalued dollar.

We have gone too far.

Our leaders fail to see the warnings. There is no easy way out. We start by taking the issues in our hands.

For renewal, we need to show the colors, celebrate our national values, reconsider who we are on our holidays, and show how we support America. Promote our ideas and values. Buy for America. To bring balance, grant a 10 percent preference for American goods and services, and ask our companies to make the same commitment.

Our leaders are against changing free trade to fair trade. To promote that key change, we have to participate by voting and by getting information to political leaders everywhere.

We need to commit ourselves personally to the task, to renew that unique American value of grace with courage.

The most important and least expensive front is about our values. We won the cold war and assumed we had no further problems. The ongoing war of words, however, shows the statists are still hard at work.

We are still fighting the cold war.

Take another look at the values missing from globalization:

- integrity—in a corrupt system that is writing the same rules, we insist on being trustworthy

- respect—we honor and support family, friends, community and nation—and other nations
- charitable—we assist others on an unmatched scale, aiming to help wherever workable
- open to all—we honor and respect all people who come in peace
- understanding—we are courteous and respectful to all people and we bring a sense of humor too hard to find on the global scene
- peaceful—we help where we can and do so without violence to the maximum extent possible
- law-abiding—we find in law and order the power and the peace we must maintain
- conservative—respecting property we save for our future by protecting the environment
- strong—we realize power is necessary to preserve the peace and to maintain law and order
- reverent—we acknowledge a higher calling, a higher Being and we respect that quality in others, even those denying any higher responsibility than self and intent on denying us that same right

Be assured these values are universal. Some may even recognize the source.

Change is a given. But change to what?
Hope is a given. What are the specifics?
We know what is made in the USA works.
God bless America.

AFTERWORD

What do I know about globalization?

The growing-up years: I was born in Cuero (for rawhide), Texas, and then had no permanent home following my father's "doodle-bugging" career, looking for oil worldwide.[1]

I had many trips abroad in those early years, and I learned from the start about global issues. For example, I was asked to look out the airplane window to spot German submarines in the Caribbean (although I never saw any). Some traumatic events—including a passenger airline crash in Mexico City—added to my ever-widening perspectives. Standing in the middle of flames taller than me, unable to run any farther and experiencing the heat but not the pain, new understandings opened up for me in ways not possible anywhere else—seeing what few ever imagine, including the value of life. As I stood immobilized, unable to see where to flee, an adult running to survive picked me up and carried me to safety.

There was more danger, something today's children seldom experience. Those events were not considered dangerous but fun—canoeing alone in uncharted swamps, swimming in rapid rivers and hoping to catch the training rope before floating down to the alligators, and moving sixty-pound crates of dynamite in a boiling hot barge. These and many more were very real experiences in a very real world. We find we can do the impossible. We experience personal responsibility.

Learning Spanish almost as a first language in those early years in Maracaibo, Venezuela, was also broadening. If I wanted a glass of water, I had to say, "Un vaso de agua, por favor." I learned those words and many more.

High school in San Antonio included being class president with standing ovations, participating in school plays, high grades, meritocracy and more.[2] Playing Casey at the bat in a real baseball game. Life guard, hiking New Mexico, ample time out of doors working at an "exotic game" ranch and shooting deer when needed, canoeing Canada with all supplies on our backs, and months in Los Angeles during the early 1950s.

Higher education: An interest in all things global stayed with me through college. I graduated with a liberal arts degree plus a special degree in international studies with honors. I also won two writing awards, the O. Henry short story and Williams Jennings Bryan essay contests.[3] My senior thesis recommended reorganizing the Department of Defense. In Law School, my senior law thesis focused on competition in the then-emerging Common Market.[4]

My college years included a student exchange program with Chile. The State Department's briefing beforehand recommended we show empathy. Good word. In Santiago I addressed the campus communist party and brought down the house with my literal translation to Spanish of that American phrase, a hot bed of communists. Humor works in mysterious ways. I was also accused of being CIA. If so, I would appreciate the now long past due salary.

Under the leadership of Frank Cooksey, I and other students met with the Board of Regents to recommend advances in integrating the university.[5]

My military career included three semesters in AFROTC. The colonel excused me when I told him of planning a professional career. He said, "We will get you anyway." We were at peace and I was never called back.

Superlawyer: A very active legal career introduced me to the inner workings of power in Washington. My deeper understandings came, at least in part, from those cases.

My active law years included inside information at the deepest level of federal price regulation for natural gas. I presented the case that wiped out regional pricing.[6] The result also increased my client's value from eight dollars a share to one hundred seventy dollars a share, in one month.[7]

A battle to save a park from a highway resulted in birthday gifts to Senator Tower, who later denied ever signing a letter authorizing withdrawal of federal highway funding.[8]

Cases before the Railroad Commission of Texas took my understandings to the deepest levels of the oil production and pricing procedures that we taught the Saudis. The Texas regulatory scheme showed how to limit the production of oil to obtain the highest prices possible. The process started in Austin, Texas.[9]

In litigation between Exxon and Mobil Oil, the case turned on pulling strings to get the trial judge to overturn key regulatory principles and save Exxon billions. The oil was produced from the massive King Ranch in south Texas.[10]

There were many more similar abuses of the courts.

Conspiracy disclosures: Most writers assume there are conspiracies in what elected officials do.[11] Be assured they are dead on. Stated motives are never true, economic advantage is usually at the foundation of decisions, and greed is everywhere. The title for this book should perhaps be "power, prestige and money." As we have seen, those three goals have been the focus of globalization by political leaders worldwide.

Knowing what I know about "superlawyers,"[12] the so-called powers that be in everything political and economic, I also know that those same lawyers have new powers. Today's "super-sized lawyers"[13] get anything done and demand far too much for their clients to access the halls of power. This corrupt access is vital for good results in Washington. The same access is vital for corrupt foreign leaders seeking money and free trade rights for globalization. We have corruption on corruption, of foreign leaders getting huge cash grants from DC then coming to DC and retaining super-sized attorneys to get still more dollars.

Interestingly, payments to these super-sized lawyers are not unlike the corrupt payments required up front in too many foreign capitals. The corrupt nations just need to say how to get things done with some "weasel words" from silver-tongued lawyers and charge accordingly.[14]

There is "balance" to the super-sized lawyers, the new and improved model for superlawyers. There are super-sized lawyers for the impoverished. The great lawyers know a very important fact: there are at least two sides to any court case.[15] There is balance. Consider those attorneys who become billionaires by "serving" the poor. The corruption of the legal system is unavoidable when such huge sums are available for such powerhouse lawyers. The real winners in cases for impoverished clients are the lawyers, not the impoverished victims.

Power, prestige and money: Compare globalization's "power, prestige and money" to my *Blood, Money & Power*,[16] showing politics at the lowest, most venal and devastating level. Be prepared for the sequel, *JFK versus LBJ*, driving the conspiracy world to a resolution.

The voting public understands that conspiracy theorizing is everywhere. Roberts is going to the Supreme Court to reverse abortion rights when his basic philosophy is to enforce the Constitution and reduce rampant judicial activism. Iraq was invaded for oil, not for unanswered issues about a corrupt criminal guilty of crimes against humanity, reports of weapons of mass destruction and evidence of support for Al-Qaeda. Oil stability remains vital to world commerce but the danger always is blackmail by curtailing oil. Congress grants money for public needs when in fact we know "pork" is what those "earmarks" produce. The list goes on and on, *ad infinitum, ad nauseam.*

Despite the gap between words and reality, we have to focus on what people say. If an insider discloses the reality, we have "the goods" to go forward with investigations or any other available resources. We should have listened to Hitler. We listened to Stalin, Khrushchev and Mao. We need to listen to what the current crop of two-bit dictators are saying.

The answer to corruption of globalization is to promote America and our core values. For globalization, this means not free trade, but fair trade. Full disclosure is also required. We must have transparency. We have to know who our leaders are talking to, how much they are paid and the disclosure of their income. Our leaders and leaders around the globe complain of life in a goldfish bowl. They do not live in any bowl—but they should.

Fact-checking: Despite the conspiracies, I have confidence in the legal system for presenting the facts. Unlike peer review with meritocrats of a similar mind-set at our institutions of higher learning, the courtroom hears from all sides. Even more challenging is making accurate presentations to conferences packed with opponents. Try these esamples for peer review:

- a proposal to unite five Texas counties for oil production, opposed by everyone but my client and taking on all of them
- a settlement conference with city and county attorneys from most of north Texas, trying to reach agreement on price increases
- a report to a conservation group on the problems with a case where the members were split down the middle

The facts are developed and practical solutions are reached. Try defending a doctoral thesis to a group of fervent dissenters, including at least one peer as knowledgeable on the facts as you are. That process will produce the facts needed. Current defense at peer review time appears to center on not upsetting anyone, apparently meaning that all should be politically correct.

The groups planning world control without democracy are similarly situated to "peer review" by the ivory tower occupants of our universities. They avoid fair debate. In a democracy you have to take the issues to the voters and you have to let the voters be heard. You encourage discussion to get agreement. In a democracy you talk with everyone or at least give them the opportunity to speak up.

The democratic system works best when there is maximum discussion.

Politics: I have been involved in politics almost from the beginning. The real world of local, state and national politics works best when we out the vote. Without the vote and the promotion of voting, democracy fails to reach its maximum potential.

I also know the cost of politics. I am still owed for leasing the Austin Municipal Auditorium in 1968.[17] In our democracy, the secret to winning, after all the speeches have been spoken and the voters take their turn, is to get out the vote. That places any candidate on the phone, getting the voters to the polls on election day. As we all know, that takes money. Little else is needed to know about the process.[18]

I know the power of politics. My senior partner was the most powerful man in Texas and was the only man the president trusted.[19] I was his attorney in his successful effort for a bonus for making Johnson president.

Also, for one year I had a TV program named *The Law and You* for broadcast Sundays before football's game of the week.

Writing: My first major writing effort was about capital punishment and the World Court. While "Thirty Days in November" remains in manuscript form, entry in international competitions resulted in interesting reviews—I knew nothing of law, or the opposite, I knew what I was doing and where I was going.[20]

In addition to the death penalty, authors should address love and romance. The hand-written pages of *Orchis Dialogues* are on the boards for word processing later this year, to bridge the gap with the monologues out there. A book on humor is in the long-range planning. The outline is there but the sequence of hilarious stories needs work. When done, the *Jokemaster,* inspired by the composite character for Zeke, will be on the street.

A note on writing and publishing, intended for the humor. I know what is required to be an "author."[21] When the book contract is signed, the term is used for the first time. My writing career consisted of college essays and stories, contest entries, legal briefs and reports, stories for my children and the usual humor shared with friends. I accepted Hemingway's advice to experience the world to write about it.[22] All this vital creative effort culminates with the contract. The title of "author" is at the end, where the contract is signed. Sign a book contract and become an "author."

All the best to every writer. Experience life to the fullest, write a lot, develop an interesting story, write the story, complete the manuscript, sign that contract, get the book on the streets and then, to make a living, sell, sell, sell. A publisher once cautioned me that "authors" are usually people who are well known in the community. Learn some public speaking, get an active sense of humor and talk and write anywhere and everywhere. Get known.

In the final analysis, how do you write a book? One word at a time, ten pages minimum daily. Get started and find the book takes on a life all by itself. The book has to be well written, real and emotional. Be considerate to your readers and make their task as easy as possible.

Values gene: Values have a special importance to me. Some geneticists believe there is a religious gene or a charitable gene or a kindness gene in everyone.[23] My grandfather was an ordained preacher. A great-uncle was mayor of New York. He had some successes against the corrupt Tammany Hall and was even reelected, always a challenge in this city.[24] Of course, his father was a general of the Union army who ruined his resume by running against Lincoln. Still and all, there may be a genetic connection to universal values over and above the personal, "me" and "only me" values of the "me generation."[25]

I have always been active in the church and found biblical reading to be an excellent source for our common values as well as an extraordinary foundation for understanding life itself. Much of our legal system is based on the Bible. Any person without a basic understanding of what the Good Book teaches is missing what we represent. Understand the historic and evolutionary developments of civilization from the pages of the Bible. Understand the basics, the universal values all people support. A commitment to a higher authority, love for family, respect for others, a respect for private property, and a deep recognition of the value of life. And be truthful.

My current attention to the Bible centers on the *Book of Job*. The wisdom reflected in that debate about why bad things happen to good people is most profound. So are the guidelines for reducing and perhaps even eliminating the bad things that happen.[26] Perfection or an approximation may be necessary. I have stumbled enough to know you hope for forgiveness and understanding and then keep on stumbling forward, still seeking resolution and a better world.

Family: What about family?[27] First, the children. I have noted their importance from my childhood experiences. Part of "child rearing" is to globalize their education and experiences. Recall that as the twig is bent, so the tree is inclined. This education includes early experiences with words and music. A plastic alphabet is something for them to chew on, and commit to memory. Travel is broadening and a child's mind is particularly open to needed insights, to mind-expanding adventures. Go places and meet people to teach networking at an early age. A foreign language is helpful. I gave a foundation by teaching the Greek alphabet.

And the stories. One example. Coming home one evening after a long flight from Washington, I found my children had first learned of *Star Trek.*[28] Settling down with all of them, sprawled across two beds, I related how Captain Kirk started his career at cadet school, in that place and time so far away. Bedtime stories are excellent to firm up the parent and child relation and to develop that mutual respect vital to family.

For the emotional side, the loving side, lullabies not from machines but from parents are excellent. And those beautiful prayers to hum to your baby and to watch the inevitable sleep in peace—that is priceless.[29]

Even more important, to die for.

Last and first and always, for me there is my beloved wife, my friend over the many years, who knows what marriage, bonding and true love really mean. Watching her sleeping peacefully, even appearing to grin, is almost too emotional.

And then, at the end of the day, you sleep, that "sweet sleep" that lets you sleep well.[30]

APPENDIX

A. Addresses to Contact Us

We welcome your ideas, stories and comments. Many have remarked that the United States needs to tell what Americans are like. We know everyone has a story to tell. You have seen how some of our greatest went through fascinating personal adventures at every level in middle America. We are the heart in the heartland and your stories and comments are most helpful to show what it means to be for America.

To the email address:
BarrMcClellan@att.net

To the publisher's address:
Hannover House
1428 Chester Street
Springdale AR 72764

We will keep all letters and stories confidential. There will be no publication of what you say unless you okay it. If we make changes for the sequel, we will get your approval in advance.

Please comment also on what you were doing or what was most memorable to you during the many high dramas and tragedies that happened since 1945.

We look forward to hearing from you.

B. Globalization and the Adverse Impact on America

1. Current World Economic Powers.

Nations of the world and their economic size based on gross domestic product, the value of the goods and services each nation produces. Some notes:

1. The United States is the world leader.
2. Some lists place the United States second, behind the European Empire; however, Europe is still working on the non-democratic process of placing member nations in the new Empire.
3. All members of the European group are listed (some lists include each nation and the Empire, in a process called double-dipping).
4. The European Union is correctly an Empire. Voters in several nations rejected membership. Those nations are being forced into the new European Empire.
5. The list includes recognized nations and related organizations on a list compiled by the CIA. Many of the smaller "nations" are part of larger nations.
6. The smaller nations and "organizations" are included in the ten existing or emerging regional unions.

Rank	Nation	GDP
1	United States	13.84
2	China	6.99
3	Japan	4.29
4	India	2.99
5	Germany	2.81

Rank	Nation	GDP
6	United Kingdom	2.14
7	Russia	2.09
8	France	2.05
9	Brazil	1.84
10	Italy	1.79

Rank	Nation	GDP
11	Spain	1.35
12	Mexico	1.35
13	Canada	1.27
14	South Korea	1.20
15	Turkey	0.89
16	Indonesia	0.84
17	Australia	0.78
18	Iran	0.75
19	Taiwan	0.69
20	Netherlands	0.64
21	Poland	0.62
22	Saudi Arabia	0.56
23	Argentina	0.52
24	Thailand	0.52
25	South Africa	0.47
26	Pakistan	0.41
27	Egypt	0.40
28	Belgium	0.38
29	Malaysia	0.38
30	Sweden	0.33
31	Venezuela	0.33
32	Greece	0.32
33	Ukraine	0.32
34	Colombia	0.32
35	Austria	0.32
36	Switzerland	0.30
37	Philippines	0.30
38	Hong Kong	0.29
39	Nigeria	0.29
40	Czech Republic	0.25
41	Norway	0.25
42	Romania	0.25
43	Chile	0.23
44	Portugal	0.23
45	Singapore	0.23
46	Algeria	0.22
47	Vietnam	0.22
48	Peru	0.22
49	Bangladesh	0.21
50	Denmark	0.20
51	Hungary	0.19
52	Ireland	0.19
53	Israel	0.19
54	Finland	0.19
55	Kazakhstan	0.17
56	UAE	0.17
57	Kuwait	0.13
58	Morocco	0.13
59	New Zealand	0.11
60	Slovakia	0.11
61	Belarus	0.11
62	Iraq	0.11
63	Ecuador	0.10
64	Angola	0.09
65	Burma	0.09
66	Syria	0.09
67	Bulgaria	0.09
68	Sri Lanka	0.08
69	Sudan	0.08
70	Puerto Rico	0.08
71	Serbia	0.08
72	Tunisia	0.08
73	Libya	0.07
74	Croatia	0.07

Rank	Nation	GDP	Rank	Nation	GDP
75	Azerbaijan	0.07	107	Bosnia and Herze.	*
76	Uzbekistan	0.06	108	Paraguay	*
77	Guatemala	0.06	109	Turkmenistan	*
78	Ethiopia	0.06	110	Cambodia	*
79	Dominican Rep.	0.06	111	Botswana	*
80	Oman	0.06	112	Bahrain	*
81	Lithuania	0.06	113	Trinidad and Tob.	*
82	Kenya	0.06	114	Malta	*
83	Qatar	0.06	115	Jamaica	*
84	Slovenia	0.05	116	Senegal	*
85	Yemen	0.05	117	Georgia	*
86	Cuba	0.05	118	Gabon	*
87	Tanzania	0.05	119	Albania	*
88	Costa Rica	0.06	120	Brunei	*
89	Lebanon	*	121	Congo (DR)	*
90	El Salvador	*	122	Madagascar	*
91	North Korea	*	123	Macedonia	*
92	Latvia	*	124	Burkina Faso	*
93	Bolivia	*	125	Armenia	*
94	Cameroon	*	126	Mozambique	*
95	Luxembourg	*	127	Zambia	*
96	Uruguay	*	128	Chad	*
97	Cyprus	*	129	Nicaragua	*
98	Afghanistan	*	130	Equatorial Guinea	*
99	Panama	*	131	Mauritius	*
100	Ivory Coast	*	132	Mali	*
101	Ghana	*	133	Congo (Repub)	*
102	Honduras	*	134	Laos	*
103	Estonia	*	135	Macau	*
104	Nepal	*	136	Iceland	*
105	Uganda	*	137	Benin	*
106	Jordan	*	138	Papua New Guinea	*

Rank	Nation	GDP
139	Tajikistan	*
140	Haiti	*
141	Namibia	*
142	Guinea	*
143	Malawi	*
144	Kyrgyzstan	*
145	Moldova	*
146	Niger	*
147	Rwanda	*
148	Mongolia	*
149	The Bahamas	*
150	Mauritania	*
151	Montenegro	*
152	Swaziland	*
153	Somalia	*
154	Barbados	*
155	Togo	*
156	Jersey	*
157	Fiji	*
158	Gaza Strip	*
159	West Bank	*
160	French Polynesia	*
161	Bermuda	*
162	Suriname	*
163	Kosovo	*
164	Sierra Leone	*
165	Eritrea	*
166	Bhutan	*
167	New Caledonia	*
168	Cent. African Rep.	*
169	Lesotho	*
170	Guyana	*

Rank	Nation	GDP
171	Burundi	*
172	Netherlands Antilles	*
173	Andorra	*
174	Guernsey	*
175	Isle of Man	*
176	Timor-Leste	*
177	Guam	*
178	Belize	*
179	Aruba	*
180	Zimbabwe	*
181	The Gambia	*
182	Cayman Islands	*
183	Saint Lucia	*
184	Liechtenstein	*
185	Djibouti	*
186	Cape Verde	*
187	Maldives	*
188	Virgin Islands	*
189	Antigua and Barbuda	*
190	Seychelles	*
191	Liberia	*
192	Comoros	*
193	Grenada	*
194	Greenland	*
195	Gibraltar	*
196	St Vincent & Grenad.	*
197	Samoa	*
198	Faroe Islands	*
199	Monaco	*
200	Mayotte	*
201	Solomon Islands	*
202	N. Mariana Islands	*

Rank	Nation	GDP	Rank	Nation	GDP
203	Vanuatu	*	216	Palau	*
204	Br. Virgin Islands	*	217	Marshall Islands	*
205	San Marino	*	218	Angujilla	*
206	Guinea-Bissau	*	219	Falkland Islands	*
207	Saint Kitts & Nevis	*	220	Nauru	*
208	Dominica	*	221	Wallis and Futuna	*
209	Tonga	*	222	St Pierre & Miquelon	*
210	American Samoa	*	223	Montserrat	*
211	Kiribati	*	224	Saint Helena	*
212	Micronesia (Fed)	*	225	Tuvalu	*
213	Sao Tome & Principe	*	226	Niue	*
214	Turks & Caicos Is	*	227	Tokelau	*
215	Cook Islands	*			

Source: Adapted from *CIA World Fact Book,* 2007.

Note: GDP in trillions of dollars.
*Under $0.06 trillion.

2. Nations Competitive Standing in Globalization

Who in the world is ready to do business, honestly? The following list is for nations with economies and laws set up to compete fairly. The United States is ready to compete. Only the top forty nations are listed.

1	United States	21	Malaysia
2	Switzerland	22	Ireland
3	Denmark	23	Iceland
4	Sweden	24	New Zealand
5	Germany	25	Luxembourg
6	Finland	26	Chile
7	Singapore	27	Estonia
8	Japan	28	Thailand
9	United Kingdom	29	Spain
10	Netherlands	30	Kuwait
11	South Korea	31	Qatar
12	Hong Kong	32	Tunisia
13	Canada	33	Czech Republic
14	Taiwan	34	China
15	Austria	35	Saudi Arabia
16	Norway	36	Puerto Rico
17	Israel	37	United Arab Emirates
18	France	38	Lithuania
19	Australia	39	Slovenia
20	Belgium	40	Portugal

Source: Adapted from "Global Competitiveness."

3. United States Trade Deficit

1960	+3,508
1961	+4,195
1962	+3,370
1963	+4,210
1964	+6,022
1965	+4,664
1966	+2,939
1967	+2,604
1968	+250
1969	+91
1970	+2,254
1971	-1,302
1972	-5,443
1973	+1,900
1974	-4,293
1975	+12,404
1976	-6,082
1977	-27,246
1978	-29,763
1979	-24,156
1980	-19,407
1981	-16,172
1982	-24,156
1983	-57,767
1984	-109,072
1985	-121,880
1986	-138,528
1987	-151,684
1988	-114,566
1989	-93,141
1990	-80,864
1991	-31,135
1992	-39,212
1993	-70,311
1994	-98,493
1995	-96,384
1996	-104,065
1997	-108.273
1998	-166,140
1999	-265,090
2000	-379,835
2001	-365,126
2002	-423,725
2003	-496,915
2004	-607,730
2005	-711,567
2006	-753,283
2007	-700,258
2008	-677,100

Source: US Census Bureau.

4. United States Trade Deficit—graphic presentation

- for the period 1970–2007; adapted from prior list
- total deficit almost one trillion dollars
- cost: 20,000 jobs per one billion dollar deficit

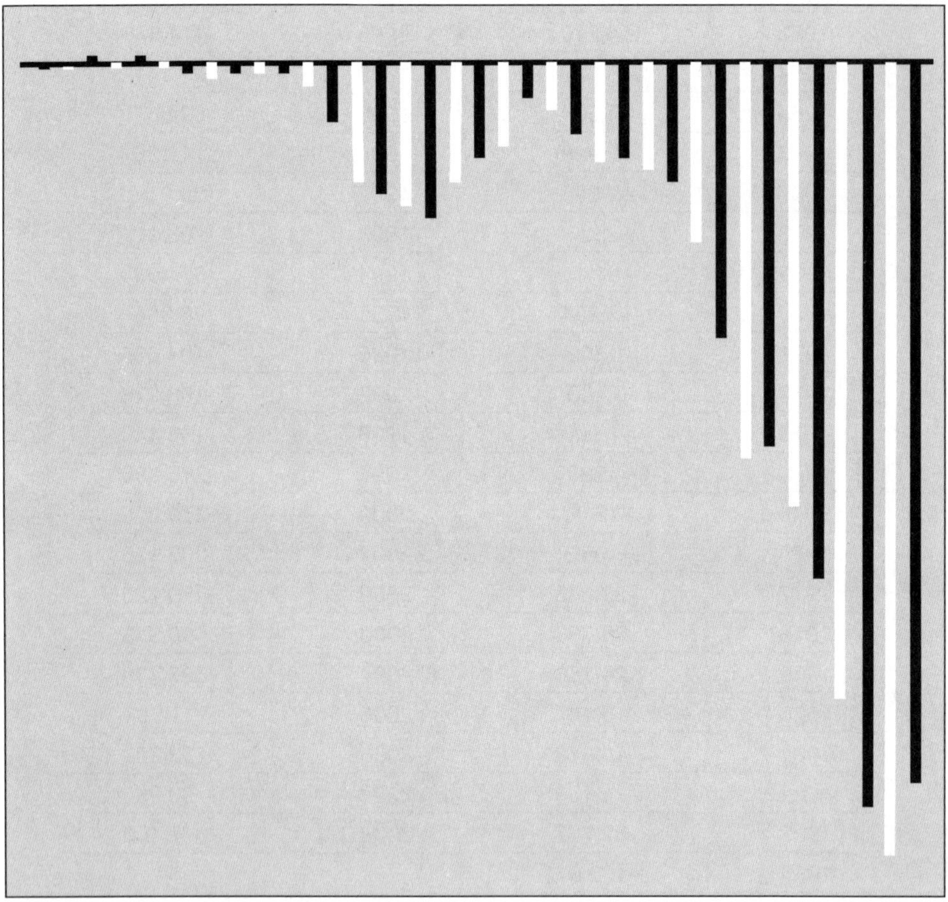

Source: Adapted from US Census, Historical Series.

5. Global Imbalance of Trade

The following shows America's trade results on the global scene. Nations with a positive trade balance are not trading only with the United States. The totals are for all nations trading with one another. China tops the list in what it gains from others. The United States is at the bottom among our trading partners. Compare this list to the corruption map. The more corrupt the nation, the more taken from us.

China	363,000	Libya	11,710
Japan	201,300	Argentina	11,154
Germany	185,100	Belgium	11,040
Saudi Arabia	88,890	Indonesia	10,210
Russia	74,000	Brazil	10,200
Switzerland	67,890	Philippines	9,040
Netherlands	59,280	Thailand	8,619
Norway	55,820	Chile	8,184
Kuwait	51,490	Iraq	7,802
Singapore	41,390	Azerbaijan	7,535
United Arab Emirates	36,110	Israel	5,941
Algeria	31,500	South Korea	3,700
Sweden	30,190	Egypt	3,115
Canada	28,460	Peru	2,045
Malaysia	25,930	Bolivia	1,325
Taiwan	23,800	Turkmenistan	689.3
Hong Kong	19,870	Bangladesh	683
Iran	19,000	Morocco	433.9
Finland	17,120	Paraguay	-82
Venezuela	17,020	Uruguay	-100
Nigeria	14,610	Tajikistan	-102
Austria	12,610	Haiti	-184.8

Honduras	-446	New Zealand	-9,973
Cuba	-750	Ireland	-12,600
Nicaragua	-754	South Africa	-16,280
Panama	-861	Poland	-18,130
Kenya	-980	India	-18,530
Vietnam	-1,199	Portugal	-18,530
Costa Rica	-1,259	Romania	-20,950
Dominican Republic	-1,993	France	-35,940
Syria	-2,160	Turkey	-36,270
Lebanon	-3,337	Greece	-36,400
Ukraine	-3,890	Australia	-50,960
Kazakhstan	-4,643	Italy	-57,940
Colombia	-5,132	United Kingdom	-111,000
Mexico	-5,414	Spain	-126,300
Pakistan	-6,477	United States	-987,100

6. The Corruption Index for the World's Nations

We have our worst trade balance with many of these "corrupt" nations; the worse our trade balance, the worse the corruption. Results have to be compared. The results show we are losing more to the more corrupt nations.

This loss status must be corrected. The prospect is that we will balance our trade by insisting the more corrupt nations clean up their act.

The requirements to reduce corruption are

1. Disclosure—open your records so we can evaluate what you are doing

2. Adopt business ethics—clean up your judicial and your business rules to assure fair trade

The top twenty most corruption free:

1	Denmark	11	Australia
2	Finland	12	Luxembourg
3	New Zealand	13	United Kingdom
4	Singapore	14	Hong Kong
5	Sweden	15	Austria
6	Iceland	16	Germany
7	Netherlands	17	Ireland
8	Switzerland	18	Japan
9	Canada	19	France
10	Norway	20	United States

The more corrupt nations, listed from worst to improving:

3. Key results:

China gets the best advantage in trade.

Nations that are competitively corrupt benefit from America's trade deficit.

176	Myanmar (Burma)	79	Saudi Arabia
178	Iraq	72	Mexico
175	Uzbekistan	72	India
172	Sudan	72	China
168	Laos	72	Brazil
162	Venezuela	68	Colombia
150	Tajikistan	64	Turkey
147	Nigeria	61	Poland
143	Russia	61	Cuba
131	Philippines	60	Kuwait
131	Libya	46	Costa Rica
123	Vietnam	43	South Korea
118	Ukraine	41	Italy
105	Egypt	41	Czech Republic
105	Bolivia	39	Hungary
99	Argentina	34	United Arab Emirates
99	Mongolia	34	Taiwan
99	Lebanon	30	Israel
99	Algeria		

Source: Adapted from "Global Competitiveness" Report, World Economic Forum.

7. Countries with the Highest Number of Migrants

USA has over 3X the nearest nation.
USA is 35X global average.

Rank	Nation	Immigrants
1	United States	38,355,000
2	Russia	12,080,000
3	Germany	10,144,000
4	Ukraine	6,833,000
5	France	6,471,000
6	Saudi Arabia	6,361,000
7	Canada	6,106,000
8	India	5,700,000
9	United Kingdom	5,408,000
10	Spain	4,790,000
11	Australia	4,097,000
12	China	3,852,000
13	Pakistan	3,254,0000
14	United Arab Emirates	3,212,000
15	Israel	2,661,000
16	Italy	2,519,000
17	Kazakhstan	2,502,000
18	Ivory Coast	2,371,000
19	Jordan	2,225,000
20	Japan	2,048,000
21	Iran	1,959,000
22	Singapore	1,843,000
23	Kuwait	1,669,000
24	Ghana	1,669,000
25	Switzerland	1,660,000
26	Malaysia	1,639,000
27	Netherlands	1,638,000
28	Argentina	1,500,000
29	Turkey	1,328,000

Source: Adapted from Nationmaster.com; globalpolicy.org.

8. Global Military Expenditures

European Empire total: $313 billion; NATO: $850 billion

1	United States*	276,700,000,000	16	Turkey	8,100,000,000
2	China	55,910,000,000	17	Canada	7,861,000,000
3	France	46,500,000,000	18	Taiwan	7,574,000,000
4	Japan	39,520,000,000	19	Netherlands	6,500,000,000
5	Germany	38,800,000,000	20	Greece	6,120,000,000
6	United Kingdom	31,700,000,000	21	North Korea	5,217,400,000
7	Italy	20,200,000,000	22	Singapore	4,470,000,000
8	Saudi Arabia	18,300,000,000	23	Sweden	4,395,000,000
9	Brazil	13,408,000,000	24	Argentina	4,300,000,000
10	South Korea	13,094,300,000	25	Egypt	4,040,000,000
11	India	11,520,000,000	26	Mexico	4,000,000,000
12	Australia	11,390,000,000	27	Poland	3,500,000,000
13	Iran	9,700,000,000	28	Colombia	3,300,000,000
14	Israel	8,970,000,000	29	Norway	3,113,000,000
15	Spain	8,600,000,000	30	Belgium	3,077,000,000

Sources: Adapted from the CIA *World Fact Book*; NationMaster.com.

Note: Figures not comparable; some sources use the CIA *World Fact Book* but misstate totals (different years reported; yearly totals not consistent with fiscal year; political purpose to overstate USA and understate others; Cuba excluded in most research).

9. The Numbers on America's Standing

The United States is the globe's greatest economy and most productive. We are also the most competitive nation, ready, willing and able to meet any other nation on terms of fair trade.

We have supported globalization with huge trade deficits, almost one trillion dollars. The loss has been in large part because many nations are corrupt. We need fair trade, with competition on a level playing field—without corruption.

Until we have major reforms we need to halt further globalization.

We are the nation most committed to globalization in many ways. For example, on migration, more people move to America than to any other nation. We have to reform our open borders. Another example: we dedicate more to maintaining world peace than any other nation.

We need parity in world trade. Our commitment to globalization must be matched by other nations. Until that happens, we have to stop further trade agreements and reform those we have.

The high price for oil adds to the deficit. If known reserves were produced, 29 billion barrels means $4 trillion. Recoverable reserves of 497 billion barrels is $70 trillion. Note that the UN wants to add $10 more per barrel.

In these times of change, we don't need to go the UN's statist route.

We need renewal of America and our systems—values that are proven to work.

C. Why and How to Support America: Ten Ways to Stand Up for America

1. Support America and promote our values.
    - "I ♥ the USA" stickers, shirts, etc.
    - wear red, white and blue
    - wear the colors
    - display the colors
2. Buy America.
    - obvious ones are tough, like autos, gasoline, banks, medicine
    - go to local stores for service and products
    - buy America on E-Bay
    - support American-owned corporations
    - see the Simmermaker lists
3. Promote America.
    - on-line offers countless ways to support America
    - boycott media distorting America's values
    - get politicians to support America
    - celebrate America
4. Insist on the 10 percent rule (NYC form attached).
    - local politics should adopt the rule (subject to legal approval)
    - use for bids
    - for business, insist on this preference
5. Insist candidates support fair trade.
    - demand a level playing field
    - expose corruption abroad
    - State Department must certify corruption-free
    - amend all trade agreements for parity
    - working conditions with parity
    - safety at work and with products
    - importers to pay costs
6. Control the borders—register all visitors.
7. Demand open government (the "goldfish bowl").

- from candidates
- all national, state and local officials
- at the United Nations and all nations
- write for America (letter or email)
  —president, White House
  —senators, congressmen and women
  —other governments (governors, state representatives, council members, county officials, parish leaders, school boards)

8. Bring humor to the world.
   - an American rule: laugh, or at least smile
   - being friendly clears many boundaries
9. Stand up for American politics.
   - keep winning the cold war with our values
   - oppose statism at any and all levels
10. Keep the faith and talk for America.
    - letters, emails (including forwarding good ones)
    - attend meetings and talk up
    - at least clap or groan
    - enjoy the process (really is humorous)

Send us your stories.
  Email BarrMcClellan@att.net.
  Mail responses to Hannover House.
  Use any format—email, letter, etc.

MOST IMPORTANT: Support our democracy—register and vote.

- You gotta tell 'em.
- They gotta know.
- You gotta vote.

D. Advisory Committee of Business Leaders
(recommended)

Globalization has resulted in unacceptable losses for the United States. Leaders who know the importance of getting results should be requested to advise on improving the status of the United States in the current globalization process. Possible choices include the following:

Governor Arnold Schwarzenegger
Mayor Mike Bloomberg
Bill Gates
Warren Buffett
Donald Trump
John Bolton

E. Ten Percent Application

Buy New York City Vendor Questionnaire [5% preference]

BID TITLE: ____
______________________________ PIN: ________________

1. Principal place of business in New York City
   a. New York City location ____________________________
   b. Location where bid item is manufactured or produced
      ____ % in NYC ____ % outside NYC
   c. Percentage of total purchases bought from NYC-based businesses? ____ %
2. Total number of employees ___________
   a. Percentage of employees working in NYC ____ %
   b. Percentage of employees residing in NYC ____ %
3. Amount of NYC taxes paid by your company in prior tax year:
   ___ $1 to $2,000 ___ $2,001 to $7,000 ____ $7,001 to $15,000 ___ over $15,000
4. Describe any additional factors in making the award to your firm which would contribute to the social or economic well-being of New York City:

a. ____
b. ____

The statements made on this form are accurate to the best of my knowledge.

NAME OF FIRM __________________ ________________
Signature of officer

ADDRESS ________________________ ______________

Title

________________________ ______________

Date

PHONE ________________________

Any misstatement of facts may result in the removal of your firm from the bidder's list.

Please use other side for additional information. [Form adopted from NYC HHC.]

F. Buying What Is "Made in the USA"

Roger Simmermaker: *How Americans Can Buy America* (Rivercross 2005). A listing of USA made products with an outline of what a consumer should do to promote America. One of only a few endorsing this very difficult task of favoring the world leader for progress. Most other nations are enjoying taking from us.

Simmermaker: *How Americans Can Buy America* (2008). Simmermaker has four books on buying America. This is the latest. The series should continue with updates.

Cheri Sicardi: *Great American Handbook* (Berkley Trade 2002). Excellent source for citizenship and for supporting America, not just purchasing but standing up for the USA.

Suggested Websites to Buy America

There are many. One place to start: "google" the term "buy USA." Several examples:

Madeinusa.org	usstuff.com
Buydirectusa.com	buyamerican.com
Stillmadeinusa.org	howtobuyamerican.com

NOTE: Check the FTC for "made in USA" for inaccurate claims.

G. Suggested Readings

Tom Brokaw: *The Greatest Generation* (Delta 2001). The lives and times of the generations that survived depression and world war and then built modern America. He also wrote *Boom! Voices of the Sixties* and *The Greatest Generation Speaks*

Lou Dobbs: *War on the Middle Class* (Viking 2006). Recommended in the text, this book looks at the direct impact on Americans.

Joseph E. Stiglitz: *Making Globalization Work* (Norton 2007). Covers the international monetary system with a look at tailor-made solutions for national economies by IMF, WTO and the World Bank. Also by Stiglitz, *Globalization and Its Discontents* (Norton 2003), calling for equity in many specific globalization situations.

Mark Steyn: *America Alone* (Regnery 2008). If the predictions do not happen, a hilarious look at where America is going as we face a national decline in will through the modern apologists.

Newt Gingrich: *Winning the Future* (Regnery 2006). The former Speaker updates his brilliant contract for America with new proposals, and calling for throwing the power and control hungry in Washington out with a grass roots uprising.

Thomas L. Friedman: *The World Is Flat* (Farrar Strauss and Giroux 2005). Important insights and concepts for grasping globalization and how quickly acceleration is occurring. Not a quick read but a solid insight into the subject.

Dick Morris (with Eileen McGann): *Outrage* (HarperCollins 2007). Covering a wide agenda of corruption including many on the global scene. Solid insights from an insider.

Pete Navarro: *The Coming China Wars* (FT Press 2006). Highlights not just the threats China presents but also the problems it faces in changing from communism to capitalism. One wonders if democracy is far behind in a huge nation going modern in the freedom of information age aka the Net.

Senator Byron Dorgan: *Take This Job and Shove It* (St Martin 2007). The North Dakota Senator tackles globalization's impact on America but, as a political slam, ignores immigration, meaning open borders are okay meaning free trade all the way.

H. Letter Package Requesting Interviews

Form Letter

Barr McClellan
xxx East XXth Street #AA
New York NY 10000
212-000-0000
BarrMcClellan@att.net

July 20, 2007

Name
Address
City State zip

Dear ___________________:

In association with Hannover House publishers, I am completing a book on doing business with American companies and their goods and services.

The book is scheduled for national release next April and should receive excellent coverage. Media appearances are already pre-scheduled.

We are inviting several well-known leaders to share their views on America, on buying USA, and on globalization. These views may be as a statement or in an interview format. In whatever format you choose, the remarks will be yours.

May I include you as a leader with your comments on this very important subject?

Unless I hear otherwise, I will follow up this letter with a call in the next few days.

Enclosed is an outline for your consideration.

I look forward to your comments.

Sincerely,

Made in the USA: Suggested Considerations

1. American Leadership

In America we overcame the Depression, won WWII and prevailed in the cold war, and we prevailed with ideas for freedom, democracy and a stable peace for the world economy to prosper. We did not claim territory or tribute; we succeeded on the strength of our ideals and then pulled back to let the world do what was best.

2. The USA Is a Generous Nation

To assist our friends, we were generous to a fault. Mistakes were made but our determination was to help based on our values, which have been repeatedly proven to be sound. We also provided the military to maintain the peace, and our Navy was dedicated to preserving the lanes of commerce. Make no mistake. We were dedicated to the job and we relied on values that are uniquely American.

3. Globalization

Now several major nations or regions are making excellent progress based on our system. The European Union is virtually our size; China is moving quickly to match and exceed our success; India is advancing with great strides; the British Commonwealth remains strong and stable; Russia is having serious problems but is working with these world powers; and the oil nations are showing forward movement. We can appropriately talk of globalization with benefits for all nations choosing to participate.

4. Problems for America

But there are problems for America. We have shouldered the heavy load these last eight decades. We have provided the military defense, the economic stability, the example for others, the ideals cherished by so many in the world, and much more, all at our cost. We have a balance of trade that is not balanced, we have a declining dollar value, the level playing field is far from flat, our jobs are outsourced or in-sourced, and health and environmental progress is not followed by our major competitors. The outlook is not good.

5. Our Biggest Problems

Corporate Greed. The big companies are the global ones, founded and based in America but determined to cut the best deal at whatever the cost to America.

Tax Laws. Our government has been giving away our advantages at break-neck speed, assuming we can easily afford the loss. This misguided thinking keeps Americans from competing fairly. What the tax laws prevent, the treaties and informal agreements have ever greater costs.

Exporting Our Future. We began before WWII and we have not let up exporting our future. For many decades we benefited mutually. No longer. We cannot continue ruining American business and its goods and services. We have to end both sending America's business out of the country and allowing outsiders to take over our businesses.

6. Steps Forward

What should America do? One suggestion is to concentrate purchases in the USA. Another is to require parity and reciprocity with our trading partners. Treaties should mandate compliance with as level a playing field as possible. But the giveaways now in place are hard to change.

Private citizens and companies will take important steps by favoring America and our businesses. Our state and local governments should direct their needs for goods and services to

America. We have to right the balance and flatten the playing field where our national leadership cannot.

One additional small step would be to dedicate our support by display of the American flag and red-white-and-blue icons.

Requests for Comments

The Honorable Trent Lott
United States Senator (now retired)
509 Third Avenue, SE
Washington DC 20003

Senator Kay Bailey Hutchinson
284 Russell Senate Building
Washington DC 20510

The Honorable Charles Schumer
United States Senator
Washington DC 20510

Jesse Ventura
Baja California Mexico
(current address not available)

Paul Wolfowitz
American Enterprise Institute
1150 17th Street, NW
Washington DC 20036
202-862-5800

Mayor Michael R. Bloomberg
City Hall
New York NY 10007

Alan Greenspan
Greenspan Associates
Washington DC 20007

Donald Trump
The Trump Organization
725 Fifth Avenue
New York NY 10022

Bill Gates
Bill & Melinda Gates Foundation
Seattle WA 98102

Warren Buffett
Berkshire Hathaway Inc.
Omaha NE 68131

Governor Arnold Schwarzenegger
State Capitol Building
Sacramento CA 95814

Colin Powell
Alexandria VA 22314-1556

The Honorable John Conyers Jr.
2426 Rayburn Building
Washington DC 20515

John R. Bolton
American Enterprise Institute
1150 Seventeenth Street, NW
Washington DC 20036

Honorable Patrick Leahy
United States Senate
Washington DC 20515

Lloyd Doggett
Member of Congress
Washington DC 20515

NOTES

Completing footnotes was once the most difficult, tedious and important part of any book. Since my last book was printed five years ago, there has been a sea change.

Call it Google. You mention a subject but cannot recall the source. Get on the Net and "google" the word or phrase. You have at least a start, if not an answer. Peter Navarro, in *The Coming China Wars* (FT Press 2006), acknowledges the Internet as a research source. The colleges and universities struggle to accept the Net and still require students go to the library. Net citations are okay so long as they are "reliable" and do not use *Wikipedia*.

Basic information for fact-checking used to rely on encyclopedias. Now *Wikipedia* gives enough of an answer to at least provide a start and for corroboration. Google is not the only research source. There are many search engines and several online encyclopedias.

What is happening is the globalization of information and the sources for that information. The results amount to a version of future shock. Call it "global shock" for basic research. Research actually becomes easier.

Efforts should be directed to making writing easier. There are sound reasons.

Word processors require wrist action that may result in carpal tunnel syndrome (cts). Abbreviations, reduced use of capital letters, fewer commas, fewer "it" and "its" and other shortcuts have been used, in due disregard of style manuals and to lessen cts.

Citations to the Net are challenging. Web addresses are shortened by omitting the http and the www because search engines no longer need those identifiers. The ongoing problem is webpages disappear or change. Fact-checkers will have problems.

Phonetics must do better to help. They should start with the new name: "fonetics." The Internet generation with text and instant messaging are way ahead in developing shorter words.

To reduce cts, references have been abbreviated to the maximum. If more detail is needed, drop an e-line to barrmcclellan@att.net.

Preface

1. Having experienced an upwardly mobile America, I avoid "middle class." Middle America refers to those of us in the middle of America based on income, ownership and experiences moving up and down with some ease.

2. *Blood, Money & Power: How LBJ Killed JFK* (Hannover House 2003). The initial rise to the top of the bestseller lists was for history and for nonfiction on Amazon. The *New York Times* showed an initial nineteen rating adjusted to twenty-two for all books.

3. Amazon.com lists the top thirty globalization books based on release date, starting with most recent. Barnes & Noble (bn.com) lists over 300.

4. "Google" globalization and get over 22 million hits.

5. My globalization experiences, both personal and professional, are in the Afterword.

6. Some may note biblical sources for these values. Note the statements are intended to be, and are, also universal.

Introduction

1. This example and six others are taken from news reports and conversations with associates. Police reports or trial results will be in the sequel.

2. Thomas Friedman's *The World Is Flat* (Farrar Strauss Giroux 2005, 2006) refers to products from abroad and assembled in

America, typically in free trade zones (FTZs). As used here, in-sourcing includes migrants working in the United States and exporting funds to another country.

3. See chapter 4, "Greed." The loss refers to trade imbalances leaving America with a huge deficit.

4. Tom Brokaw, *The Greatest Generation* (Random House 1998).

5. At reagan.utexas.edu/archives/speeches/1989/011189i.

6. At un.org/aboutun/history.htm.

7. United Nations optimistic planning; on hindsight, naiveté. UN Charter, Art 47, Military Staff Committee ("essentially dormant"). At *usunnewyork.usmission.gov/Issues/msc.* The MSC is "mandated to do nothing." At *globalpolicy.org/security/peace-kpg/reform/2001/msc.*

8. At winstonchurchill.org/i4a/pages/index.cfm?pageid=429.

9. The "hope" is dictators will accept human and civil rights. Standing alone, such "friendly persuasion" fails. Direct challenges might help. See reaganlibrary.com/reagan/speeches/wall. ("Mr. Gorbachev, tear down this wall.)

10. I was told this during a private event at the United Nations' Secretariat Building, New York City. The need for anonymity is obvious. The person was an intermediate-level administrator. Disclosure in an organization as secret and corrupt as the United Nations would ruin his career. The name has been disclosed to my publisher and meets the *New York Times* most recent revised standards for anonymous sources (editorial page, 6–10–2008).

11. "Statism" describes control by the state, the "big brother" world of George Orwell's *Nineteen Eighty-Four* (Secker and Warburg 1949) [*1984* hereinafter]. The movie is Michael Radford (director), *1984* (Umbrella-Rosenblum Films 1984).

12. Conspiracies are necessarily limited to a few people who have illegal purposes. McClellan, op.cit., p. 1.

13. George F. Russell Jr., "The Power of Globalization," National Bureau of Research, Vol. 16, No. 2 (November 2005).

14. For present purposes, "empire" includes adding territory by coercion rather than democracy. The term has been widely abused for political purposes. See Max Boot, "American Imperialism?" *Council on Foreign Relations* (5–6–2003), cfr.org/publication.html?id=9394; cf. Jan Zielonka, *Europe as an Empire* (Oxford 2006).

15. Critics suggest democracy cannot be "transplanted." See M. P.

Maggay, "A Derelict Democracy" (5–23–2007), mpmaggay.blogspot.com/2007/05/derelictdemocracy. Key examples to the contrary are Germany and Japan since 1945.

16. American experience in the First World War resulted in isolation. Leave Europe to fight its wars. James MacGregor Burns, *Roosevelt: The Lion and the Fox*. (Harvest Books 1956). (FDR promised he would "not send American boys into any foreign wars.") For our determination to protect American families, see Stephen Spielberg's "Saving Private Ryan" (Paramount, Dream-works 1998).

17. The terms include the national government "taking care of" citizens, usually at the expense of others who worked and planned to take care of themselves.

18. *Time,* "The Silent Generation" (11–26–1951), time.com/time/-magazine/-article/0,9171,821852,00.

19. Controversies over human rights and civil rights lead some to deny any greatness to America. We had problems and provided solutions, through democracy. Cf. Tom Brokaw, *Boom: Voices of the Sixties* (Ballantine 2007).

20. The Internet started with government and university computers interconnecting in the mid-1970s. The Internet and the World Wide Web were well underway by the 1980s.

21. The term is singular. There would likely be only one exchange of nuclear weapons.

22. See "State of the News Media 2006," stateofthenewsmedia.org-/2006/narrative_radio_audience.asp?cat=3&media=9NPR survey, March 2006; cf. American Society of Newspaper Editors Ethics Code, asne.org/index.cfm?ID=886.

23. Anyone who would deliberately kill an innocent person has psychotic issues that separate them from a population seeking peace. The value of a human life cannot be compromised. See BBC, "Talking Points: Is violent protest ever justified?" (6–27–2001), news.bbc.co.uk.

24. James Carville is credited with the term. *The War Room* (Hegebus and Pennebaker, documentary, 1994). For politicians, the significance of the economy has never been lost. Cf. Charles A. Beard, *An Economic Interpretation of the Constitution of the United States* (1913, new edition, Macmillan Company, 1952).

25. See wordreference.com for the significance of "meeting payroll."

26. Hamilton's recommendations were made as our first secretary of the treasury acting under the new Constitution. Duties included printing money, imposing tariffs, assuming debt, providing the common defense and conducting foreign affairs. See, e.g., law.umkc.edu/faculty/projects/ftrials/burr/HamiltonBio.

27. *Stanford Encyclopedia of Philosophy*, "Globalization" (2002, revised 2006), plato.stanford.edu/entries/globalization.

28. The "KISS" system is widely used in business. Typical overburdened sentences need simplication. William Zinsser, *On Writing Well* (Collins 2006). See also Stephen Hoch and others, *Wharton on Making Decisions* (Wiley 2004).

29. The book *1984, supra,* and the movie are classics. Orwell predicted a new world order with three regional governments, constantly at low-level war, mainly intent on controlling all thought.

30. The devil is in the details, for investigators to state facts correctly and for writers to provide accurate text. In business, service must be accurate. See usinenglish.com-/links/Detailed/1820.

Chapter 1: *Pax Americana*

1. The statement is so fundamental, so important and so elusive that it seems utopian, impossible, even trite. Efforts continue. See, e.g., carnegieendowment.org. When queried, Google yields 38 million hits.

2. The Cuban Missile Crisis is a modern example of preemptive action to prevent a foreseeable threat. For a basic approach to the realities of war and peace, see Morgenthau, *Politics Among Nations* (McGraw-Hill 1985).

3. Progress is being made. See, for example, Andrew Mack, "Peace on Earth? Increasingly, Yes," *Washington Post* (12–28–2005).

4. Brokaw's follow-up books are listed in the Appendix.

5. See Introduction, note 13.

6. There are several towns in northeast America named Levittown. Some 17,000 homes were built virtually overnight to take care of the postwar housing boom. At levittownhistoricalsociety.org-/history.

7. For further perspective, see tigger.uic.edu/~pbhales-/Levittown.

8. Cell phones are rapidly replacing land-line phones in the home (also being replaced by voice-over Internet services).

9. US Census Bureau. census.gov/history/www/through_the_decades. Compare 1860, 1900 and later.

10. The early relief programs of the New Deal were struck down by the Supreme Court. Leuchtenberg, *Franklin D. Roosevelt and the New Deal, 1932–1940* (Harper Perennial 1963). Zeke cared less about the politics; his stomach pain ended.

11. Americans are very perceptive about politics. We know "pork" and revenge in "the profits and the perils of voting." This particular instance was understood and accepted. See, e.g., Stephen Earl Bennett, "Political Ignorance Revisited," publicopinionpros.com/features/2005/dec/bennett_ns. Cf. "aggregation" in chapter 6, "Leaders."

12. Donald Trump was interested in investing in casinos. Gulfport was not ready for the huge investments promised. The neighboring city of Biloxi was ready and landed the casinos (none from Trump).

13. Lynching was a horrific crime against humanity. The terror lasted until late in the 1950s. Since then, there were isolated murders for many years. See law.umkc.edu/faculty/projects-/ftrials/ship/lynchstats.html.

14. The story of retail in America shows how one successful chain after another started up and became established. William Leach, *Land of Desire: Merchants, Power, and the Rise of a New American Culture* (Pantheon 1993).

15. An essential part of Lockheed, the "eggheads" (now known as "geeks") did the thinking outside the box.

16. The moon base is yet to be built. The foundation planning is complete. The details are in blueprints.

17. Many plays are developed in the Manhattan crucible for Broadway. This delightful romance was a true stroke of good fortune for Belle.

18. The situation occurred twenty years ago. The client is now deceased. The details are not disclosed, yet. There are no unauthorized disclosures.

19. The secrets are fully protected, not just by confidentiality agreements but by federal law.

20. For the "generations" in America, see timepage.org/time.
21. See "State of the News Media 2006," journalism.org.
22. The island was well concealed. Even Google missed it.
23. This major undertaking eased travel between downtown and the medical center. Local politics slows the works.
24. The media attention to violence—"if it bleeds, it leads"—should be down-played because of "copycat" behavior.
25. The initials were for Thomas Jefferson. The name was not particularly welcome in some areas of the South after the Civil War.
26. Peace is the basis for commerce, and our Navy does the job. See, e.g.,news.navy.mil/search/display.asp?story_id=36409 (promote maritime peace).
27. Problems include island ownership, oil rights and maritime commerce. China and the United States have cooperative training underway. See navy.mil/search/display.asp?story_id=26570.
28. With the embedded tradition, there are some effective controls on early release of data. BBC News, "How Embedded Journalsists Are Handling the War" (3–25–2003), news.bbc.co.uk-/1/hi/uk/2885179.stm
29. Federales are the federal police. Over the years, Mexico has reorganized the group several times. Corruption has been a problem.
30. The tradition has encouraged many a prospector and investor to lose money. See John Huston's *Treasure of the Sierra Madre* (Warner 1948).
31. Many of the stories are in the books mentioned; however, none is disclosed, not yet. The working titles may change.
32. Changes had been made between Worth's career and the life Thad survived. We move forward. Washington Post.com, "Rice: Obama's Run shows Black Progress" (2–25–2007); washingtonpost.com/wpdyn/content/article/2007/02/25/AR2007022500456.
33. When speaking of the faith of our fathers, the mother has to be included. See, e.g., christianitytoday.com/ch/2007/-001/6.43.html.
34. The overlap of cultures and nations is globalization. The process has been underway for many centuries.
35. The eradication of yellow fever has been credited to Walter Reed. In fact, the leadership came from Maria's grandfather. mcat-master.com/medicine&war/yellowfever.htm.

36. See abanet.org/intlaw/hubs/programs/Annual0316.0316.06.pdf.

37. At multied.com/Bio/presidents/Lincoln for an account of the president's trip when he was nineteen.

38. Stanley Kober, *The CIA as Economic Spy* (12–18–1992), at cato.org/pubs/pas/pa185.htmlss.

39. This information is suppressed. Cuba may open up but is still pursuing nuclear rights. Cf. babalublog.com/archives/003799.

40. Alvin Toffler, *Future Shock* (Random House 1970). New developments will result in ever greater changes as information moves ever faster. See Standford, op.cit, Introduction, n. 27.

41. Naming the generations often results in overlapping years and confusion. These generations are defined to explain behavior and more. Here we have the greatest generation, covering 1929 to 1945. The "greatest generations" is plural, for 1945 to present. Perhaps we need the Internet Generation, or the Practical Generation, or the *Pax Americana* Generation, or even the Global Generation.

Chapter 2: Trillionaires

1. For a review, *see answers.com/topic/dot-com-1?cat=biz-fin.*

2. See Matthew Miller (ed.), "The 400," *Forbes* (9–20–2007).

3. Membership in "the club" fluctuates from year to year as newcomers move to greater wealth and as the stock market moves up and down.

4. The international scene hosts several "clubs" such as the "Club of Rome." The national leaders also gather in the Group of Seven or Eight, more or less.

5. Luisa Kroll, "The World's Billionaires," *Forbes* (3–5–2008).

6. Peter Bernstein and Annalyn Swan, "Vast Wealth," *Forbes* (10–08–2007).

7. There has been litigation over Microsoft's business practices. Groklaw, "Microsoft Litigation Page," groklaw.net/-article.php?story=20041228040645419.

8. The Net started with military planning and then included support from major universities for research. Thirty years ago a researcher friend gave me an advance briefing.

9. Bill has many critics. See Dylan Tweney, "So Long, Bill Gates, and Thanks for the Monopoly," *Wired* (6–27–2008). Webmasters in the Rockies have their special memento to Bill.

10. Bill Gates, "Strengthening American Competitiveness," Senate Committee on Health, Education and Welfare (3–7–2007); at microsoft.com/Presspass/exec/billg/speeches/2007/0307Senate.mspx.

11. Competition is reviewed in chapter 4, "Greed," and chapter 5, "Parity."

12. We are dealing with globalization; "globe" will be used routinely.

13. The gifts are covered in chapter 4, "Greed." The *Columbia Encyclopedia* reviews the history and current status of the foundation which started in 1994. See answers.com/topic/times-topics-bill-and-melinda-gates-foundation. With subsequent mergers the "Bill and Melinda Gates Foundation" has resulted. Total assets in 2006 were $30 billion plus. Warren Buffett added $31 billion that year. See berkshirehathaway.com/donate/bmgfltr.pdf (the letter commitment).

14. The recommendation at the World Economic Forum is for "creative capitalism." See Microsoft.com, remarks by Bill Gates, "A new approach to capitalism in the 21st Century" (1–24–2008). microsoft.com/Presspass/exec/billg/speeches/2008/01-24WEFDavos.

15. Bill candidly tells what works. His main interest remains computer and technology advances. Speeches at the annual technological conferences are worth reading. See microsoft.com/presspass/exec/billg/default.aspx?tab=speeches.

16. With a healthy sense of humor, *Forbes* notes the race. Bill would be ahead of Warren but Microsoft bid for Yahoo. See forbes.com/2007-/03/07/billionairesworldsrichest_07billionaires_cz_lk_-af_0308billie_land.

17. For the "Oracle of Omaha," see berkshirehathaway.com.

18. The term is Warren's shorthand description for his investments. See Motley Fool, "Priceless Investment Advice" (2–11–2008), fool.com/investing/value/2008/02/11/warren-buffetts-priceless-investment-advice.

19. Warren is paid only $100,000 per year. He strongly opposes super-sized benefits to executives. Based on personal experience, my recommendation is for the chief executive (as the person responsible for business development) to improve corporate performance (results) and earn through equity ownership. Pay would be kept at a minimum; dividends would be earned.

20. His views are stated in several forums. His message to stockholders is a good start. Always laced with humor, Warren is very open to telling others what he does. See Berkshire Hathaway.com. Life in a "goldfish bowl"?

21. The Walton family fortune, when combined, is the largest in the trillionaires club, with a total at $65.7 billion. forbes.com/lists/2007/54/richlist07_The-400-Richest-Americans_Rank.html. For information on Wal-Mart, the website is best. At walmart.com.

22. This small insight is from personal experience.

23. Kim and Mauborgne, *Blue Ocean Strategy* (Harvard Business 2005). Their recommendations have been practiced by business leaders for many years.

24. See walmart.com/catalog/catalog.gsp?cat=542413.

25. See, e.g., wakeupwalmart.com.

26. The patent office remains a key for the protection of innovation.

27. *Scientific American*, cited at Boeing.com.

28. See boeing.com/companyoffices/aboutus/.

29. From Al Capp's Dogpatch, a potent "white lightning" fermented from unmentionable sources. See lil-abner.com/Dogpatch. Rennie was with Lockheed, not part of Boeing but a key part of America's aerospace team.

30. To paraphrase Wendell Willkie in his campaign against FDR for "one world" or "globalism." See Alan Farbhan, "Global or just Globaloney" (6–27–1994), money.cnn.com/magazines/fortune/fortune_archive/1994/06/27/79450/index.

31. See flightspeak.co.uk (4–20–2008) "English is now the mandated language of aviation." Today we see "globalization" one step at a time in many areas. See Ramona Binder, "One Country, One Language" (9–29–2006), at worldpress.org-/Europe/2509.cfm (problems Europe has teaching three required languages).

32. The "club" is no longer limited to men. In 1922, a senator's wife was named senator, serving for one day. The first woman elected to a full term was in 1932. See senate.gov/artand-history/history/common/briefing/women_senators.

33. See *Forbes*, supra, n.16.

34. The few who practice full disclosure are to be congratulated. Far too often government service leads to great wealth. Disclosure

would be an improvement and may be happening. See Ellen Miller, "Congress Fails When It Comes to Disclosure" (7–7–2008), rollcall.com/issues/54_1/guest/26408-1.

35. Lott is no longer a member of the Senate. He retired one year after reelection.

36. Friedman uses a different meaning, for our companies bringing goods into America, working on them here, and then selling them here or taking them foreign again. His example is a UPS undertaking where their planes arrive here, products needing more work are completed and then delivered here or overseas. Friedman, supra, Introduction, n. 2. Our term is for a direct comparison to outsourcing. Comparable terms are exports and imports.

37. Hurricane Katrina hit hard. Trent's home was destroyed. Ingalls Shipyards is now part of Northrup Grumman Ships. A Navy base near Trent's home has been closed.

38. See *Herding Cats: A Life in Politics* (HarperCollins 2006).

39. See Kay's webpage, senate.gov/~hutchison/bio. She has several books on women in politics, two with other authors, one on her own. See *Leading Ladies: American Trailblazers* (Harper 2007).

40. General biographical information is available at Lloyd's webpage. See house.gov/doggett/about.

41. Voting records are available at Congress webpages. Considerable information is available on each politician including mail and email addresses plus phone contacts. See clerk.house.gov/legislative/legvotes. (House of Representatives); senate.gov/pagelayout/legislative/-a_three_sections_with_teasers/votes. (Senate). Several private webpages include voting records.

42. See ontheissues.org for details. Several webpages are interactive on issues for decision. See chapter 6, "Leaders."

43. Senator Schumer strongly endorses global leadership for New York. For a full report, see *schumer.senate.gov/SchumerWebsite/pressroom/special_reports/2007/NY_REPORT%20_FINAL.*

44. Conyers webpage did not mention free trade. See house.gov/conyers. His Detroit district includes autos and their union. He has taken leadership to reform our free trade policies.

45. See Leahey's comments at Davos disclosing this interest in more taxation. Topix.com. He also appears at youtube.com/watch?v=qVabbOBjRKA.

46. The reform party calls for many restrictions on free trade. At americanreform.org/platform.

47. A disclosure. I appeared on Jesse Ventura's talk show. He later retired to Baja California and could not be contacted for an interview. His new book, with Dick Russell contributing, is *Don't Start the Revolution Without Me* (Skyhorse 2008).

48. See rightweb.irc-online.org/profile/972 for John's profile. He is presently with the American Enterprise Institute in Washington, DC.

49. Chez Nadesha, "In defense of John Bolton" (8–28–2005), not a fan but conceding the "bum rap" he faced. See cheznadezhda.blogharbor.com/blog/_archives/2005/8/28/1175345. See also Anne Applebaum, "Defending Bolton" (3–9–2005), washingtonpost.com/wp-dyn/articles/A18706-2005Mar8. See Condoleezza Rice, "UN Needs Reform" (April 2005), washingtonpost.com/wp-dyn/articles/A18706-2005March.

50. Congress has made several efforts to improve the United Nations, with few results. See "Reform at the UN" un.org/reform/mgmt_reform.

51. United Nations commitments remain "no disclosures" and "more governance." See review in "Cato Handbook for Congress," cato.org/pubs/handbook/hb105-51.

52. John addressed the NYC Rotary Club and I was fortunate to attend. I shook hands to thank him but did not otherwise visit with him.

53. Some apologists state violence is okay, that the call for "law and order" is only to prevent needed rebellion. Peaceful demonstrators are often pushed forward by violent organizers. Others become terrorists and attack facilities with loss of life. Some remain committed to violence and killing others. See *New York Times* interview (9–11–2001).

54. See *Forbes*, Jeffrey Sachs, "The Forbes One Billion" (10–08–2007). Forbes.com/free/2007/094. The standard for poverty is income of less than one dollar per day.

55. World Bank, "world poverty," at worldbank.org/WBSITE/EXTERNAL-/TOPICS/EXTPOVERTY/0,menuPK:336998~pagePK:149018~piPK:149093~theSitePK:336992,00.

56. The report states the results are "phenomenal." See "Trillionaires," n. 13. The United Nations and its affiliated groups

have accomplished nothing comparable. They want more money and oppose any business efforts. See Bill Gates, at "Trillionaires," n. 14.

57. Critics are everywhere, particularly opposing proponents for America. The ongoing war of words with the statists and meritocrats will not end until they admit losing the cold war.

58. See "Defeating Global Poverty," defeatpoverty.com (5–27–2007). The results are studies and more studies; then more overhead and even less results.

59. Similar to the courtroom, facts must govern debate. When facts are misstated, corrections should be made. When facts are not reported, the omission must be added. There is a huge failure to present "fair and balanced" facts. See chapter 7, "Values."

60. A meritocrat is a person who has scored highly on their SAT and believes themselves anointed to say whatever they want to reach a statism objective, more and more government and more and more taxes. The sublime belief and arrogance is that, without any direct experience in the business of running the economy and commerce, they know more that the hands-on owners and managers. See, e.g., answers.com/topic/meritocracy.

61. At accd.edu/sac/j-p/comfort.

62. See, e.g., Matthew Kerbel, *If It Bleeds, It Leads* (Westview 2001).

63. At journalism.org there are annual reports on "the state of the news media." See also stateofthenewsmedia.org/ and enter the year.

Chapter 3: Econofacts

1. See Michael Wheeler, *Lies, Damned Lies and Statistics: The Manipulation of Public Opinion in America* (Dell 1977).

2. See newsroom.com.

3. Samuel H. Williamson, "Six Ways to Compute the Relative Value of a U.S. dollar Amount, 1790 to Present," at measuringworth.com/calculators/uscompare/index.php measuringworth.com, 2008.

4. For my friends with ASPCA, a "lie-dog" is a sleeping dog. One that is sleeping cannot be running.

5. In March 2008, economists split on whether we were in a

"recession." Todd Wallak, "Recession is here" (3–15–2008) boston.com/business/articles/2008/03/15/. For discussion, see National Bureau of Economic Research, "Recession." At nber.org/cycles/recessions.

6. Psychologists have their standard manual. See allpsych.com/disorders/dsm.html. Economists should develop a similar foundation. The National Bureau of Economic Research has definitions routinely defied by its own members. See Wallak, supra.

7. See nobelprize.org/nobel_prizes/economics/laureates/-1970/samuelson-bio.html.

8. For Samuelson quotes, see thinkexist.com/quotes/paul_a.-_samuelson.

9. See Kenneth R. Hoover, *Economics as Ideology* (Rowan & Littlefield 2003).

10. See Murray Rothbard, *Keynes, the Man* (Praeger 1992).

11. The quote was used by Galbreath to suggest the founders opposed all taxes because of personal greed. The likely motivation is they did not trust government. Why pay someone to take your money? As usual, both motivations and more may have been involved. Economists are not good psychoanalysts.

12. For Friedman's Nobel Prize, nobelprize.org/nobel_prizes-/economics/laureates/1976/friedman-autobio.

13. At nobelprize.org/nobel_prizes/economics/laureates/1974/press.

14. The plan to reduce taxes and stimulate the economy was written on a cocktail napkin. Arthur Laffer, "The Laffer Curve," (6–1–2004) heritage.org/Research/Taxes/bg1765.cfm. The plan worked, and has worked ever since. A broader view is the economic report showing how business has reduced poverty, not the government dole. George F. Russell Jr., "The Power of Globalization," National Bureau of Research, vol. 16, No. 2 (November 2005).

15. Reagan used the phrase often. Perhaps we have a complete answer to Galbreath?

16. There is some leeway in accounting; however, IRS review prevents inaccurate or ambiguous books. Generally Accepted Accounting Principles provides those guidelines and is a solid testament to business ethics. See gaap.net. Keep honest books. See business values in chapter 2, "Trillionaires."

17. The balanced budget has been tried for decades. Congress required a balanced budget in 1997. Balanced Budget Act 1997, thomas.loc.gov/cgi-bin/query/z?c105:H.R.2015. Results have not been "balanced."

18. Paul Volcker, ny.frb.org/aboutthefed/PVolckerbio.

19. Volcker, pbs.org/fmc/interviews/volcker.

20. Remarks, Alan Greenspan, federalreserve.gov/boarddocs/speeches/2000/20000825.

21. At nndb.com/people/164/000023095.

22. Ben Bernanke, federalreserve.gov/abou http://www.foreign-policy.com/story/cms.php?story_id=2747&popup_delayed=1tthefed /bios/board/bernanke.

23. Any suggestion of improving free trade is instantly called isolationism. Senator Leahy is an example. Others support debate on the issue, emphasizing that improvements are needed. The support for free trade is very powerful.

24. Ron Blackwell, AFL-CIO testimony, Congress, January 2007.

25. Id, testimony on China trade, Congress, May 2007.

26. See gallup.com for polling results.

27. Economic History, oxford-economichistory.com/LOGIN?-sessionid=526da4dbfd4f8dbc213c5980d13a3037&authstatus-code=400.

28. A similar comparison with the world economic product shown, tracks the first one at academicinfo.net/econhist.

29. See census.gov/econ/census/.

30. There are several excellent websites working to improve statistical reporting and analysis. NationMaster.org has procedures for researchers to develop their own special reports. There are charges. Statistics are not available for totals to show each nation's economic commitment to globalization. Charitable contributions and faith-based support are difficult to track. Some would omit defense spending. Others exclude administrative costs. The International Standards Organization (ISO) is reportedly making some progress. See so.org/iso/iso_catalogue/catalogue_ics/catalogue_ics_browse.-htm?ICS1=01.

31. Military totals are reported with great detail, usually with the political purpose of showing how the United States spends too much and is therefore a warmonger. Peace must be maintained and

American defense efforts have provided that foundation for *Pax Americana*. One interesting result is the total for members or prospective members of the European Empire. They now spend more. Consider also the support to NATO. The point would be to unite in assuring global peace, with contributions from all nations on parity.

32. The cost of globalization to the United States is denied by the free traders. In fact, the deficit in trade and the budget relate to globalization. The net loss each year is divided among all Americans for the loss figures. The family loss is calculated at four members.

33. Dobbs, *War on the Middle Class* (Viking 2006), 233.

34. Lou may disagree with comparisons to FOX and the radio hosts of Radio Free America (personal description); however, if both political parties call for lower taxes, whoever in the respective parties promotes lower taxes should be of no consequence. Values have no copyright.

35. See NationMaster.org.

36. Greenspan, federalreserve.gov/boarddocs/speeches/2005/20050204/default.

37. The short thesis was released recently. The "gloom and doom" sounds like Orwell but has not been supported by any detailed studies. See Parag Khanna, "Waving goodbye to hegemony," *NY Times magazine* (1–17–2008).

38. Results support this unstated but assumed motivation. America was determined not to have another war. Also, we recognized the economic suffering and were determined to do something about it, by improving the economies and providing jobs.

39. See *Brought to you by the Wonderful People who Bombed Pearl Harbor*. By 1970 we had moved ahead from 1945, and humor was at least beginning to appear as the economies improved. A measure of globalizing humor?

40. US Census Bureau, country specific report, census.gov/compendia/statab/cats/foreign_commerce_aid.

41. Economists tend to support or reject Adam Smith on philosophical grounds, either statist or commercial democracy. Smith believed the market worked from individual buy-sell transactions and concluded "an invisible hand" kept the economy going. See United Kingdom, free trade group, adamsmith.org/.

42. See lehd.did.census.gov/led/index.

Chapter 4: Greed

1. *Federalist* No 39 p 125, yale.edu/laweb/avalon/federal-/fed39.

2. "Thomas Paine," quotationspage.com/quotes/Thomas_Paine/.

3. See 'Lectric Law, "Sovereign immunity" lectlaw.com/def2-/s103. "legal fiction," legal-dictionary.thefreedictionary.com-/Fiction.

4. See, e.g., Robert Cassidy, "Failed Expectations of US Trade Policy" (6–4–2008), fpif.org/fpiftxt/5274.

5. "Invisible Hand," InvestorWords.com, Webfinance, Inc. (7–14–2008), investorwords.com/2633/invisiblehand.

6. Peter Elstrom, "Outsourcing Uneven Impact," *Business Week* (12–22–2007), businessweek.com/bwdaily/dnflash/content/feb2007/-db20070221_427240.

7. US Census, historical statistics; see Appendix for chart and graph.

8. Peter Morici, "Why the trade deficit is so large and why it matters" (10–11–2005) chinacurrencycoalition.org/presscenter/p_morici_101105.pdf+trade+deficit+subsidies&hl=en&ct=clnk&cd=21&gl=us.

9. "Conspiracy," lectlaw.com/def/c103.

10. George Russell, "UN Coming Cleaner?" foxnews.com (5–20–2008).

11. See for George Bush, John McKenzie, *Absolute Power* (Century Foundation 2008); for Bill Clinton, see David Limbaugh, *Absolute Power* (Regnery 2001).

12. Excellent equity principle; see Blackstone, *Commentaries*.

13. IRS made several raids based on "apparent wealth" and was very successful. Congress promptly made the practice unlawful.

14. Alan Harding, "Origins of the Crime of Conspiracy" (Royal Historical Society 1983), jstor.org/pss/3678991 (fee required); compare, "conspiracy theory" encyclopedia2.thefreedictionary.-com/Government+conspiracy; distinguish "conspiracy theories" tpiccraze.cp,/rew?d=Government_Politics/Politics/Conspiracy_Theories [theories without admissible facts].

15. See *Blood, Money & Power*, 302.

16. Internet theft, identity theft, copyright infringement; see *USA Today*, "Tech" (5–23–2001) usatoday.com/tech/news/2001-05-23-id-theft-solutions.

17. See foxnews.com, "UN Development Program Violated Law" (6–11–2008) foxnews.com/story/0,2933,365676,00.

18. See BillandMelindaFoundation.com.

19. NGOs are unique "non-government organizations," many promoting United Nations policies with support from the UN. See ngo.org/index. Compare NGO defined, nonprofitexpert.com/ngo.

20. See berkshirehathaway.com.

21. Per Bill Gates speaking for his Foundation, no government or charity. Warren Buffett agrees.

22. Walmart.com.

23. See, e.g., settlement reached by Boeing to pay $615M (5–16–2008); corpwatch.org.

24. Boeing donations could not be located and verified.

25. The standard Christian tithe is 10 percent. Bill has done far more, nearly one-third of his personal fortune.

26. Philanthropists raise questions about actual help. Paul Maidment, "Giving It Away," *Forbes* (3–5–08).

27. Note that billionaires have lifted millions out of poverty, a continuation of the Laffer principle, that business provides jobs. See, e.g., "China's growth contributes to poverty relief" (4–9–2005) chinaembassy.org.nz/eng/xw/t210186. The United Nations record is unacceptable. Those "tea party" diplomats need to learn how to communicate and how to convince by addressing all peoples in the world diversity. United Nations "Handbook on poverty statistics" (7–21–2004) still a work in progress? unstats.un.org/unsd/,ethods/poverty/chapter7. No statistics show actual relief (results). Congress routinely withholds United Nations dues to encourage reform. See CNN.com (6–18–2005).

28. Corrupt governments get the money which is then given to individuals. Too often dictators leave office with huge sums in Swiss banks. Corruption correlates with the United States trade deficit. See Appendix for chart.

29. Micro-credit works ("teach a person to fish"). Stefan Lovgren, "Nobel Prize goes to micro-loan pioneers," *National Geographic* (10–13–2006); nationalgeographic.com/news/2006/-10/061013-nobel-peace. There are many similar programs getting results.

30. The transparency report on global corruption is in the Appendix. Most of the world is corrupt beyond certain minimum standards.

31. The United.States is in the top twenty. See Appendix.

32. See totals, chart in Appendix.

33. Global competition shows the nations ready to compete and at what level. World Economic Forum, 2007 Report. See Appendix.

34. Sunlight Foundation, "Exposing Earmarks," sunlightfoundation.com/exposingearmarks/.

35. Global Integrity report 2007, report.globalintegrity.org.

36. Mike Moffatt, "Balanced budget," economics.about.com/cs/ economics.about.com/cs/economicsglossay/g/balanced_budget.

37. Corruption at the State Department. Several books by David Casavis. See, e.g., afsa.org/fsj/julaug06/books.

38. State under investigation. Cnn.com/2007/POLITICS/ 09/18/-state.dept.fraud.ap.

39. Transparency and full disclosure require "the goldfish bowl." See Transparency International "Time for transparency," transparency.org (several reports). The principle should apply to all in government at all levels of government.

40. See US Agency for International Development, "Fighting Corruption," at usaid.gov/our_work/democracy_and_governance/ technical_areas/anticorruption/aid.gov.

41. See Jack Gage, "Best Countries for Business," *Forbes* (6–26–2008) forbes.com/business/2008/06/26/denmark_ireland_finland-biz-cz_jg_bizcountries08_0626bizcountries_bestcountries.

42. US Census, statistics on China trade, see Appendix.

43. US Census, Canada and Mexico imbalances, see Appendix.

44. Overall trade deficit shows the United States at the bottom, dead last. See chart in Appendix.

45. CRS Report "New World Gold Mine" (8–27–2006), ncseonline.org/nle/crsreports/mining/mine-9."

46. Based on personal experience.

47. See Appendix.

48. See Appendix on Immigration.

49. Our Global Neighborhood (Oxford 1995). Several members were from nations considered corrupt. There is no diversity con-

forming to world populations. The proposals include adding $10 per barrel of oil (about 25¢ per gallon of gas). Compare Henry Lamb, "Our Global Neighborhood" sovereignty.net/p/gov/ggaanalysis.

50. The North American Union is under development and some versions include a common currency referred to as the "amero." See Andrew Marshall, "North American Monetary Integration" (1–20–2008) at globalresearch.ca/index.php?context=va&aid=7854.

51. Thomas Paine, quotedby.com.

52. Thoreau, Thoreau.eserver.org.

Chapter 5: Parity

1. The series is owned by the Dogpatch USA; however, the park is not operational. Lil-abner.c/dogpatch.

2. "Lil Abner," Broadway play (1959); musicalheaven.com.

3. "Level playing field" defined at investorwords.com/2783/level-playing-field.

4. Several organizations are promoting a level playing field. Some concepts are developed from privatization efforts. See Lawrence Martin, "Determining a Level Playing Field for Public-Private Competititon" (11–99) 64.233.183.104/search?q=cache:SiUaQy_IdCQJ:management.energy.gov/martin.pdf+level+playing+fielddd&h2=en&ct=clnk&col=12&gl=us.

5. At internationalcompetitionnetwork.org/.

6. This point is implicit in the discussions and in what followed. Business looks to results. We understand the underlying policies that supported our doctrine of globalization. That doctrine has never been stated explicitly; however, the results prove the doctrine.

7. Some agreements reflect the problems for labor unions regarding wages, hours and terms of employment. Some concentrate of improving environmental issues. Even with NAFTA, side agreements acknowledge issues but have no enforcement. See cec.org/pubs_info_resources/law_treat_agree/naaec/index.cfm?varlan=english.

8. See weforum.org, at tab "General Competitiveness Report."

9. Full disclosure is a vital feature of government. This basic quest for freedom of information is blocked everywhere. Even New York City's alleged dedication to "open" values shows required disclosures are not made. "NYC Foil Requests: Satisfaction Not

Guaranteed" (March 2003) nyccouncil.info.pdf_files/reports/foildreport/Report to the City, 2003.

10. This commitment has not been investigated. Some statisticians are developing the database needed to make the comparisons. Until we have full and open disclosure, the necessary numbers for guidelines are not possible. Some agencies still rely on those numbers.

11. This commitment will include the funds needed to maintain a world economy and work toward global political solutions. If the hope remains that the United Nations will reform, firm plans with effective law and order must be adopted. An alternative is for the ten regions to develop their enforceable legal systems for fairness and disclosure, then work with the global trade organizations to enforce the needed commitments. Finally, in keeping with the territorial expansion of the European Empire, nations can form new alliances for political union. This step would be most difficult but outlines are there for the United States to admit Canada, Mexico, and a few other candidates. Even the United Kingdom and the former British Commonwealth would be well-served to re-unify with the "colonies" rather than fall again into the European imperial projects. The suggestion is that the United Kingdom will be better off here than there. See, e.g., themediaroom.com/election2004/issues/statehood/Canada. Of course, this will not happen without full agreement among the nations involved.

12. The European Union, with an aggressive policy of admitting more and more nations has become an empire in every sense of the word. The latest economic reports show Europe's gross imperial product is more than that of the United States. With the continued unification under NAFTA, a larger North American economy is emerging. The definition of sovereignty is properly questioned. See plato.standford.edu/entries/sovereignty. Compare Jan Zielonka *Europe As Empire* (Oxford 2006). Democratic elections must be included in the process.

13. See ftc.gov/bcp/online/pubs/buspubs/madeinusa.

14. See internationalcompetitivenetwork.org.

15. At weforum.org, at tab "Global Agenda Councils."

16. The missing numbers are primarily contributions to and/or by charities, apparently included with non-government organizations

(NGOs). The totals need development and then they need uniform standards. These are not yet available. Consider the military expenditures by the United States and the European Empire. The United States has a readily available total. The European nations have similar budgets and their total military budgets exceed the United States budget. Obtaining comparable figures for all categories and all nations in the ten regions is simply "not readily available at this time."

17. This impact on each American is calculated from the deficit for 2007. The total deficit since 1980 shows each American lost $55,700. There is a direct cost to every individual. As a government cost for free trade, another word for the loss is tax, a global one.

Chapter 6: Leaders

1. Presidential debates are available online. For 1992, see debates.org/pages/history.

2. Winston Churchill, House of Commons (11–11–1947), wais.standford.edu.

3. See Constant Contact (1–24–2005), enterstageright.com.

4. For issues and selection suggestions see selectsmart.com; vajoe.com; issues.2008.org. There are many similar webpages.

5. Early elections in the United States were vicious. Tough debates are to be welcomed. We debate to arrive at a better understanding and a better democracy. Accept "the heat in the kitchen." See, e.g., Bernard Weisberger, *America Afire* (HarperCollins 2001).

6. For aggregation see, for example, Erikson, MacKuen & Stimson (2002).

7. See gallup.com/poll and select the subject and the year.

8. Eisenhower, "Six Qualities That Make a Great President," *Time* (6–14–1963).

9. Presidential qualities, survey of 100 historians, comments by Vijai Sharma on study by three psychologists, mindpub.com-/art377.

10. Hedley Donovan, "Job Specs for the Oval Office," *Time* (12–13–1982). time.com/time/magazine/article/0,9171,923131-2,00.

11. Karl Rove, "What Makes a Great President," hnn.us.1529 (6–30–2003).

12. Joel Klein, *Primary Colors* (Random 1996).

13. Sissela Bok, *Lying* (Pantheon 1982).
14. Gallup on big issues—globalization. See gallup.com.
15. UN report and adoption; governance report approved; UN General Assembly (9–8–2000).
16. "Consensus" means "what?" The idea is to assemble people of like mind and get a report. Any reports of global consequence should be representative of the global population and should exclude representatives from corrupt nations.
17. Proposed taxes include levies on oil produced, financial transactions, communications and more.
18. "Core values" are not defined. There is no specificity involved but the Bill of Rights would be useless.
19. The proposed European Union needs a constitution. After rejection by voters in several nations, a treaty format is being submitted, without voter participation. In other words the government is being imposed without approvals by the democratic process. The people most directly impacted have no voice or vote.
20. Paul Farhi "Elitist: The Rarefied Term That's a Low Blow" *Washington Post* (4–18–2008)washingtonpost.com/wp-dyn/content/article/2008/04/17/AR2008041703990. For "meritocrat" see thefreedictionary.com/meritocrat.
21. Bill Gates at World Economic Forum (1–25–2008), supra, Trillionaires, n. 14.
22. Reagan remarks on change, reaganlibrary.gov.

Chapter 7: Values

1. One humor study is Giselinde Kuiper, "Globalization of Humor," giselinde.nl/research; see also onderzoekin-formatie.nl (2004–2008).
2. The book declares the "end of history," that is of the war between state control (socialism) and individual freedom (democracy). Francis Fukuyama, *The End of History and the Last Man* (Free Press 1992).
3. The latest popular forecast for *1984* returns. See Parag Khanna, "Waving Goodbye to Hegemony," *NY Times Magazine* (1–17–2008). See also Parity, supra, n. 15.
4. "Core values" is a term the "governance" report does not

define. A better definition would be the values listed at the end of each chapter in this book. A better term would be "universal values" but the statists reject "universal" yet find "core" values. They are the same.

5. Used in the broad sense of politics, not criminal conspiracy.

6. American College of Trial Lawyers, *Code of Petrial and Trial Conduct* (2002) see actl.com/AM/Template.cfm%3FSection%DAll_Publications%26Template%3D/CM/ContentDisplay.cfm%26ContentfileID%3D59+trial+conduct&hl=en&ct=clnk&cd=1&gl=us.

7. "Propaganda" means the deliberate omission of facts. That is also a definition of the lie or at least the half-lie. Too often, the major media are very good at this propaganda; however, any broadcast or article will show signs of this bias. The media would serve everyone, including themselves, with the Hannity-Colmes format, both determined to present diametrically opposed viewpoints. Very informative except for "everybody talking, nobody listening."

8. The United Nations reports seek consensus but no veto. Consensus means full agreement. If one person or nation disagrees there is no consensus. The veto continues. The consensus is reached, however, among like-minded representatives carefully selected in advance with no consideration for diversity of opinion or background.

9. Requirements for political and economic unification, see "union" at thefreedictionary.com/union. See also sovereignty at plato.standford.edu, supra.

10. The United Nations charter provides for a united military command. See Article 47, Charter. The provision has never been used. New efforts are underway to set up a "quick strike" military force. See governance proposal, supra.

11. See above re "Canada Statehood."

12. For strong opposition to the proposed North American Union see Daneen G. Peterson, Ph.D, stopthenorthamericanunion.com.

13. The New York preference is by county and city but with mixed enactment and enforcement. New York City has it subject to review, again. See Betsy Gotbaum, Public Advocate, NYC, "Procurement in New York City: A Strategy for Local Economic

Development" (June 2003). A sample of the application for the preference is included in the Appendix. Many states have adopted similar provisions. See eva.state.va.us/buyer_only/news/alerts/pr.pdf+ny+State+preferences&hl=en&ct=clnk&cd=1&gl=us.

Chapter 8: Results

1. Even to mention results seems sophomoric; however, few policy advisers or decision makers in politics acknowledge the importance of results. Economists and their politician friends are so often wrong and never called to account that the issue must be highlighted. Results means being right—like in the biblical reference that "by their fruits ye shall know them" Matthew 7:15. Prophets speaking to results must produce results. Checking the economists and finding their errors should be the true test; what have been your results? Politicians need not be included in this critical test. Their promises (predictions) are simply too often wrong. There are outstanding politicians, of course, especially those who get results such as knowing how to meet a payroll without printing more money.

2. The problems for economists are their lack of standards and the politization they practice, analyzed in chapter 3 on "econofacts," at pp. 111–36.

3. The classic remark remains, "It's the economy, stupid." Too many ignore the basics of the economy such as accurate accounting, the necessity for a profit, meeting the payroll, and generally running a business by the rules for business. Washington, clear up your books. Get jobs going the old-fashioned way.

4. To be productive, the usual measure is making a profit. Government avoids that term but the point is good results must be achieved. If there is no profit and there is no work, something must be done. The National Academy of Sciences is proposing standards for evaluating efficiency. See report, "Research Needed in how federal government evaluates efficiency ..." National-Academies.org; 1–31–2008. Legislation is pending. See HR478, Federal Agency Performance Review and Efficiency Act, 111th Congress. For progress, we need jobs and we need profits.

5. American economic policy after World War II was to prevent another war, period. Economic support for progress centered on

Europe and a common market. Globalization and regionalization resulted from careful planning, virtually a day at a time, case by case. See pp. 20, 81, 121, 132, supra. On hindsight, this "doctrine" is apparent.

6. The "cost to America" represents many deductions. In addition to the cost of "free" trade, there is foreign aid, excess costs from overseas corruption, private gifts, etc.

7. The latest annual loss figures for "free" trade are 2008. The loss is $677.1 billion. See p. 263, supra.

8. The trade deficit has soared to a total over the years of $9.13 trillion. See "Five Short Blasts" forum, petermurphy-wordpress.com.

9. See US Trade Deficit Commission, report issued November 14, 2000, at govinfo.library.unt.edu/tdrc.

10. The downturn had several sources: trade deficits, family income declines, mortgage foreclosures, the price of gasoline, and more.

11. See chapter 5, at pp. 160–75. The concept is not just purchasing power parity but overall trade balances with no one nation carrying the deficit. The 2008 downturn shows America cannot afford colossal unilateral losses to support trade.

12. Consider the imbalance for key nations. China leads the list for a positive trade balance. See p. 265, supra. China is also one of the most corrupt, tied with Brazil, India, and Mexico, all important trading partners.

13. Comments by Peter Mandelson, British labor leader, secretary for business and Europe Union trade commissioner. BBC News, 10–17–2007. Mandelson remains a "free" trader. See TimesOnline, 3–16–2009. Bipartisan support is emerging for open and fair trade. See Jamail Afridi, "Twenty Agendas at G-20, Part II," Council on Foreign Relations, backgrounder, 9–23–2009.

14. G20, final statement, endorses "a level playing field" but nothing is done to expedite a solution to the crisis, the needs by so many for jobs. See MinnPost.com, 9–28–2009.

15. See Appendix, Item 6, p. 267.

16. Several federal agencies are part of key commitments to economic progress. The Council of Economic Advisers was established by the Employment Act of 1946. The National Economic Council was established by executive order in 1993. See

whitehouse.gov/administration/eop/[at cea and nec]. Economic advice is provided by many agencies and individuals. Disclosure: my son was a member of the CEA.

17. Fiscal policy centers on interest rates, or the cost of money to banks. See pp. 117–18.

18. See elections.foxnews.com/2008/10/16: "Joe the plumber is the nation's every man ..."

19. See Gordon Shelton, "Role of Government in Promoting Homeownership," Economic Review (July/August 1990); see also "A Brief History of Home Equity Loans," felixsalmon.com, 8–15–2008; Louise Story, "Live Richly," 8–14–2008; nyt.com.; equity ownership includes stock market holdings; see Lillian Woo and others, "Measuring Ownership in America," sf.frb.org/publications-/community/investments.

20. In an address to the Bank of England, the problem was underscored by noting bank officers made loans on traditional business assurances such as value of the property, income history, and more. But, salesmen in the bank then discounted the loan for a healthy commission. The pressure was underway to make loans as soon as possible. The bank lenders need to be separated from the bank salesmen of those loans.

21. Efforts should be directed to improving the trade balance. Some steps are underway. Listen to business leaders. FedEx, Cisco, and Office Depot expect slow recovery; they also support corporate tax cuts. See Reuters, 9–20–2009. After one year in the doldrums, expedited recovery is needed. Cutting taxes ala Laffer would find scant support among the Keynesian economists now promoting more government control. Many economists call for a corporate tax cut. See Chris Edwards, "The U.S. Corporate Tax and the Global Economy," Cato Institute, Tax and Budget Bulletin, September 2003. For parity, reduce the corporate tax to the lowest among our major trading partners. An example: be Ireland's 12.5 percent, from the 40 percent imposed on American companies. See also Ambassador Terry Miller and Anthony B. Kim, "High Corporate Taxes Undermine U.S. Global Competitiveness," Heritage Foundation, Web Memo #2065, 9–18–2008.

22. With rapidly changing economic reports in a politically charged climate, updated statistics are difficult to select. Even reliable

sources are proving to be politicized. Henry Clay noted, "Statistics are no substitute for judgment." Oil prices converted to pump prices are a good example of the need for judgment. We know the price at the pump exploded.

23. Statistics are best reserved to experts to permit them to try to prove their divination; some graphs support our judgment. For the huge decline in manufacturing jobs, Bureau of Labor Statistics, "Manufacturing Employment." For the decline in family income by $1,000 per year, Census Bureau, "Current Population Survey, 1963–2008." For the increase in subprime lending and subsequent declines, Census Bureau/Harvard, "Statues on Nation's Housing, 2008." For gasoline price increases for six years, see website at dogreatgood.com, "Gasoline Prices, 1979–2009." For foreclosure increases 2007 through 2009, RealtyTrac Press Releases, "US Foreclosures Market Reports." And for the trade deficit increasing until 2009, then falling slightly but still leading other nations, Census Bureau, Annual Reports. To summarize, jobs declined, family income declined, subprime lending supported high-risk mortgages, gasoline prices took away any possibility to recover and foreclosures rose. The economic decline was inevitable.

24. For still another recent approach to easing the adverse economic impact, MadeinUSA.com is for patriotic spending with recycled dollars. The webpage lists American companies and products made in the USA. A key point is one added American job means five to eight related jobs added. A job loss means the reverse. Saying the trade deficit is not a problem and that buying America is the answer, leaders for American products are furniture, acrylics, food and clothing. The webpage overlooks key issues to build productivity and jobs. Identifying higher business costs, the need for parity, for reducing those costs to spark American productivity, is downplayed. America is the world's most powerful consumer market. We should buy USA to show the need for fair and open trade.

25. The popular federal measure of inflation, the "consumer price index," is misleading. There are several measures of inflation and none agree. Expensive errors result. See, e.g., "The great inflation cover-up," money.cnn.com/2006/03/31/.../-spiers_cpi.fotune/?.

26. Bear Stearns, Bloomberg 4–2–2008; Financial Times, ft.com-/cms/.../00077b07658, 5–29–2008.

27. The collapse in September 2008 resulted from government intervention in trade, homeownership, control of oil production, and more. The explanations depend on the economist and the politician. After one year, the main point is the failure to recover. The initiatives suggested would put Americans back to work and let business go back to work. Two back-and-forth, only slightly partisan discussions are in Wikipedia.com, "Economic Policy" and "Economic Collapse."

28. General Motors and Chrysler benefited from a federal "bridge loan" recognized as a bailout. See, e.g., "Behind the Bailout," pbs.org/now/shows/438/index.

29. See Nick Gillespie, "Tea Party March ... draws ... between 2 million and 60,000 ..." reason.com, 9–13–2009 (ABC reported 75,000, then reported 2 million); see also dailymail.co.uk-/world-news/article/up-million-march. Milt Shalla, a dear friend provided me on-site information; a huge turnout.

Chapter 9: Free America

1. See usdoj.gov/usao/pressreleasemarch09. In addition, Madoff was ordered to forfeit $170 billion in assets. See washingtonpost.com/ar2009026605642 (6–26–2009).

2. Do not let Congress set accounting standards through politics, Financial Accounting Standards Board, "Don't politicize accounting rules," TheDeal.com, 10–2–2008. How do Americans rely on any projections, particularly by politicians not interested in the facts?

3. See article by Laffer at heritage.org/research/taxes 6–1–2004. Compare, Hale Stewart, "Art Laffer Is Wrong on [sic] Inflation," *Huffington Post,* 6–11–2009.

4. The applicable quote in the private economy, "That's close enough for government work." Refers to poorly done work. See en.wiktionary.org/wik.

5. See Commission on the Private Sector & Development, un.org especially webapps01.un.org/nvp/frontend!policy.action?id=662.

6. See Caroline Baum, "Obama Goes Postal, ..." Bloomberg.com, 8–18–2009.

7. See americanbankingnews.com/2009/10/07.

8. Disclosure: my son headed Medicare, 2004–2006.

9. The promised transparency was "dealt a severe setback." *New York Times,* 10–4–2009 (search at nyt.com).

10. Business is based on sound accounting principles. Washington relies on the power of the purse, to print money whenever. A fundamental principle of the American economy, insisted upon by Alexander Hamilton, was to have a sound dollar. No more.

11. Business needs some reassurances. Instead, every business has to look at a huge deficit requiring taxes, at healthcare plans to require huge business costs, and a sense of *mea culpa* to the international community, suggesting continuation of trade deficits. Business needs assurances but has none. Instead, they invest in gold.

12. The necessity for the goldfish bowl has been emphasized. See pp. 16, 95, 150, etc.

13. Personal experience based on review of opportunities in Honduras; analysis showed payroll costs were no longer an advantage, due to local wage laws.

14. "2009 National Trade Estimate Report on Foreign Trade Barriers," ustr.gov/about-us/.../2009-nationaltradeestimate ..., 10–9–2009.

15. His auditor has been indicted. AP, 9–30–2009, msnbc.msn.com-/id/31964977/ns/business-us_business. Personal experience: attorneys appear to be routinely excused in corporate fraud situations, even as board members. This protection must end.

16. "Nuclear Power in the USA," world-nuclear.org/info/inf41, 10–1–2009.

17. Id.

18. Sheila Gaquin, "ANWR Oil to Reduce Gas Prices?" Americana-ffairs.suite101.com/article.cfn/..., 5–14–2008.

19. Larry West, Autos account for half of global warming, environmental.about.com/od/globalwarming/a/autoemissions.

20. UN: "US workers are the world's most productive," AP, 9–3–2007 at msnbc.msn.com/id/20572828; "most generous," answer.yahoo.com/question/(see index); 5–21–2007 (US per OECD is twice any other nation); hardest working (UN Report, id.); and competitive (caution: the World Economic Forum in its report for 2009–2010 concludes Switzerland has replaced the United States. This is not accepted because Switzerland is, through extensive bilateral agreements, a de facto member of the European Empire; the

ranking is not accurate). Cf. "The Global Competitiveness Report 2009–2010," weforum.org/en/initiatives/gcp/Global% 20Competitiveness% ... (9–10–2009). With this explanation, the United States is the most competitive, hardest working, most productive, and most charitable nation in the world. Hello, Washington; just turn us loose.

Afterword

1. The trip into early childhood adventures was undertaken by Freud. Trying the same trip is interesting and helps understand the foundations for "knowing thyself."

2. For the meritocrats—those with the ability to govern without the need for elections—my academic results from many years ago are available on request; however, you have to rely on actual experience, not some theoretical testing in an ivory tower milieu.

3. The cash was very helpful in that senior year at the University of Texas.

4. Reportedly, the paper was the first article for an international law journal at Texas. I never saw it. I headed to Washington DC for a paying job.

5. As I recall the meeting was a first ever between students and regents. Little success but the start was made.

6. AOG, Docket RI71-144, FPC 1971 (original filing no longer available).

7. Royalty company takeover in stock purchase fight.

8. The case went to the Supreme Court, *Named Members* v. *City of San Antonio*, et al, 400 US 939 (1972).

9. See *Government Regulation and the Economy* (Lexington 1980), declaring the Railroad Commission to be the most powerful regulatory agency in the world, or, for present purposes, on the globe.

10. The facts and references are in *Blood, Money & Power* (Hannover 2003) at 238.

11. Journalists have to learn to probe deeper in their investigations and questioning, and to seek all the insights possible from the two or more sides active in most cases. Take whatever "spin" you prefer, but present all the facts.

12. The term is from Goulden, *Superlawyers* (1972).

13. The term is mine. The high-priced and high-powered DC

lawyers are over-valued. The money in globalization too often justifies the extraordinary payments "because of the heavy responsibilities involved, I must have compensation to cover the trust and the risks involved."

14. The needed disclosure would be only a start. The actual use and abuse of the power need disclosure.

15. Based on personal experience. As a DC lobbyist, you quickly learn what is really going on just by seeing who is registering to visit key powers in the White House and in Congress.

16. Released in September 2003 by Hannover House. Sales reached bestseller status by November.

17. Humphrey's campaign with war protestors present in strong numbers.

18. One very close election depended on calls on election day until late in the afternoon, then driving to pick up a few more voters. The race was decided with less than one hundred votes separating winner and loser.

19. See *Blood, Money & Power*, at documents 24.

20. The letters commenting on the entry were sharply divided. The two contests are yearly.

21. "Author" is defined (not without controversy) at several websites.

22. Hemingway is a source. Getting experience is good practice. Meritocrats should try a regular job, 9–5. Better yet, open a business and work 24/7.

23. The religious gene is still being explored as more and more instincts are found to determine behavior in the human genome. See McKee, "Genes contribute to religion," *New Scientist*, May 24, 2005.

24. George B. McClellan Jr. was mayor from 1904 to 1908. See *New York Times* article, January 2, 1904.

25. One of the generations included in the greatest generation.

26. Several popular books consider the subject. See especially Kushner, *When Bad Things Happen to Good People* (Avon 1983).

27. Divorced once with four sons from that marriage, all doing very well, thank you. A son and daughter from the second, both doing very well, thank you. My second marriage is in its thirtieth year. Most of all, thank you to a very understanding and supportive wife.

28. The popular series started in 1964 and was re-released in 1973. The story I invented was just that, there was no Star Trek episode on cadet school.

29. Borrowed from the VISA ads.

30. "Sweet sleep" was a high-quality state of rest reflected in several Greek stories. Must have been hard to find back in those early days. Still is.

INDEX